SELENA AND HER MYSTERIES

WRITTEN BY
MOIRA DARRELL

ISBN: 978-1-7781408-1-5 (ePub)
ISBN: 978-1-7781408-0-8 (print)

Cover artwork by Nancy-Lynne Hughes with permission
Book layout by Human Powered Design

Find me at Facebook Page:
Moira Darrell Books

Contents

PROLOGUE

I CAN'T ASK AUNT JENNY.

Honestly, is there nothing that I believed five days ago that actually is what I thought it was?

Should I begin a list of what I have discovered in these recent days?

Would it make me feel more or even less in control? There are so many strange things, so many mysteries.

Backing away as she had instructed herself, yet hesitating, Selena moved to the door and closed it hearing a firm "click". With precision, she locked the door with the key she had found.

Remembering back to that afternoon, she also remembered another afternoon, another child.

Now she knew who they were; where they had come from; how far they had travelled; and what happened in the years between.

But there were those remaining mysteries, still unsolved.

PART ONE

1

Who Were They?

SELENA STRAIGHTENED HER ROOM as usual before leaving. As she came down the hallway, she noticed some unlevel photos on one wall.

She smiled to herself while glancing at them. The garden photo made her think of Laura Waters, her best friend since they were 13. While playing all those years ago, Laura had looked up the meaning of Selena's name. Laura told her jokingly that the name "Selena" was a Greek name for *Goddess of the Moon.*

Today, this thought made her stand up straighter, remembering that she had stood up then, and, in a condescending manner, had glanced mockingly at Laura in her own imitation of a Goddess. Then Laura looked Selena up and down and surmised, "You could be a Goddess, you know. You're pretty. At 5'8", with naturally wavy, light caramel coloured hair falling to your shoulders, yep, a 13-year-old Goddess." Selena's eyebrows formed a questioning expression, setting off her blue/green eyes and dark eyelashes.

Continuing with the train of thought as a 13-year-old, Selena remembered inquiring of Laura, "As I am Goddess of the Moon, will you bow down to me when there's a full moon, Laura?" And so, Laura practiced bowing not so gracefully at first, and they both had a giggle.

As she touched a wall photo of Aunt Jenny with her fingertip, Selena recalled her aunt saying, "Selena, you are creative and resourceful, yet you are a dreamer, with a colossal imagination and always, always suspecting mysteries that are simply not there."

Aunt Jenny may say I am imagining mysteries that aren't there, but I suspect she is covering up stories that I deserve to know about.

From a habit of muttering when she was alone, she quietly stated, "I know that inquiring and asking questions is who I am. There're so many mysteries about Aunt Jenny's life that I can't solve. So many things brushed under the carpet, not answered in the 12 years I have lived here .... Not answered yet!"

Selena straightened a photo on the wall, reminiscing about some events in her life. She thought about the terrible family tragedy of losing both her parents.

Most of my family have passed away. I'm ticked off that I know barely anything about them, and Aunt Jenny absolutely refuses to talk about family no matter how often I ask. How the heck can I get her to talk?

Her thoughts continued to roam as she left the room and headed to her bedroom to get ready so she could catch the bus to her morning university class.

I'm well aware of my aunt being an eccentric and private lady who does not mix with people of the town. I'm concerned about Aunt Jenny's mounting reclusiveness. There're no friends with whom she associates. The neighbours are polite. But no one comes to visit her.

Then a memory popped into her mind:

Wait! Except for that couple and their children. Who were they? When I was 9 or 10, a young couple came to visit Aunt Jenny with a baby girl. I'd been upstairs reading. I remember coming downstairs to get a glass of milk and some cookies. I came into the living room, and a couple and child were with her.

"Selena, it is so wonderful to see you again. How are you?"

Nice to see me again? That was an odd comment. Who are these people?

"Oh, I'm good. How are you?"

"We are well, thank you. We just came for a quick visit. We have to leave soon."

Selena got her glass of milk and cookies. She returned to the living room with an extra cookie in hand.

"May I give this to your baby?"

"That would be lovely. You are always so thoughtful."

Thoughtful. Always. Huh? They know me?

Selena spent a few minutes playing with the child while also listening to the adult conversations.

I've found out nothing from listening to them. These people seem to really know Aunt Jenny.

There was a ping in Selena's memory as she studied the couple, but she could not dredge up an actual meeting with them. Her Aunt Jenny seemed genuinely happy and friendly while the couple visited.

Her Aunt Jenny had sent Selena outside to play, so she had not been in the house to say good-bye when the couple and baby left. Upon returning to the house, Selena came into the kitchen to see what the noise was. Aunt Jenny was clattering dishes in the sink, muttering to herself and appeared extremely agitated. Her movements were jerky. Selena feared dishes would be broken!

"Aunt Jenny, is everything okay? Where did the people go? Who are they? They knew who I was. I didn't know them."

"Just someone I knew from long ago, that's all." Selena saw fresh tears at the corners of her Aunt Jenny's eyes. She was going to quiz her aunt more, but her aunt had totally turned away, rigidly, from Selena to wipe the dishes.

"But …"

"I'm busy, Selena."

Many years after, near Selena's 13th birthday, the couple visited again, this time with a different baby in tow, and no little girl which Selena would have expected.

What have they done with the other child?

This time the couple again felt familiar to Selena in some indistinct memory she could not conjure up.

But something's definitely off with that memory of them. I'm confused, but oh well, I'm glad Aunt Jenny has someone visiting her.

"Good afternoon, Selena. Would you like to get a cookie for the baby? I know he would like one." The baby grabbed the cookie and grinned at Selena. "Oh, look how he adores you, Selena. I am extremely pleased that he likes you so much. We are glad that you got a chance to meet him. Please hold him for a little while."

Well, they're cute, for sure, even fun to play with. I like them, but why is there a different baby each time?

When this couple in other years came to visit Aunt Jenny with no baby at all, Selena remembered feeling curious, but unconcerned. Being a teenager, Selena did not spend a lot of time thinking about it. However, now that she was an adult, it was another mystery to add to her heap of mysteries. She did wonder where the people and their children lived and if they'd come again.

Do they live in this neighbourhood? I haven't met up with them in my walks.

As usual when questioned, her Aunt Jenny would say nothing about the couple except that she had known them many years ago, and they had come to see how she was.

Aunt Jenny should have known I'd just keep speculating. Who were they? They're vaguely familiar. I wasn't introduced, yet they seem to know me.

The last time they visited, Selena overheard her Aunt Jenny talking to them just prior to her being asked to take the dishes away into the kitchen. Her Aunt Jenny was crying and saying, "Please, will you come back for another visit sooner?"

Selena did not hear what the young couple answered, but she clearly heard her aunt's forlorn response. "All right. I will see you there then."

'I will see you there then.' Where would she see them?? Here in Ottawa? Was she going somewhere? Am I going somewhere?

Now, with her memory flashing back to these mysterious visits, Selena had questions in her mind. She remembered coming from the kitchen only a few minutes later and being surprised that the young couple had left.

I didn't hear the creaky door open. After each visit, Aunt Jenny's needy of me. Their last visit made her sad again when they left. What do they have to do with Aunt Jenny? Why do they make her sad? What the heck!

Selena forcefully brought her mind back to the present. "Enough! I want to grasp more meaning from those memories, but I've got to leave. All these thoughts rushing through my head will make me late."

2

Austin — The Beginning

Her Aunt Jenny had given Selena a diary for her 15th birthday. It remained blank until after she turned 16 and started her driver training.

This entry was added to her diary:

"Aunt Jenny gave me this lovely, embossed diary on my 15th birthday. I was extremely excited to get it. It has my name in gold letters. It feels very special.

Until today, I didn't have anything to put in here. Now I can tell you, dear diary, all my secrets.

I hope I am not being too obvious in wanting to spend more time getting driver training. With the neighbours next door, Theodore could take me, but I always wait for Austin to be free. Do I think he suspects me? I love how he looks. He's nice."

Two weeks after:

This entry was added to her diary:

"He asked me to sit beside him at lunch today – right during class, he leaned over to speak to me. The

other girls in class are giving me looks. They noticed something is going on between Austin and me. He is so good looking."

Four weeks later:
This entry was added to her diary:

"The first time he kissed me, I felt like my feet had left the ground!!!!"

Bud Semple, their next-door neighbour, sighed and shook his head each time he saw Selena. Since her Aunt Jenny was not an outgoing person, he took pity on Selena.

For the 12 years that Selena had lived next door to them, Mr. Semple would make comments, such as: "Um, are you going to the new movie at the theatre tonight, Selena? Karen and I are going, and we'd like to have you come with us." (Aunt Jenny did not believe in moviegoing). "Will you get your driver's license this year? Karen and I'd like to teach you when we teach our boys." (Aunt Jenny did not feel Selena needed to drive around, wasting time).

Selena had been friends with their twin boys, Austin and Theodore, since she moved in. By the time she was 16, the relationship changed for her. Her chest fluttered at the thought of seeing Austin during driver training.

Karen and Bud Semple did take Selena driver training. In the end, her Aunt Jenny said that if they wanted to do it, it would be good to have Selena be able to run errands. When either Karen or Bud were coaching their own boys to drive, they invited Selena along. It became quite a lot of fun to be there when the boys were driving and to share driving lessons.

After both boys obtained their full licences, Austin took Selena around the neighbourhood streets and parking lots to practice. Karen and Bud still ensured that Selena had proper driving instruction by training her themselves.

By then, Austin and Selena were dating and often stopped for ice cream or to go for a walk in the park.

This entry was added to her diary:

> *"We enjoy being together other than driver training these past years. He's out of high school now and taking a pre-firefighting course. When I graduate, we may be thinking of something more serious than just dating. I could marry him."*

3

Rufus and Caylie

Although Aunt Jenny was distant to Selena, Selena does not doubt that Aunt Jenny loves her in her own way.

This entry was added to her diary:

"I feel a love of sorts from Aunt Jenny. She shows affection to me with pats to my shoulder, a smile, a hand squeeze. I need to feel that affection. And we are both fond of Aunt Jenny's sweet little Poodle/Cocker Spaniel dog named Rufus. I know that dog loves me."

Selena giggled now as she thought of Rufus. She walked the eight-year-old dog faithfully every day. Rufus loved the walks, and Selena loved walking him. Rufus was attentive and obeyed 'Sit, Down, Stay, Heel, Come, Do You Want To Go Outside, Do You Want To Go For A Walk' and most excitedly, 'Do You Want A Treat'?

"Rufus, would you like to go for a walk?"

"Ruff, ruff, ruff, ruff!"

"Oh, Rufus Goofus, you have such a personality! I'll call you Curly Joe today. Just look at your fur! You do need a good brushing." Rufus didn't care what she called him because he just wanted to be with her. He wagged his tail when Aunt Jenny approached him; however, Rufus ran to Selena and became enthusiastic to see her.

The cat was another, much newer, character in the house, for character was the only way to describe her. The cat had been hanging around their garden and side door. She did not mind Rufus at all and came right up to him. Rufus thought the cat would make a good playmate. The cat was a lot more hesitant toward Selena and her aunt than she was to Rufus.

Neither woman thought they needed a cat in the house. However, after a week of putting up photos of the stray cat at stores around the neighbourhood, calling veterinarian clinics and checking with the Humane Society, her aunt brought the cat into the house as a stray. As her Aunt Jenny shook her head at the kitty, her short brown curls bobbed this way and that.

Aunt Jenny said in her determined manner, "Since this kitty seems to be here to stay, she needs a bath. She is quite grungy. She also needs proper feeding – too skinny, and her fur looks very thin." So, Aunt Jenny volunteered Selena for the task of bathing a cat that did not want to be bathed.

A little while later, after blowing her hair out of her eyes, Selena held onto the kitty tighter.

"Sweetie! Yeah, I'm sorry you don't particularly trust me or like water, but look how smart you are. You're frightened, but you don't put your claws out. What a good kitty." When the bathing and drying was over, this was the prettiest cat Selena had ever seen.

"In fact, I've been reading about an Irish celebration and it's also a word for companion called a Ceilidh. It's pronounced the same as Caylie. Since we don't have a name for you, pretty girl, I formally christen you, 'Caylie Ceilidh Pretty Lady.'"

"Purr, purr, puuurrrrrr".

As she petted the newly named cat, Selena called out, "Rufus, come see your new friend. Rufus, meet Caylie Ceilidh Pretty Lady. Oh, look at you two!" The dog sniffed, almost knocking Caylie Ceilidh Pretty Lady over in the process. The cat purred loudly. "You're going to get along just fine."

Selena sometimes underestimated her Aunt Jenny. Out came a

cat tray and litter, a couple of cat toys and a little harness and leash.

"What!" Selena exclaimed.

"Well, you just never know what I might have stored away, do you?" No other explanation was given even after several questions.

She's full of surprises.

Selena made an appointment with their veterinarian for after work that day. She would also pick up some proper cat food even though the kitty didn't mind the leftovers she had been given in the meantime. Selena decided to take both Rufus and Caylie Ceilidh Pretty Lady to the veterinarian.

Her Aunt Jenny then produced another animal crate when Selena brought out Rufus' travel crate.

"There you go again. I thought I'd have to put them both in Rufus' crate. That'd have been an adventure."

"Never you mind. I have my secret stashes all over this huge house. There are nooks and crannies everywhere. I am not the only person to have lived in this house in over 55 years." Then Aunt Jenny's face closed, and she walked away.

Conversation over!

The Vet's office was just a few blocks away. Selena took her Aunt Jenny's Ford Escape. Pulling up to the outside of the Vet's office, she always appreciated the colourful outside stucco, overpainted with pictures of cats, dogs, even guinea pigs and a few birds. After checking in with the receptionist and waiting for a few minutes, she was ushered into a check-up room. The Veterinarian, Dr. Josephine Owens, a few strands of her hair gone astray with dark strands falling out of the clips, entered and greeted Selena and the pets.

"Selena, so good to see you again."

"Hello, Dr. Owens."

"I keep telling you to call me Josephine – even in the office. You've been coming here long enough, and we're friends."

Introductions of the kitty, Caylie Ceilidh Pretty Lady, ensued. After doing the check up on both animals, Dr. Owens looked at the chart and announced, "Good health, good teeth. I've given Caylie Clady Pretty…"

Selena politely interrupted, "Nope, both names are pronounced the same."

Dr. Josephine Owens tried again with a laugh, "I've given Caylie Ceilidh Pretty Lady her shots and examined her. She's slender, indicating that she's been on her own for a while. Rufus is also doing well. He didn't need his shots yet but examining him regularly is always smart because he's running around in your woods. Best to do two for one. They get along well, don't they?"

"I think they'll make a good team. Ceilidh means 'celebration' and 'companion'. I'm happy that Rufus and Caylie will be companions. I've become excited to have her in the household. She's cute too."

"Yes, those blurred spots on the kitty, the fact she's so tall, long and slim, the size of her feet and ears and that little spacing in her cheek fur indicate she's part Bengal as well as part tabby. She's a beauty!"

"Oh, I wondered about those spots!"

"I'm delighted to see Rufus again and to have someone as compassionate as you are to bring in a new pet for examination. I'll text in a couple of weeks to see how you're getting along with Caylie."

Once out in the reception area, Selena requested good quality cat food. Payment was made and a thank you given.

When Selena arrived back at her Aunt Jenny's house, she set about feeding the newest arrival and preparing supper for herself and her aunt. Rufus wagged his tail.

"Oh you! Rufus, would you like a treat?" Selena could almost hear him, "Well, what do you think, Selena?" Instead, there was "Ruff, ruff" wag, wag and scampering across the floor to lick her outstretched fingers.

Selena began tidying the kitchen. Something popped into her mind, unbidden. It startled her:

It would be nice to have my own place to clean.

She pushed any idea of moving out of her mind, and she began to dance and sing an Ed Sheehan song while wiping the countertop. The yellow loose-fitting wrap skirt she wore bounced along with her beat. Every time Selena danced and sang, Rufus howled along with her.

"Baby, I'm dancing in the dark"

"Howw Howwwwwwl, hooowwwl."

"With you between my arms"

"You're hilarious, Rufus. Sing."

"Howw, howwl, howwwwwwl, hooowwwl."

She ended with her singing, "Darling, you look perfect tonight."

This entry was added to her diary:

> *"Should I get a place of my own once I turn 20 in August? I like my life with Aunt Jenny, and I'd miss her company and interesting conversations about history and geography. I'm fine here. I love Aunt Jenny and she's my family."*

Afterward, when supper was cooking, Selena took Rufus for his daily walk, which was so much more than a walk because Rufus loved the paths, the smells, the detours and, um, the bushes. Rufus loved the bushes. His lead was retractable. Usually, since no one was around, his lead was let out to the longest length or even off leash completely. Rufus was happy to run ahead.

"You are so curious, Rufus Goofus. They say, 'curiosity killed the cat'. Your nose will get you in some trouble someday."

She let Rufus off his leash. He appreciated having more to smell and less restriction. Selena loved these walks as well. She had lots of time to think at home, but the thoughts she thought out walking in the woods with the fresh air were quiet and pleasant. Selena also loved the scent of the wood, the drying leaves, the new aromas of spring emerging. Birds call, and a trio of Blue Jays swoop overhead. She smiled, sighing contentedly.

The wind picked up, blowing in different directions. Rufus put his face into the wind, smelling all the good dog smells of the woods. Suddenly, the wind shifted again and stirred the branches, whisking Selena's long hair toward her face. A moment later, it was almost calm.

With the wind swirling in different directions, a poem struck her.

I need to put this in my diary before I forget it.

She made up the poem as she went along, reciting it to Rufus. He stopped to look at her, listening politely and then to sniff the air and leaves whipping around him.

"Okay Rufus, home we go."

"*Awww,*" said Rufus in Selena's imagination. However, Rufus just did an about turn, came to get his leash on, sniffed the leash, then her shoes, the bushes, the rocks and everything on their way home, and, with several stops, they arrived back at Aunt Jenny's house.

After supper, her aunt simply said before disappearing, "I will be in my room for a couple of hours Selena. I have some reading to do."

"All right, Rufus, that leaves you and me to entertain ourselves. What'd you have to say for yourself? What've you been up to today? Did you rake up the leaves like I asked you to?"

Rufus replied as usual, "Ruff, ruff" (I love you too). Selena translated the different inflections. Selena knew what Rufus meant when he barked.

The poem she created on her walk was added to her diary:

"The wind is on the tear
Blowing on my face and hair.
Through the grass and all the trees
I see clearly each little breeze

Making its familiar rendezvous
Over the hills and every slough.

Yesterday the wind did whistle
Tossing every flower and thistle
This way and that way in its haste
Giving the world a tiny taste
Of the scorn it holds for everything,
Letting us know who is the king.

Today there is no wind at all.
I cannot see him though I call.
I know he will be back again
Bringing along either sun or rain.
But, today, the world is still –
Not a breeze on land or hill.

Tomorrow the wind may be a baby
Cooing softly as if he is happy.
Patient fingers will move through the grass,
To show to us its peacefulness.
Slowly the flowers will move left to right
On a day consisting of a wind so slight."

4

Closet Mystery

THE CONVERSATION AT SUPPERS followed a trend. Selena spoke about her day, but the conversation came back to Aunt Jenny's books. Jenny Jenkins was an author who had written numerous history and geography books, several of which have been published.

I've read all Aunt Jenny's books. I enjoy them so much. She's engaging and knowledgeable. The public also loves the books. They sell wildly.

"I don't need to publish every book I write. My other books are just for my own personal satisfaction. I am making great progress with this book, Selena. I have over 200,000 words so far, and I have done revisions to the previous chapters as well. I have so much more information in my head that I am extremely excited about."

"That's great, Aunt Jenny. Where do you come up with all your information?"

"Here and there, Selena. It requires a lot of research." Then her aunt hurried off to her bedroom again.

As Selena sat at the table, she pondered her aunt's personality.

Aunt Jenny is always busy, always locking herself away in her own bedroom, writing one of her books, researching or reading. She's very private.

This entry was added to her diary:

"There are mysteries that have happened in this house. One of these days, I'll get to solve the mysteries I keep envisioning. If only I had more answers than questions. If only ... What? If only I had an aunt that answered questions."

Aunt Jenny told Selena many times that she did not mind when Selena had friends in the house. Selena did the cooking and cleaning up. Her aunt would put in a perfunctory appearance, have supper with her friends and chat a little. Then she would say a 'good night' as regular as clockwork.

"Well, that was a nice supper and good company. I am glad that you came over tonight, but I have some research and writing on my book that I need to get to." Her friends were happy with Aunt Jenny's company, but the conversations always flowed in a more spirited manner afterward.

Selena could understand why Aunt Jenny did not mind being in her own bedroom. It was really a very private suite with an extensive sitting area used as a study, bookshelves galore, bedroom and a four-piece bathroom.

In another indication that her aunt preferred her privacy, Aunt Jenny always closed her closet door when Selena knocked and came into the bedroom. That was one more thing that Selena noticed that seemed peculiar as Selena walked into her aunt's bedroom. It might be nothing, but her aunt consistently shut her closet door when Selena knocked.

Surely, that is odd to always rush to close your closet door. I see that as a mystery. But Aunt Jenny would change her expression toward me showing her irritation at this subject of a 'mystery'.

Selena glanced toward that closet as it was being closed. She did not want to appear too prying. She entirely respected Aunt Jenny's privacy, but deep down she *knew* there was something mystifying about that closet. What she saw with her eyes was just an ordinary tidy closet. What she saw with her *mind* was a mystery!

"Maybe there is no mystery at all, but I don't believe it. Something is up with that closet. Maybe a sign of Obsessive Compulsive Disorder? My aunt does have some interesting characteristics, but she is who she is."

Selena was very aware that she tended to make up too many stories about happenings and that she should leave it at that.

Aunt Jenny has told me that for so many years. But I can't stop my mind being awhirl with the mysteries around me.

"What's in your closet?" Selena had asked when she had just come to live with Aunt Jenny at age 7. "You're so very tidy, auntie."

"Well, Selena dear, I like to keep everything in its place. Do not wonder about my closet. It is my own private affair. You are not to enter my closet where I keep my personal items. Ever. You may call me Aunt. I do not prefer auntie at all."

"Okay, Aunt Jenny. I won't go there."

Still ...

Aunt Jenny's house was continually a source for Selena's imagination. There are 17 rooms, not all of them used. Many are totally shut up and some rooms locked.

Selena had also inquired once, "Why are the rooms shut up? I'd like to be able to explore them. There's so many places I can't go."

In her matter-of-fact tone and stern manner, Aunt Jenny said, "They are not to be looked into Selena. Everything is cleaned. All the furniture is covered. There is no use keeping those rooms open. No one is going to use them anymore."

This entry was added to her diary:

> *"I'm so darn polite. I'd love to snoop in the closed-up rooms. But I can't do it without Aunt Jenny's permission. There's so much that I can't see here. I love to explore. Someday when Aunt Jenny has time or is done her latest book or feels better or realizes how curious I am, then I*

can be shown into those rooms.

In the meantime, I just have to make up all the stories.

Selena remembered her aunt telling her that her father, Grandfather Arthur, had been an architect and her Grandmother Olive, a decorator. Whenever Selena asked Aunt Jenny about family, Aunt Jenny would compress her lips and not answer.

I appreciate Aunt Jenny telling me that little tidbit. That was some info at least.

Recently, Selena had brought up the subject again. "Really Aunt Jenny, I feel that I have lived here for so many years now. It must be time that you can share our family stories."

Aunt Jenny said, "Selena dear, there is nothing to tell."

"Aunt Jenny!"

"Then know this. My own mother may as well have been an only child as her sister went back to Russia 25 years ago, and we have not ever had communication. My own father had no siblings either. Your father and I had no siblings except ourselves. Your other grandparents on your mother, Anne's, side had no siblings. We are not a prolific family. All your grandparents are gone. As you see, I had no husband or family myself. Your mother and father have passed away. There is only you and I left in this world."

Selena started to speak, but she was silenced by a stern look. "They are all gone. There is absolutely nothing, nothing more to ever say on the subject of family."

Her aunt then immediately walked away, muttering to herself with shoulders rounded, her head down, and Selena noticed her footsteps were heavy and listless.

That was that, as Selena knew from experience – there was no additional information coming from Aunt Jenny. Selena loved stories and there had to be stories here. There seemed to be hidden, untold stories and mysteries in many aspects of her Aunt Jenny's life.

This entry was added to her diary later:

> *"I really do get frustrated that I live here and yet I know nothing more and cannot get a more personal answer when I ask a question. What the heck is that about? But that's the most information I've ever heard.*
>
> *I'm convinced someday I'll get more information out of her. There's much more to find out."*

"Someday, she'll think I'm old enough to know." Imagining that eventuality, Selena thought of so many questions that needed answers, and she felt she would sit Aunt Jenny down with a cup of tea and some fancy pastries – then answers might be forthcoming.

Soon, I hope. Only a month ago I approached her, and my queries were put off again. It's time!

This entry was added to her diary:

> *"I'm going to keep track of these queries I have for Aunt Jenny. Maybe it's childish, maybe there's nothing being kept from me. But what about:*
>
> - *My grandparents lived here for about a year after I came. Aunt Jenny won't talk about them.*
> - *What were my grandparents like?*
> - *How did my grandparents die? = I was young, but why can't I remember anything?"*
> - *What about when Aunt Jenny and my father, Elliott, grew up in this same home?*
> - *What information should I know about when my parents died?*
> - *Why don't I have memories of visiting before I came to live here?*
> - *What was my father like when he was a baby, as an adolescent?*

- *What was Aunt Jenny like?*
- *Was she always this private and stern?*
- *Who were that couple?*
- *Where do they live?*
- *Where are the children?*
- *Did my grandfather build this house? = He was an architect*
- *Did my grandmother decorate this house with the ornaments and painting? = She was a decorator*
- *Who would have stayed in which room?*
- *Had there been parties here with friends and family over?*

As Selena stood at the window, a smile gracing her face, she gazed out at the yard and outbuildings, and she reminisced about the years living with her Aunt Jenny as she often did.

I love living here with Aunt Jenny. My adventures outside are wonderful memories. Looking out over the yard and woodlands that I see from my window always make me appreciative of being here.

Ever since Selena was a little girl when she came to live in this wonderful setting, she loved to explore the yard, the garden, the woodlands and the outbuildings.

Those three outbuildings have always fascinated me. They were fodder for all sorts of imaginative thoughts for a 7-year-old. A toolshed with all its implements, gardening tools and old riding mower was one of the first things that got my imagination working.

There were stories to make up about the old tool shed as Aunt Jenny said there used to be a full-time gardener. However, Mr. Eric Brisbane, the current gardener, worked part time. He came over every week to do yardwork and mow during the growing season and several times a year to do the arduous work, particularly in spring and fall. He seemed to know exactly when to show up to do the pruning, hoeing and weeding during the various seasons. Selena laughed at herself, remembering that when she was younger, she used to imagine that the other gardener had died or was killed in a gardening accident, maybe he had fallen off the mower and that he was buried under the garden shed.

Maybe I used to be over imaginative.

There was a second shed which from the time Selena had arrived, remained empty. Of course, this had set her mind wondering too as to what purpose it had. There were burn marks on the walls and ceiling. Again, she remembered her thoughts as a young child:

Was there an explosion? A fire? What had been in that shed? What had it been used for? Smuggling? Why was it cleared out? Who used it?

Selena and Laura had played in that shed and used it for many made-up games. They had dragged in scrap wood and fallen tree branches from the woodlands to make pretend furniture for a playhouse. They had built pirate ships, corrals for the animals; they pretended to be the animals, wagon trains…

Such fun times! Laura was the best childhood friend!

Her Aunt Jenny had an interest a few years ago in pottery, and she did not mind if Selena puttered around in the old pottery studio built as a huge shed in the back yard. Almost a year ago, Aunt Jenny had said, "If you can get some use out of the equipment and supplies, please do. I had been going to donate the whole works to the local high school. If you use the equipment and supplies, then that will save me the trouble of contacting the high school to arrange for them to pick everything up."

Selena found that she was frequently daydreaming about creating things. She relayed to her aunt how excited she was to discover this pottery studio.

"How come you stopped making pottery?"

"I thought it would be rewarding, but it takes too much patience for anyone to take it seriously."

Her aunt had surprised Selena several weeks ago by saying, "I just ordered and had delivered three boxes of clay that you can use. They are in the pottery shed. It will keep for a couple of years if it is cool in the studio, and you ensure that the boxes and bags are kept tightly sealed. The glazes in the pottery studio will be dry from age and neglect, but if you can figure out how to get them into useable order again, they are all yours. Add a little water to each dry jar and mix them up. All my tools and equipment are there. If you ignore using the items and equipment, then I shall dispose of everything eventually."

Selena was delighted that day, over the moon in fact. She and Rufus danced a little jig. Selena had taken the jars of glaze, opened each one and found that they were not dry as bone. She added only a little bit of water, depending on the amount of glaze left in the jars.

When I mixed the contents, the jars should be good enough to glaze something with. I need advice on whether I should be adding more water. I'll just keep them a little moist until I learn if more water and mixing is required.

Hoping to figure out the pottery on her own, Selena attempted to make little bowls with just her hands. She was not even considering tackling that pottery wheel. Selena found that her little bowls cracked after the second day, and they would be no use to anyone. However, she kept them on one of the many shelves. Recently, after several attempts to create something that did not crack, Selena gave up the idea of figuring it all out on her own. She decided that the library may have hobby books and that there should be something on pottery.

That should be a simple solution.

It seemed to Selena that her aunt was missing out. Selena has imagined Aunt Jenny instructing her how to use the wheel properly and to sculpt the clay. Surely, she knew how.

5

The Clinic

As Selena walked up to her workplace after her morning class, she cast an affectionate glance at the building's sign. *THE CARING MEDICAL CLINIC. That's what the sign reads, but we all say, "the Clinic."*

Many entries before and after were entered, but these were her entries for the Clinic.

At age 17, this entry had been added to her diary:

> *"Dear Diary, I'm excited. Now I'm volunteering during high school at The Caring Medical Clinic. I think the name is a play on words because the main doctors are named Carey."*

At age 18, this entry had been added to her diary:

> *"Now, I have been working part time at The Clinic while attending University of Ottawa.*
>
> *It's a pre-requisite to get my degree. They are fantastic people. The Doctors are professional, but nice."*

The first staff member Selena encountered that afternoon was

Elizabeth Wheale. Elizabeth kept the patients coddled and gave support to them in her maternal and protective way.

"Good afternoon, Selena. You're here early. Are you ready for more fun and games with the patients?"

"You're funny. I'm trying to imagine you asking Dr. Carey Senior that!"

"Holy schmoley, I think I'll keep that comment just for you. I doubt I'd even ask young Dr. Kev that question. You're the youngster here. I can tease you."

"You are a big tease, Madam Receptionist."

As Selena left the friendly receptionist behind, she dissected her feelings, surprised at them.

I'm feeling a little testy, darn. I know that I'm the youngster here.

Selena entered her little cubbyhole office and perused the files laid out for her with patient names from this morning as well as who would be in this afternoon. She continued to contemplate her situation off and on while getting ready for the afternoon. It had been agreed by her bosses that every Monday morning Selena would spend the morning taking one of her demanding university classes. She also has Wednesday evening classes, and the doctors were pleased to see her further her education.

Elizabeth was just teasing. I like her so much that it shouldn't bother me.

This entry was added to her diary later:

> *"I was annoyed at Elizabeth today – She called me the youngster! I should have thicker skin. I'm younger than most of my university classmates and the same at my job. It's because I was accelerated in early grades. It shows how hard I worked. Since graduating from the international baccalaureate program, I've attended classes at the University of Ottawa for two whole years.*

Aunt Jenny says I need to help pay my way through university. I don't mind. It's good for me to learn about money and saving."

Today Selena set up patients' tests, assisted in analyzing the results, kept a neat, typed computer record of each patient's visit and recorded what the day's problem was. As Selena went about her work, she knew the time might be coming for her to change her employment.

I could think about changing jobs. I'm eager to do more testing. I want to be able to use all my training, to do research in medical sciences, molecular studies and treatment of human diseases.

I'd previously looked into the details about the degree I want. I need to get a bachelor's degree in a physical or a forensic science to complete the degree in Biology.

When Selena was not busy with her work and activities (the Clinic, university classes, homework, cooking, daily home tidying, checking out travel information), then she was avidly reading medical crime novels. The Clinic also had shelves of books, manuals and pamphlets for her evaluation.

Weekly, Selena spent time at the library to discover more medical mysteries to solve, along with her passion for old records and medical information. It was common to find her on her hour-long lunch, poring through those de-identified medical records that Dr. Brent Carey had retained for the 30 years of his practice. The office procedure was to keep them until they ran out of room upstairs. Selena looked through these records randomly. There were no identifying names; however, she liked the medical history involved as she attempted to understand the stories.

One report stood out for her. The woman from a small neighbouring town had come to see Dr. Carey Sr. regularly. Mrs. "X" always reported having fallen; bumped into open cupboard doors in the night; or being careless in some manner or another. The notes that Dr. Carey, Sr. wrote down indicated that he did not believe her. He had suggested that she and her minister husband attend marriage counselling.

On Mrs. "X" last appointment, Dr. Carey Sr. had advised her that she needed to report these "accidents" to the police immediately or that he would call them. Mrs. "X" had stopped coming to Dr. Carey Sr. at that point.

What a horrible situation for this Mrs. "X" to find herself in.

There was a newspaper article someone had slipped inside the file with the names blackened out. "REVEREND FREED – NOT GUILTY VERDICT". The gist of the article was that this minister had been verbally and physically abusing his wife for ten years. He was released when many of the parishioners made personal declarations emphasizing his amicable and virtuous personality, stating he was a respected and dignified citizen.

The townspeople had organized a public outcry, and the newspaper reporter felt the congregation had manipulated the small-town Judge. The minister and his wife had quickly moved away and had not been back.

I can't get her story out of my mind. It makes me incredibly sad, but I feel reassured with the sense of how happy my mother and father had been through their marriage.

An important enjoyment about being in the Clinic was the at-work friendships. The staff was not sizable – there were three doctors, one nurse, a bookkeeper, an office receptionist and a medical assistant.

Selena remembered determining, on her first day, that the senior partner was a no-nonsense doctor. Dr. Brent Carey told patients what he believed they should change to help themselves with their own health – in no uncertain terms. Dr. Carey had been coming out with a patient to the then empty reception area when Selena was arriving that first day.

"Your diabetes will indeed get better with this prescription. However, as I advised you, you must change your eating and living habits for your health to substantially improve. I want to see you in two months."

"Sure, Dr. Carey. I will follow your instructions."

Indeed, Selena recalled, that the patient came back looking ruddy complexioned and healthier after two months. This afternoon, Dr. Carey Sr. poked his head into her work area.

Abruptly brought back to the here and now by Dr. Brent Carey saying to her, "Good afternoon, Selena. How are you today? How was your class this morning?"

"Good afternoon, Dr. Carey. I'm well, thank you. You know I love my classes. It went well. How are you?"

"Today is another good day for our clinic. We had the usual Monday morning patients. Right, there are two more patient reports that need doing immediately. Have a good day, Selena." The door closed behind him.

And poof! He's gone back to work.

That afternoon, Selena spent two hours working diligently through her work files and doing up reports. She had also assisted with the 14 patients the three doctors had seen that afternoon. At the staff break, Selena gingerly entered the staff room.

Seeing the petite and fit, bronze-haired, Mary Chen and Elizabeth, she admonished, "That scent! Have you guys brought baked goodies again?"

"We can't resist attempting to give you some smothering mothering, Selena," was Mary's quick reply. "Besides being the office manager, I also manage the baking department."

"You're just trying to fatten me up," complained Selena, eating another pastry.

Dr. Kevin Carey strode into the lounge. Selena admired the way Dr. Kev (as all the junior staff secretly call him) handled his patients. Dr. Kevin Carey was different from his father in his manner toward his patients. He had a friendly smile and a sympathetic ear for each of them.

This entry was added to her diary later:

> *"I think Dr. Carey, Jr. is genuinely concerned in a brotherly way for his patients and co-workers, taking an interest in everyone. I think he's a saint.*
>
> *His patients respect and adore him.*
> *As do all the staff.*
> *As do I..."*

Mary and Elizabeth had their own grown-up children about the same age as Dr. Kev. Mary chuckled, "And we'll make sure young Dr. Carey ends up with half a dozen of whatever we bring on any day."

Patting his lean stomach, he replied earnestly, "Thank you. I always enjoy your muffins, biscuits and tarts. I'll never complain about your pampering us all."

Listening to this banter reminded Selena of Dr. Kev's good friend, Jeremy McGregor. Dr. Kev had gone to medical school with Jeremy McGregor's older brother, Daniel. Jeremy was now Dr. Kev's best buddy. Jeremy owned his own computer company, and he appeared to think that life was a lark, which, with him around, it was. Jeremy and Dr. Kev made a good pair, complementing each other – Jeremy, being a comedian and Dr. Kev being serious.

Jeremy often showed up at the Clinic to get together with Dr. Kev for lunch. When Jeremy visited the Clinic, he always made time to chat with Selena, asking how she was doing and discussing an eventual purchase of a computer.

"Come into my shop at any time, Selena. I'll take good care of you, even give you a deal. Let me know when you're ready. We'll find you exactly what you need."

"Yep Jeremy, I'll be in one of these days. It's getting closer to final term exams. A laptop would be helpful for exam preparation and in my classes. If you're a good salesman, you'll be able to make a sale."

Always, after speaking with Selena, Jeremy headed over to visit with Bethany Kothare, the newest doctor in the clinic, and Penelope Sanchez, the clinic's nurse. His conversations were somewhat like, "Come on ladies, let's go for lunch. I can stand up old Kevin today and instead take all three of you ladies out for a fantastic lunch. I may even pay."

Turning her mind from those musings, a smile brightened her face as she pictured her Aunt Jenny's enchanting house, garden and surrounding forest. Selena's mind settled on a thought of her Aunt Jenny sitting on the patio, discussing gardening with Mr. Brisbane. Feelings of great fondness for her Aunt encompassed her.

Selena tidied up her teacup and pastry plate.

Now to get back to work.

6

A Real Mystery

When Selena came home from work, Aunt Jenny was walking very slowly down the stairs.

"Aunt Jenny, is everything all right? Are you feeling okay?"

Her Aunt Jenny's stiff-lipped reply was, "I am on my way to see Dr. Robertson. I did not have an appointment. I called, and he will see me."

"You look quite tired. I'll drive you."

"No, I will be fine, thank you."

"But…" Selena started to argue, but, seeing a familiar unwavering look on Aunt Jenny's face, she knew any further conversation was forbidden.

Rufus met Selena at the stairs, tail wagging hopefully. "We'll do our usual walk in a little while, Rufus."

"Rrrrr, ruff!"

The house was large enough that Aunt Jenny had a housecleaner come in one day every two weeks to do a massive clean, but after work each afternoon and before supper, Selena did a quick tidying up of the house. After she had done a little tidying and set out what she would make for supper, Selena climbed the stairs. She knew her own room was clean. This was an instilled habit borne from Aunt Jenny's having drilled into her head that it must be tidied each morning.

Selena entered her aunt's bedroom, knowing to clean just in the bedroom suite, not the closet – as per previous instructions.

Aunt Jenny mustn't have been feeling herself. There's a lot more stuff out of place! She's usually quite meticulous.

She bent to retrieve a photo album which must have fallen from a shelf as it was now propped on the floor beside the bookshelves in an unceremonious fashion, some pages askew. Engrossed in her own thoughts, Selena picked it up, turned a page or two.

Muttering to herself, "Hey, this is great! I haven't seen this album before. There's dates shown on each bottom right corner showing these are relatively recent photos."

Suddenly, her eyes moved from the current dates to the photographs themselves. Something flashed in her mind – that implausible, unsettling feeling of déjà vu. Selena's eyes seared each photograph. She was looking at a photograph of the young couple who had visited.

What? But this photograph is a decade ago, not recent!

"I'm sure of it. Aren't I? I know this is the same couple. There is the baby girl. But… Is that the only reason they look familiar to me? I can't grab in my mind what's nagging at me. I hate it when that happens."

Continuing to turn page after page, Selena found more photographs of that same couple looking older. Then her Aunt Jenny appeared in some photographs. Aunt Jenny was holding the little girl and a baby. Then there were photographs of the little girl growing older as well as the baby boy and more photographs as he grew into a small child. But these dates are crazy! These dates do *not* match the time frame of the people in them!

Selena checked the dates on all the photographs again. Some photos appeared to be from a different camera and just a different picture style. She slammed the album shut, set it down for half a second. Then, picking it up, she looked again at the photographs. She strode to the window, still holding the photo album, looked at the album again in the light from the window.

Aloud, she said, "Well, this isn't possible! Holy Christmas! Some photographs have a framed calendar sitting on the mantel. The calendar clinches the years these photographs were taken!"

"What the blazes is happening here?" she shouted to no one present.

What have I gotten into? What the heck? I can't be losing my mind.

Selena found herself plopped on a bedroom stool; her eyes were closed tight. She took a deep breath and then another. She opened her eyes, started again at the beginning of the album, turning page after page, again becoming overwhelmed, her breath coming in small gasps. Selena turned the last page. She felt panic-stricken.

Where has my scientific mind gone? These photos aren't possible.

She closed her eyes, shook her head to clear it. Opening her eyes, she glanced around the bedroom. Her gaze settled on the closet door. She was stunned that her aunt's closet door stood a few inches ajar.

"I'm not supposed to look in there."

Surprised and sitting still, but keeping her gaze glued on the closet, Selena slowly became aware that through the opening between the rows of her aunt's clothing, there was another door at the back of the closet.

Oh my gosh. Now what? Is my mind playing tricks on me? My aunt's closet door is never open. After the shock of the photos, I'm not certain I want to see anything more. But what's the second door?

Aware she should not be snooping, but curiosity compelling her forward, she pushed the clothes aside farther and there indeed was a door. Finding the knob and attempting to turn it, she discovered that the door was locked!

Of course, it's locked. This is what Aunt Jenny doesn't want me to see. Where does this door lead?

Still unable to stop herself, she reached up above the door frame to see if a key was there as above other doorways in the house. Selena did not find a key. Glancing around, she saw beside her a large ornate lion ornament.

An ornament I've never seen before.

She reached in and again no key. With her fingers still in the mouth of the lion, Selena had an image of her aunt's face looking as fierce as the lion, admonishing her. She realized with a jolt what she was doing.

I can't do this. Here's a real, actual, not imagined, mystery! It'll take some thinking about how to approach Aunt Jenny since she guards her life stories so closely. I must know.

When her aunt arrived home, Selena was eager to approach her. However, she could see that she would need to wait until tomorrow. Her Aunt Jenny was very distant and distracted. She was obviously upset, and Selena did not want to upset her further. Her aunt barely ate her supper.

"Aunt Jenny, how'd your appointment go today? Is everything okay?"

"It is nothing, Selena. I will be fine. I am tired from too much researching my book today. That is all." Then her aunt excused herself with her practiced expression that allowed no further conversation.

I think there was a wince of what? Pain, discomfort?

This entry was added to her diary later:

> *"I found a photo album today. This can be added*
> *to my mysteries. The house décor is not possible! These*

pictures show a different rug and wallpaper, although it's this house.

And a calendar showed dates that would have made Aunt Jenny young, but she's the same age she is now in the photos. Those children are growing older, but she's staying the same. This is surreal.

I think Aunt Jenny is wearing clothes that she purchased recently."

Added: "The dates must be wrong!"

"Aunt Jenny had an unscheduled doctor's appointment today. She seems very tired. She's so young, so it can't be anything serious – I hope not. She's a good person, and I love her. Dr. Robertson will take care of her.

I'll chat with her tomorrow. Hopefully, she'll be feeling better. Then I'll ask about that photo album and mention the hidden closet door. I can hardly stand the suspense until then."

7

Jenny Jenkins – Months Ago

T*HESE MEETINGS TOMORROW WITH Julian and Tessa are very important.*

Through the elevated window, Jenny Jenkins noticed the sun was setting, the sky tinted in pinks and orange, the clouds high in the sky. She jotted down the instructions that she would review with her accountant and her lawyer at tomorrow's meetings. Her chestnut brown hair was becoming peppered with gray, her physical appearance looked trim, her face slightly thinning, and the wrinkles had been held at bay.

Under her breath, she said, "Soon winter will be over. We will be into spring. A time of life and regrowth. Will I be here? I can't leave until I speak with her."

- Update my Will;
- Change ownership of house;
- Insurance;
- All bills and accounts.

I hope she will not be disappointed or angry with me. How can I expect her to understand why I am doing all this? I am trying to sort it all out before I go away. I will explain everything to her. I am just so drained living in this manner. I need to get back there very soon. Where I was happiest. She must understand. That is all there is to it.

- Make notes of how to use this room.
- Tell her why I am making these choices.

I must write the letter as well. Just in case.

8

Not Aunt Jenny

The next morning as Selena opened the blind in her room and peeked out her window, she saw that the sky was a gorgeous shade of blue with only wispy clouds hanging high above.

A glorious day. Spring is here. Not even a breath of wind.

Selena knocked on her aunt's door, wanting to check how she was this morning before heading into the Clinic.

She called through the door when her aunt did not answer, "Aunt Jenny, are you up? How're you doing today?"

"Selena, I have been up for hours." Her Aunt Jenny called out, probably from her desk several feet away. "I have a lot of writing to do today. *History in the Making* is coming along very well indeed. I will not see you for breakfast. I will eat in an hour."

It's not unusual for Aunt Jenny to be so tied up with her book that she didn't have breakfast with me. Darn it though. I wanted to see for myself how she is feeling to make certain she's okay. She sounded fine. Second of all, I need to broach the subject of the album and closet. Now I need to get to work though. I have a bus to catch.

At the staff coffee break, Selena had attempted to call her Aunt Jenny, but she could not reach her. Worried, she telephoned her next-door neighbour, Karen Semple, to ask her to check on Aunt Jenny.

Selena answered Karen's return call on the second ring. "Selena, your Aunt Jenny does seem very tired today. I'm running an errand for her. I'll see if she would like a little visit when I go back to her house."

During the morning, Selena's mind turns to her work future.

When I get home after work today, I'll ask Aunt Jenny's opinion about changing jobs. Then I need to ask her about the photo album and the door off her closet. Maybe, maybe.

Later that same beautiful spring morning with the sun shining brightly outside, Dr. Carey Jr. came to speak to her.

"Please come to my office and sit for a bit." Selena nervously followed Dr. Kev, fidgeting with her bracelet. He closed the door. She sat where he indicated.

Did I do something wrong?

"Selena, I've been asked to relay terribly sad news to you." Pausing, he continued, "Your Aunt Jenny's doctor, Dr. Trevor Robertson, has just called my father. You know that Dr. Robertson and my father are fairly good friends." Dr. Carey paused again, hesitating to add the rest of the information.

"He didn't want you to be told over the telephone. I've something dreadful to tell you." Selena could hear muffled sounds coming from other areas of the Clinic, but her mind was abuzz, worrying what was to come next.

"What are you going to say? Is it Aunt Jenny?"

He stood beside her and put his hand on her shoulder for a moment in a consoling manner. His eyes were compassionate and tender. He was used to giving unwelcome news to patients, but this was different. An employee, even a friend.

Dr. Carey sat down beside her. "I'm so very sorry to have to tell you this, Selena, but I'm afraid that your aunt has died."

"What! Oh no, n-not Aunt Jenny! No, you're wrong!" Making

herself calm down, she stammered, "What h-happened?" She started to protest again, stood up and then sat down firmly.

Not Aunt Jenny. I need her. No, it can't be possible. She's all I have.

"When did this happen?"

"I don't have any other information. Evidently, the ambulance was called, as well as Doctor Robertson, as coroner. He wants to see you to settle some details and to give you his support. In his position as coroner, he wanted us to advise you. He found it acceptable as he is also your doctor and a friend of your Aunt Jenny. Dr. Robertson asked that I drive you to his office as soon as possible to make arrangements, that he'll make time for you no matter what he's doing."

Dr. Carey was saying, "I'm extremely sorry. Please take the next week off, even two weeks if you want, so that you can take care of things that need to be taken care of. Can I take you to see Dr. Robertson now? I'll drive you to see him. I have arranged for Dr. Kothare to see my next patient."

Selena felt too distraught to think rationally about being with Dr. Kev right now.

How could he tell me that? Why would he say my aunt was dead? I had thought him so caring and thoughtful.

Selena bristled, rubbed her temples, and replied through a haze, "No, thanks. I need to walk. I'd like some fresh air, and I'll leave as soon as I gather up my purse and coat. I'll head out right away. I just need to walk."

Then he tried again, "Selena, I'd like to drive you."

"No!" Selena heard her voice saying in an abrupt manner, "Thank you for your offer. I don't want your help. I really do want to be alone right now. I'll be fine." She quickly left the room, afraid of her reactions to more loss.

How can I cope with Aunt Jenny gone? How will I stand to have lost her? I can't have lost her. I've lost too many people that I care about. She is my family, all of it.

As she reached her own office area, her mind wandered to her Aunt Jenny's instructions from about two weeks ago. Her aunt had asked Selena to put the numbers for both Dr. Trevor Robertson and Perrault & Associates Law Firm into her new cellphone. Selena did, in fact, have Dr. Trevor Robertson's number anyway as he was her own doctor.

"It would be good for you to have these numbers just in case you need to contact them."

I'm not sure it makes sense, but it seems Aunt Jenny is always meticulously organized.

Selena sat immobile at her desk for several minutes.

What am I to do?

Then, she walked hurriedly past staff and waiting patients, leaving the Clinic.

I'm imagining they're feeling so pitiful for me. They won't even know what has just happened. I should feel deeper distress. I must be in shock. I feel numb. Oh, so numb.

Selena was unaware that the day was fresh, yet warm – the fine, sunny day she had noticed when drawing back her curtains this morning. It meant nothing now as she walked toward Dr. Robertson's clinic. As it was close to noon and his clinic might close over the lunch hour, Selena decided she could stop to calm herself. She found a little café and requested a glass of iced tea, knowing that she did not want food. For a long time, Selena just sat, her iced tea untouched. She was thinking random thoughts of her life while fidgeting with the bracelet Aunt Jenny had given her.

On my 16th birthday, Aunt Jenny gave me this bracelet when we were dining in a fancy restaurant to celebrate.

I know Aunt Jenny was so busy with her writing, but I will miss her so very much. She was all the family I have, and we did have so much in common with books, history and geography.

Random thoughts rushed at her.

Gosh, Aunt Jenny has always been interested in the architecture of these old Ottawa buildings. I see that brick building and wonder what she would have to say about the inlaid design.

Selena, with tears forming in her eyes, had glimpses in her mind of having suppers with her aunt, their talks of history, geography, of Aunt Jenny petting Rufus, getting the kitty Caylie, sitting on the patio with Mr. Brisbane and then Aunt Jenny demonstrating some affection from time to time toward her, all the remembrances of interactions for the past 12 years.

So many thoughts of her life so far, of her wonderful parents, of her parents' deaths, of being seven years old and living with her Aunt Jenny and her grandparents. She openly sobbed, not caring what anyone else thought of her.

I hardly ever think of my grandparents because I was living with them in that house for such a brief time after my own parents died. They passed away so suddenly. I was only a little girl. I don't remember Aunt Jenny telling me what happened, why they died. I think I do remember them – just fleeting scenes of people who loved me – small snatches of blurry memories, almost ideas of memories – I can't get the real memories. They seem blocked out.

Selena glanced up for a moment. She was relieved that no one was near her. The waitress had come up once, saw that Selena's glass was untouched, apparently noticed the tears and had stayed away, leaving Selena to her thoughts.

Now I am so much more alone. My grandparents are gone. Aunt Jenny is gone. My whole family gone. I have painful emotions of losing my parents, of being terrified for weeks after.

As she thought of her own parents, more sadness sat on her shoulders, crawling down her spine.

I know my mother and father had been in a car accident 12 long years ago, veering from an on-coming vehicle that was on the wrong side of a winding valley road. Mom and dad's vehicle had gone over a cliff, and they had been killed instantly. That was the one thing that I always make myself feel reassured about, knowing that they had not suffered at all.

If something had to be valued out of losing my wonderful, loving parents, then that was something, wasn't it?

Selena had been an only child and she knew her parents had loved her a great deal, as she had and did still love them. Her father whom she adored, Elliott Jenkins, was Aunt Jenny's younger brother. She remembered segments of the memorial service: His co-workers conveyed how hardworking, intelligent and fun he was to work with. They said Selena's father was a man of great character, and there was not much he would not do for other people.

Her father was always telling jokes at home too and kidding around.

Even when joking, he was so considerate. I remember looking up to him. He seemed so tall, with light hair falling over his forehead, bending over me and mussing my hair, teasing me and loving me.

Selena fondly remembered her mother, Anne Jenkins, as a charming woman, of great warmth, tall, slender with fetching hair – a cinnamon colour. At that same memorial service, the speakers told of a lovely woman, a great teacher, a friend, lost in her prime.

I can still feel my mom's warm hugs and kisses, smell her perfume.

Selena could hear her mother say, "Selena, I'm turning into the tickle monster (*tickle, tickle*). I must have a BIG HUG before I can stop (*tickle, tickle*) (*giggle, giggle*) tickling you!" Of course, Selena would be giving her mom the biggest of BIG HUGs, and they would hug and laugh. Anne Jenkins had seemed to love life to the fullest.

I remember that the three of us would go horseback riding. I took riding lessons. It seems I was just tiny. Mom told me I could ride like the wind. Well, that was then. I have not ridden since.

Remembering each summer, Selena thought about herself and her parents cruising up and down the lakes and rivers of Ontario in a boat they rented from a family friend. *The Sea Lion* was the name of the boat.

She could hear her mom's voice in her head. "Hey, let's take the boat to the beach over there. Remember we were here last year? They had the best ice cream. You and your dad can stand in line for ice cream. I'll grab some milk and eggs and meet you in line."

Selena remembered fishing and camping in a tent on the beach when they did not feel like sleeping on *The Sea Lion.*

I remember my favourite place was called Lake of the Woods.

During those summers, Selena had developed a love of the water.

I had to take lots of lessons my mom insisted on, and I had to wear a life preserver.

"Selena", her dad would say, "you swim like a fish and, when you get gills, you can take off your life preserver." She would laugh at him and put on the life preserver, wishing she could grow gills just the same.

She continued to bring her happy memories forward, touching on them as she was touching on the charms on the bracelet she was fondling.

It was long ago. I do feel saddened, but also gratified to have these wonderful memories. The memories I don't have are of other family members. I know one set of grandparents lived in the U.S.A. Aunt Jenny told me they were dead.

Aunt Jenny, how could you die? Will all I have left is memories of you too?

After some time had passed, she realized that she had been sitting there almost motionless and not breathing in full breaths.

I might be ready to endure the visit to Dr. Trevor Robertson – the coroner. She shuddered.

9

Dr. Robertson

Dr. Robertson, big in stature and in voice, said, "Come in, Selena." She entered and he closed the door. "I'm extremely sorry about your Aunt Jenny. I know that this must be such a shock to you."

Upon saying that, Dr. Robertson took Selena in a gentle bear hug. This was not their usual greeting; however, she could see he was as emotional as she was. She knew Dr. Trevor Robertson very well. He had been her own doctor since she was seven when she came to live with her grandparents and aunt. Selena had not felt comfortable changing doctors to her employers because she wanted to keep her personal doctor separate from her work.

Dr. Robertson was an old, old friend of her Aunt Jenny, as was the lawyer, Gavin Perrault from around the time she went to university many years ago.

As he released her, he kept hold of her hands and said, "Your grief might be unbearable to you right now. Let your feelings go." He patted her back.

Selena started to cry.

"I know you have lived with Jenny for many years, and how much your aunt thought of you. You'll miss her."

Selena removed her stylish, yet well-worn coat, rubbed her

cheeks with both hands and choked out, "How could this happen? How did she die? I can't believe this happened."

Very calmly, Dr. Robertson explained that the next-door neighbour, Karen Semple, had picked up prescriptions from the drug store for her Aunt Jenny that morning. After Karen Semple had rung the doorbell and there was no answer, she had gone around to the side windows, checking for Jenny.

"She said that she could see Jenny on the couch in the living room. When she knocked on the window two times, Jenny still did not move, and Mrs. Semple had called an ambulance and the police. The police had called me, as coroner."

"Your Aunt Jenny had a massive heart attack, and her death was instantaneous. Your Aunt Jenny died peacefully while having a nap. There will be further reports made."

Tipping his head to get a good look at Selena to gauge her readiness to hear more, he decided she was ready. "Selena, your Aunt Jenny hadn't been well for a while. Her heart was failing her. I know she refused to tell you any of this. We had lengthy discussions about it. Jenny had been seeing a cardiologist, Dr. Keisha Attaway. They worked out a plan for medications. She was having regular checkups, echocardiograms, as well as a test called an Angiogram where your aunt's heart was x-rayed by inserting a tube and dye.

"How could I not have noticed? That much distress – my own aunt."

"I'll gather up some of the medical reports for you. Your aunt's cardiologist, Dr. Attaway, and I were attempting to get your aunt to agree to a pacemaker which would have alleviated some of the stress on her heart. All these decisions were your Aunt Jenny's to make. Selena, I'm sorry to say that her heart just gave out before she would agree to more extensive treatment."

"I'm studying to have a career in biochemistry, but I couldn't fathom that my own aunt was that ill."

Dr. Robertson continued to console her, rubbed her hand, and succeeded in taking away some of the numbness which had come upon her earlier.

While twirling her hair in a frenzy and feeling a pounding in her head, she said achingly, “I feel so sad and empty. I’m trying to understand. I’ve such guilt for not being more attentive. She was quite young, so I never guessed.” Selena was trying to resign herself to her aunt’s death, tears trailing other tears down her face. She stood up to face him. “I can’t just sit here. What should I be doing?”

His reply came swiftly, perhaps he had been waiting for her to get to this stage. “There is something that you need to do. I’ll get you a copy of the Certificate of Death to take to your lawyer. However, please sit back down for a minute so we can discuss a couple of the processes. You said you needed to be doing something. You do. You’ll be seeing Gavin Perrault. As you know, he is your aunt’s lawyer. You’ll also need to see the Funeral Director who will help you complete some documentation.”

Ensuring he had her full attention, he touched her hand. “The other thing I need you to do is for yourself. At times like this Selena, family members tend to take on a guilt or blame themselves for the outcome. It’s just the way our minds work. Some people have to blame someone, and they choose themselves. You cannot carry it as yours. It’s not yours to carry.”

Dr. Robertson leaned toward her again, gently patting her shoulder in comfort. “I will be calling Doctor Carey Sr. again. Do I have your permission for him to advise the staff of your Aunt Jenny’s passing?”

“Yes, please. I was in no frame of mind to say anything before I rushed out.”

Dr. Robertson helped Selena on with her coat, handed her her purse and walked her to his outer office door where his receptionist took Selena’s hand and told her how sad she was about her Aunt Jenny. Clutching her purse tightly to her side, clutching onto something solid, she left the building.

Dr. Trevor Robertson watched Selena go. He said sadly to himself, *Brent Carey assured me that Selena won't have to handle this loss alone, that her friends will help her get through it. I could tell Karen Semple was a great friend. I sense that she always watched over Selena. I feel she'll be there for Selena as well as her friends. I hope we're right.*

As Selena thought of going home to her Aunt Jenny's house, her thoughts centered on it being a cold, lonely house. That solitary thought made her shiver. She momentarily felt cold herself. Winter was over, but there seemed a chill in the air, a chill inside her.

Winter is gone; spring is here.
The air is fresh; skies are clear.
It is a time to go to see
Everyone who is dear to me.
But as I go from place to place,
I miss the still familiar face.

10

Getting Through

Selena trudged home with her mind sluggish, not paying attention to her surroundings, and she had walked to her Aunt Jenny's house in a daze. Her feet knew the way, and she went with them, onward. Her world was off kilter to be sure – not sitting at the right angle.

Arriving at the door to her Aunt Jenny's house, Selena stopped. She just had to sink down and sit on the step. Her head hurt, her mind hurt and she could not make herself go in knowing the house would be empty. No Aunt Jenny. No one to make supper for. No one. She felt tears at the corner of her eyes.

"Ruff, ruff".

"Oh Rufus. Oh Rufus, come here." Selena grabbed onto a bundle of his fur for his warmth and to feel life.

"Hello Selena, dear. I'm so very sorry about your Aunt Jenny. Come here love. Let me give you a hug." Karen was a generous, kind woman, tall, yet very slight in frame, short dark hair curling around blazing green eyes.

Selena stood up, facing her next-door neighbour and friend, Karen Semple.

"Karen, thanks for taking Rufus. I hadn't even thought of him. Poor puppy. Thank goodness he had you today."

"Well, we have been good company for each other, a sad day indeed. Your kitty is in the house safe and sound."

Karen and Selena became friends over the past two years. They had known each other well enough over the previous years. It seemed when Selena was done high school and Karen's twin boys had left home, that they just gravitated toward each other. Karen was indeed older, but she was fun-loving at heart, and, occasionally, Karen came with Rufus and Selena for a walk and a chat. Karen had told her husband that Selena was an "old soul". Her husband, Bud, and Selena still always exchanged a "hello" and "how are you?"

She and Karen had sat on the back patio many times sharing conversation about their day. Karen and Bud's twin boys were away at courses. Austin, wanted to be a Firefighter like his father, and Theodore was continuing courses in law enforcement. Austin had spent the first year still in Ottawa taking courses to help him get into the Toronto school. Now when Austin and Theo came home a couple of times a month, their parents welcomed and fussed over them. Karen and Bud took it in their stride, accepting that they were empty nesters, happy and content with their own marriage.

Karen seemed to want to be a surrogate mom to Selena. Selena so enjoyed that feeling, but nothing could replace her own mother in her heart.

"I saw Dr. Robertson. He explained how you found Aunt Jenny. Thank you for calling the police and the ambulance. How are you feeling? It must have been a terrible shock."

"Yeah, Selena. It was a shock. Being a nurse helped me with that. One I wouldn't have wanted you to experience. You know your Aunt Jenny wouldn't want her death to take over your young life. We'll get you through this, Rufus, Caylie, Bud and I and your friends.

"I'm preparing a nice supper for you, Bud and myself. But I want to give you a choice. Please come for supper at our home, but if you can't face anyone right now, I'll wrap up the fried chicken, garlic roasted potatoes and parmesan asparagus and bring it over later if that's your wish. Think about it and let me know in an hour or so. We really don't want you to be alone."

"Karen, you're so kind. I'll have to think about it. Right now, I just want to go in the house and bury my face in a pillow. Then I'll take Rufus for a walk. I'll call you before 4:00. Thank you for taking care of Rufus. And Karen, thanks for trying to take care of me. I really do appreciate it." They hugged again and said good-bye for now.

Karen turned to go and then rushed back for one more hug.

"Take care of yourself, sweetie. I hope to see you, but we'll truly understand if you're unable to come. If you don't come over, I'll bring the supper. Then I'll check in on you in the evening. Maybe we can get together to chat or watch a movie?"

"Karen, I'll call you before 4:00." Realizing again the empty house awaiting her, she said, "You know that having you be with me and watching a movie does sound appealing. Even if I don't come for supper, please count on the movie. That would be just what I need."

"Chat later, Selena."

Upon entering the house and closing the door, Selena greeted Caylie Ceilidh, sat on the floor rubbing Caylie's upturned tummy and gave her a hug. She ruffled Rufus' fur.

"I am grateful to have you two." After a few minutes, still sitting on the floor, feeling unable to continue to be in the house, she moaned, "Rufus, do you want to go for a walk?"

"Ruff, ruff" wag, wag and dance a gig.

"Let's take a long walk, Rufus."

The weather is still warm enough if I wear a jacket and scarf. The wind is only slightly blowing.

Grabbing his leash and attaching it to his collar, Selena opened the garden door. Sighing with relief at having a purpose and with no destination in mind, Rufus and his hero went off, one happily with sunshine in his heart and the other sad as if it were pouring rain.

Selena and Rufus returned to the patio. "I feel so alone, so desolate. I need to talk to Reverend Sherwood Badham from Aunt Jenny's church."

He has been a huge part of Aunt Jenny's life.

She tread wearily into the family room to telephone him. When he answered, she told him about her Aunt Jenny passing away. He said, "I'll be right over."

Sobbing, she sat, not really thinking, waiting for Reverend Badham. Quickly rubbing away the evidence of her tears, she answered the doorbell. He and Selena talked about her Aunt Jenny for an hour.

"I will be here to support you, yes, but who else will be here for you?"

Selena was able to tell him that Karen Semple, her neighbour and friend next door, would be with her this evening.

Reverend Badham gently manoeuvered the conversation toward the subject of the funeral. With some anguish in her voice, Selena rubbed her temples and said, "She was so young! Yet Aunt Jenny discussed this with me. I didn't feel it was necessary. She had said arrangements had been made. I just did not understand why she was telling me things that would be so far in the future." Then, in a softer voice, "I thought that then, that there was no need to tell me."

Selena glanced down, and put her hand over her bracelet, feeling like she was getting one little connection to her aunt. Tearing up again, she sobbed, "Dr. Robertson said Aunt Jenny knew something could happen to her. Reverend Badham, this is so sudden for me. I am so sad for Aunt Jenny. She had so much life left to live. What shall I do?"

"Your Aunt Jenny had also spoken to me. We had discussions on her decisions and the ramifications, yes. We had soul searching to do. She also told me she had discussed this with the law firm of Perrault & Associates. As to the funeral date, today is Tuesday, yes. I'll just look at my agenda here. Do you think that Friday perhaps 2:00 p.m. would be the appropriate date and time to have the funeral? Does that feel right for you? Whatever you need, I will help you."

Almost whining, "But do I need to *do* anything?"

"You will need to attend at the Funeral Home. I will go with you if you wish. There'll be arrangements necessary. I think that you should worry about that tomorrow. I'll call you and we can discuss what you would like said at your aunt's funeral, among other details, yes.

"I believe that you should do one more thing tomorrow and that would be to telephone the law firm of Perrault & Associates to clarify everything with regard to your Aunt Jenny's passing and ask if you should be aware of any information from them."

"Dr. Robertson said those things, but nothing registered at that time."

It was decided that Selena would call Reverend Badham tomorrow after she spoke to the lawyers. Reverend Badham gave Selena a hug before he left. "I'll talk with you tomorrow, yes."

Only a half hour later, her cellphone sounded with the song "Hello".

The cell read-out showed the name of a former doctor at the Clinic and her friend, "*Colleen Kirsch*". Colleen and Selena had been friends while Selena volunteered at the Clinic during high school, had maintained that friendship while Selena took full-time classes, and continued the friendship in the past year. She was like an older sister to Selena. In fact, Colleen said she had always wanted a little sister.

"Hi Colleen."

"Elizabeth from the Clinic called to tell me. She said that your Aunt Jenny had suddenly passed away. Selena, I'm so sorry. Is there anything I can do to help you?"

"No Colleen. I appreciate your condolences. I feel numb. I can't believe this has happened. I went to see her doctor, Doctor Robertson, this afternoon."

"How did that go? What did he say?"

"He said that Aunt Jenny has been ill with heart problems for some time – that she was avoiding having a pacemaker put in. So, for him, this isn't absolutely unexpected."

"I'm so bloody sorry, Selena. I want to see you."

"It is traumatic. Karen, my neighbour, is coming over tonight, and we'll watch a movie. Do you want to join us?"

"That would be good, Selena. What time?"

Trying to think with her muddled brain what time she should suggest, Selena said, "I'll ask Karen for 7:00ish. It'll be so good to see you again. I can use a couple of good friends right now."

"All right, Selena, I'll be there before 7:00. Again, I'm so sorry."

When Selena called Karen back, she said, "Karen, I just feel that I need time alone for a little while. Could you bring over the supper you prepared? But would you still like to watch a movie with me about 7:00 p.m.? And, Karen, would you mind if my friend Colleen Kirsch joins us? She called a moment ago. She also wanted to be with me this evening."

"Selena, I've met Colleen. Having us both there will be good for you. Tell me, have you seen the movie *La La Land*? It's apparently a fantastic love story in a musical style set in LA. It's about two people struggling through life while pursuing careers they are passionate about. I haven't seen it, and I've been planning to for a year."

Colleen and Karen arrived within minutes of each other before 7:00. Small frame, petite, with straight dark auburn hair framing her face in a pixie cut, Colleen arrived first, and her hug was achingly heartfelt. Selena knew Colleen was efficient and forthright – knew she could be fiercely protective of her – like an older sister; however, she also knew very well that underneath her blunt exterior, Colleen was very sweet.

"I've brought a bag of Cheezies and some simple cookies." After handing them to Selena, she added, "I liked your Aunt Jenny. She was always polite. She seemed glad that you had company. She made her history chats interesting."

Selena agreed. "I loved her interest as history was truly relevant to her. Because of how we filled up a lot of our conversations, my marks were remarkably high in history, geography and social studies. Thanks for bringing the cookies and Cheezies. They're my favourite snack."

Karen then arrived. Selena took Karen's hand and murmured, "Thank you for that scrumptious supper. I didn't feel like eating, but once I took one bite, it all disappeared." Turning around to Colleen, she added, "You've met Colleen Kirsch. We've been friends almost as soon as I began at the Clinic. We just clicked the day I started working there."

"And Colleen, you've met my friend and neighbour, Karen Semple."

Each said, "pleased to see you again." They gave each other a quick and pleasant smile. To Selena, they genuinely liked that the other woman was there and, most importantly, to help her at this time.

Selena added Colleen's snacks to some cut up veggies and sodas set up in the family room, and she led her friends into the room.

Not using the living room. Aunt Jenny passed away there. I can't even say died in that sentence! I need to keep it respected for now.

Selena stopped her thoughts when Karen said, "Oh, Selena, this lounge is the most comfortable I've ever sat on. The furniture in here all looks built for comfort."

She smiled stoically and left them hanging while mulling over the relatives that had sat there and passed on. Bringing her mind back, she said, "Either my grandparents or Aunt Jenny certainly knew that comfort was an important part of relaxing. Can I get both of you some soda?"

I need to set aside my anguish for a moment or I'll break out in tears.

"I have cookies, soda, veggies and Cheezies that you can help yourself to while we watch this movie."

"Thank you."

"Yes, thank you." Karen added, "When we travel to the USA, Cheezies aren't available there. They are Canadian made."

Selena served the first portions, and then they all helped themselves as the movie progressed. They had little time to chat as they watched the movie, which was just as well because Selena was glad not to chatter. After the movie, Selena acknowledged. "That was interesting and very emotional. It ended up being much better than I thought it would. I enjoyed it. Thanks for suggesting it, Karen."

Turning to Colleen, Selena advised that Karen had come over to bring items to her aunt and that Karen had found Aunt Jenny. Selena touched Karen's arm, saying again how devastating it must have been for Karen to find her aunt.

"I believe that it was good that I was the one here. You're so young. Don't you agree Colleen that if someone had to find Jenny, then it's good that it wasn't Selena?"

"I agree with you knowing you're a nurse. It's so sad that her Aunt Jenny passed away. But I'd agree with anything to prevent Selena from the experience of being the one to find her."

Karen also asked Selena if she and Bud could come to the funeral with Selena. "In fact," Karen asked, "Let us drive you there. We live right beside you, and we want to be with you on Friday. Please let us."

Selena felt relief at this offer. Mulling over the time frame, she suggested, "I would like to be there 45 minutes early though to meet with the Reverend and to say goodbye to Aunt Jenny." Karen readily agreed.

"I'm relieved not go to the church alone. The funeral home will have everything arranged, and I'll be signing their documents tomorrow."

Karen said she would contact the church ladies. Between Colleen and Karen, they would arrange for a luncheon at Aunt Jenny's home after the funeral. The church ladies would serve and clean up.

I couldn't do this alone. I know Karen, Bud and my friends will be my support.

"Thanks so much both of you for all your thoughtfulness. And for staying with me this evening. And for taking these decisions off my hands. I simply don't seem to be able to think what to do. The other day, Elizabeth joked that I'm so young. Right now, I do feel young and incapable. I need you all."

"You're welcome, sweetheart. I'm glad that you enjoyed the supper. I need to get back to Bud. He'll be looking to have some tea with me before bed. Take care, dear girl."

Selena hugged Karen again before opening the door. "Goodbye, Karen."

"Colleen, would you like to stay a little while? I haven't seen you for a couple of weeks. I'd actually love company for just another half hour."

"Selena, that'd be great. Karen is a lovely lady. I'm relieved she was there this afternoon."

"I know that it was best, but I feel terrible for her. She knew Aunt Jenny so it wouldn't have been easy." With a necessary subject change, Selena added, "Let's chat about how the renovations are going in your new home. How is your brother and his contractor friends working out?"

"Oh, they're doing a thorough job. Let me bring up some photos. See what the kitchen looks like." Chatting while she got her phone to the photo app, Colleen continued, "I knew when I bought the house that it needed work. No surprises. Look at these shots. I wanted a larger fridge, so they removed part of this wall.

Peering over to Colleen's screen, Selena said, "Yeah, the fridge looks good. I love the new island, very modern."

"This all makes it more open to my family room. They've redone the main floor bathroom. I just had them install everything new in there."

"What an amazing transformation."

They chatted about Colleen's "new" clinic and their work, avoiding her aunt's death. Colleen had stood up as Selena said, "I really wish that you still worked at the Clinic, but glad that you're satisfied with your new doctors' clinic and that you found your 'new-to-you' home. Thanks for coming over this evening."

"I'm happy I came. It's late on a work night, so I'll leave now. I won't see you before Friday. I'll call you and be thinking of you. Be good to yourself, Selena. Your aunt made decisions. Unfortunately, they affected you. I know you'll miss your Aunt Jenny. You're much stronger than you think. I know you are."

"I don't feel strong. I'll see you Friday and thank you for staying a little longer tonight." Selena opened the door. One final consoling hug and good night.

Selena was now alone. She looked around the rooms on the main floor. Silence and sadness encompassed her.

Aunt Jenny is gone – gone from my life. I've my work, my studies, my friends, neighbours, Rufus and Caylie, but, essentially, I'm alone.

The clock ticked, ticked, ticked incessantly. The room felt cold, empty, desolate.

The house feels sad, maybe missing Aunt Jenny, missing others who have passed too. Can a house mourn a loss? Is it pushing me away, telling me to leave it alone?

Selena went out to sit on the patio for a little while with Caylie in her harness and Rufus being Rufus, sniffing a flowerpot. She rubbed her arms and her bracelet. She sobbed as emotions overtook her. Rufus came and sat with his chin on her knee. Selena absently leaned over and rubbed his ears.

This bracelet is made with my birthstone, peridots inlaid in white gold, a beautiful gift from Aunt Jenny. I'll cherish this memento forever and ever.

When she opened the garden door, Rufus and Caylie ran in. Selena stalled at the door for a moment, took a deep strength-giving breath and then went back into her aunt's lonely house.

After reading a travel book for an hour to distract herself from how alone she was, she pushed away the self-pity.

I'm feeling too, too dependent on everyone else. It's time I smartened up and took on the responsibility for myself.

Selena hoped for a decent sleep. However, she tossed and turned and could not sleep for a long time before she fell into a fitful slumber.

There she stood, suddenly realizing she was totally alone, completely by herself. The dreadful thought which had been tugging at the back of her mind for several minutes sprang forth in all its horror. She was alone! It was gradually turning to dusk. Each and every tiny sound sent her heart thudding, her pulse racing. She felt cold as panic seized her. Terror stricken, she walked on. Something moved. She heard footsteps. Someone or something "coughed" a short distance behind her. She froze; she stood motionless. Although she tried desperately to move, she could not. She was petrified. A twig snapped a few feet behind her. She whispered, "Oh God, let me faint!" She became aware of a presence behind her. She screamed as a clammy hand clasped her arm. In her dream, she woke up. Her mom was standing over her and shaking her by the arm.

Selena at that moment did wake up. Remembering what the day had brought, she again saddened at her loss, missing her Aunt Jenny. Pondering about the dream that had awakened her, she was aware she had not had that dream since she was very young. No one was going to help her get over this feeling of being alone tonight.

She felt chilled, grabbed a throw blanket and rose from bed. At her desk, fumbled for her diary and wrote:

"The wind is blowing all around.
The leaves are falling to the ground.
Yellow, red or orange and gold.
Crisp and dry, so unfeeling, cold.
I want to save them in a book.
Between the pages I will look
To remember the fleeting fall
Before winter enclosed us all.

On a separate page, she scribbled:

> *I wrote a poem tonight. That's all I could do. I wrote a poem of cold, crisp falling leaves as though that will make a difference. Aunt Jenny has died. Nothing can make a difference. These words are as meaningless, cold and desolate as I feel.*
>
> *You can save leaves in a book, but I want to save my memories in more than a book. What can I do to make it better? Dear diary, there is nothing, nothing that can make it better."*
>
> *Dr. Robertson is an incredibly good doctor, and he must be a good man. He tried hard to help me today. He was kind to me. I remember his words. He said, 'Remember, please, that your Aunt Jenny was a well-read, medically informed woman. She knew exactly the choices she was making. Not telling you or involving you was one of her choices. Not getting the pacemaker was another of her choices. We all will miss her so very much, but we can't carry that guilt and responsibility on our shoulders.'*
>
> *Dear diary, I do carry the guilt on my shoulders. It is sitting there – heavy, weighing me down.*

Selena then ripped the poem page from her diary and crumpled it up. Then she absent-mindedly straightened the page out again and proceeded to shred it into minute pieces and threw them, as though scattering leaves into the wind.

11

Dr. Kevin

The next morning Selena rallied enough to call the law firm of Perrault & Associates. She shrugged out of her night clothes, dressed in a perfunctory manner and deliberately refused to think about what lay ahead in her day.

"My name is Selena Jenkins, and I wish to speak to Mr. Perrault regarding Jenny Jenkins. I'm her niece." Selena had to collect herself to go on, grabbing a breath. "My Aunt Jenny passed away yesterday. She was a client of your firm, and it was suggested I call Mr. Perrault."

"Mr. Perrault is with a client at the moment; however, Ms. O'Bryan is one of our estate lawyers. I know that Jenny Jenkins has had appointments with Ms. O'Bryan on several occasions, and Ms. O'Bryan is available. My condolences at this time, Ms. Jenkins. I'm sorry for your loss. Could I put you through to Ms. O'Bryan?"

"Hello Selena, this is Tessa O'Bryan. My secretary explained to me what happened. I'm deeply sorry for your loss. We need to meet. Would you like to come in today or even tomorrow?"

"I was aware that you had instructions regarding the burial. Aunt Jenny told me that many weeks ago. I didn't understand why she was telling me that – at the time. Yesterday, I met with Reverend Badham, and the funeral can be on Friday afternoon at 2:00 p.m."

"Selena, the funeral arrangements will be taken care of as per previous arrangements between your Aunt Jenny, Reverend Badham, the funeral home and our law firm."

It was decided that Selena should come into the office for a preliminary appointment at 1:30 p.m. tomorrow.

"Again, condolences from our firm regarding your Aunt Jenny. I'll meet you in person Thursday to discuss documentation and the Last Will and Testament. We'll have a further appointment to advise you of the entire estate once more paperwork is done. I'll be at the funeral on Friday. Take care, Selena."

I'm not going to my Wednesday University class tonight. I know I can't be in class. I'll get my assignment on-line and do a better job.

After plunging into her homework assignment, the house phone rang. As Selena took swift steps to reach the living room, she wondered if the person at the other end would hang up before she got to it.

"Hello," as she grabbed a breath.

"It's Kevin Carey. You sound as though you were rushing. How are you doing, Selena?"

Selena felt incredibly happy to have Dr. Carey phone her. For a moment all she cared about was having his familiar, friendly voice near her.

"I'm actually feeling quite numb. I think I can handle the emotions. The next few weeks will be difficult. I sent a text to Elizabeth with the funeral times and place." Thinking back to when Dr. Carey told her about her aunt's death, Selena remembered that she was a little unkind in her response to him, so she added, "I owe you an apology for my harsh outburst yesterday. I'm a little ashamed of myself."

"It wasn't that bad. I may have been taken aback at that moment, but I know that I gave you heartbreaking information. I understand. I wanted to call to assure myself that you were doing okay. How did the appointment with Doctor Trevor Robertson go yesterday?"

"Thanks for accepting my apology. Dr. Robertson was informative and kind.

"Perfect. I'm relieved to hear you're all right. Is there something I can do? I'd like to help you. How about I take you to lunch so you don't have to be in the house alone any longer?"

"Actually, my next-door neighbour, Karen Semple, and Colleen kept me company last night. Karen made supper for me, and the three of us watched a movie. You're very thoughtful; however, I'd like to be alone today. My Aunt Jenny's funeral will be on Friday at 2:00 p.m. I hope you don't mind my saying 'no'. I just need time to think this all through."

"Okay, that's fine. I understand." Dr. Carey sounded disappointed. "I'll call you again to see how you're doing. I'll be attending the funeral on Friday, along with some of the other staff. We want to pay our respects as well as be there for you. Goodbye for now."

Selena hated to let him go, but said anyway, " Thank you for calling. I probably will take a few more days off from work. Could next Wednesday be good timing to come back?"

"Selena, the other doctors and I have discussed this. You also had holidays saved up. We want you to take extra time if you need it."

"Thank you, Dr. Kev. See you. Goodbye." She gave the telephone a small smile. She had not actually said Dr. Kev to him before as it was the pet name that the staff used.

Little did Selena know, but Dr. Kevin Carey smiled into his telephone as he clicked it down. He shifted his glasses further up on his nose in a confirmation of his feelings. Sitting in his office, Dr. Kevin Carey's face showed he was touched by their conversation.

Perfect! I know the office staff call me Dr. Kev. I'm pleased that Selena just called me that. I'm surprised at myself. Maybe Selena means something to me. She's a good, faithful employee, and I do care how she's doing in these terrible circumstances.

Just then, Dr. Bethany Kothare got his attention. He had work to do.

Selena stood, momentarily pausing with phone in hand. She gently hung up the landline receiver. She realized with a pang that she liked Dr. Kevin Carey a little – *More than a little? Or just having someone familiar check up on me?* It was a good feeling that she needed right now.

Get a grip on yourself. Dr. Carey is a nice man. He's not someone I even thought of having those kinds of feelings for. Dipstick!

Selena turned around, coming back to the fact that she was at her Aunt Jenny's house and the current sad circumstances.

As if I should be mulling over things like that when my Aunt Jenny has just passed away.

She glanced around the living room where she had not been since her aunt's passing. She gazed regretfully over at the sofa.

Poor Aunt Jenny. She died all alone. Selena could have added, "as she lived her life".

Rufus came bounding into the room carrying one of his dog chews, and Caylie was lazing on Selena's blanket on the loveseat.

"What are you doing, Caylie? That's my blanket, not your blanket." Caylie was normally so good about only getting on furniture that had one of her blankets on it. Selena was so proud of Caylie knowing so many words that Selena spoke to her.

In cat language, Caylie said, "Meow."

Selena said gently, but firmly, "Get on your blanket, Caylie, not mine. Where is your blanket?" Caylie walked a few steps toward her own blanket, turned and looked at Selena and started to come back to what she knew was a more cozy and already warm blanket. "That is my blanket Caylie – my blanket. Where is Your blanket?" Caylie meowed a lower, longer syllable, "Meeoorrow" ("I wasn't doing anything") turned and walked to her blanket, looked at Selena and then lay down where she should have been in the first place, licking her paws dismissively.

"Good girl, Caylie. You're a good kitty. Are you Crazy Cate today?" Crazy Cate aka Caylie gave Selena a little scowl and then licked her paws again and started to purr like that was her plan all along.

"When in doubt, lick, right Caylie?" Selena had not been aware of a cat's repertoire for showing their feelings prior to having Caylie. It was so good having a kitty as another companion. Selena sat down with Rufus who gave up his dog chew to have his ears rubbed.

"A little sit on the patio seems a good idea with the weather outside being warm enough." Selena let Rufus out in his dog run first, and then she got Caylie's harness and leash. Selena had a glass of juice and once outside she relaxed a little more. Ten minutes passed. Twenty minutes passed.

I enjoy these guys, but the loneliness is getting on my nerves. I can't just sit here alone all afternoon!

The pets and Selena answered the doorbell at 3:28 p.m. Selena had been anxiously, or eagerly, looking forward to this time together with Dr. Kev, toying with her hair, pushing it over one ear and then the other, and not being certain which emotion was prevalent as both anxious and eager feelings interchanged.

"Hi, Selena. Oh, hello pets!"

Bending down to the floor, Dr. Kev said, "And you must be Rufus. Are you the goofus?" At this, Rufus rolled onto his back and panted, almost smiling, waiting for a tummy rub to which Dr. Kev obliged. "Yes, perhaps he is a goofus. Aptly nicknamed." Then Caylie shyly made an appearance from behind Selena, growing more friendly when Dr. Kev called to her and gave her a pat as well.

"Hello Caylie." Questioningly, inquiring, "What's the rest of the name for this lady of the manor?"

"It's Caylie Ceilidh Pretty Lady". The second name is spelled C-e-i-l-i-d-h, but it's pronounced the same as her first name. It means celebration or companion."

"Perfect. I've heard of a Ceilidh to do with St. Patrick's Day. Well, that is a long handle. They're both lucky to have you as a companion. I'm so sorry what you're going through. You've spoken fondly of your Aunt Jenny, and you'll miss her."

Selena knew Dr. Kev, with his dark brown hair and blue eyes was being genuine in his considerate manner. A tear tried to get past her eyelid, and she turned away for a second. When she turned back, she had a determined look on her face.

"I'm not sure how I'll get through this, except with friends like you to keep me busy." Catching herself with tears at the edge of her eyes, she looked away again for a moment. "I know in my heart that my aunt wouldn't want me to be so upset, but I am, and .... I'll just have to be strong. Colleen says I'm strong."

"Colleen is a good person, and I hope that she's right, but you shouldn't need to get through this alone. Your friends will keep you company. I'm relieved that you let me come over this afternoon."

Earlier Selena, feeling a need to squelch her loneliness, had glanced at her cellphone, thinking of Dr. Kev's telephone call.

"Maybe," she said. "Well, perhaps I could. I feel so alone. Why not?" she reasoned. Selena dialed the Clinic.

"Good morning, The Caring Medical Clinic. How may I help you? Oh, Selena?"

"Hello, Elizabeth. Yes, it's me. I'm calling to speak to Dr. Carey Jr. But how are things going there?"

"Things are going just spiffy here, Selena. I'm so sorry for your Aunt Jenny's passing. We're just devastated for you. The fort is being held down, and you're missed, but you just take the time you need. Are you getting on all right? I could come over after work if you need some company."

"I'm all right, Elizabeth. You know, it's hard for sure. Aunt Jenny was busy a great deal of the time, but the house is emptier without her. You know I have Rufus the Goofus and Caylie Ceilidh Pretty Lady to keep me company. A neighbour and Colleen have been keeping an eye on me. Thanks so much for offering though. Next week, I'd like to have you come over and see the pottery studio that Aunt Jenny had let me use. I haven't been having any luck with anything. I'd like you lend me your expert potter's hand, so to speak, with figuring out what I should be doing."

"Oh, you know that's right up my alley, Selena. Would you be available on Saturday afternoon? Sunday, I'm playing pickleball with Mary. Man oh man, she's in such good shape that it'll be a real workout for me." They made plans for 4:00 Saturday afternoon. "I'll put you through to Dr. Carey right now. He's in his office, and he has a light schedule this afternoon."

"Hello, Dr. Carey. I was rethinking a plan if you're still available. You're right about my needing some company. It's been an emotional time. Thanks for calling earlier. I just needed time to think. You could come over here when you're done work – you can meet my dog and my cat. We could play a game of Codenames, Sequence or Chess?"

"Okay, Selena, that's perfect. I used to be rather good at Chess years ago. I'll pick up a pack of Cherry and Cream Soda. How does 3:30 sound?"

Rufus had his walk and many a sniff. Back home, Caylie suspecting something was going to be happening had followed Selena around as she fluttered here and there preparing for company. The soda glasses were set on the coffee table in the family room. The MP3 was currently playing *Adele*. The Chess board was on the rather extravagant "card table" shamelessly made out of Ebony wood. Aunt Jenny had admitted her own parents had expensive tastes.

Selena had time on her hands and went up to Aunt Jenny's bedroom again and checked around for that missing key. She tried all the places that a key would be.

If you were a key, where would you be? Come on, where are you?

She even went through the pockets of each piece of clothing in the closet. No luck again.

How long is this going to take to find that blasted key and get this mystifying door at the end of Aunt Jenny's closet out of my mind? But I must get ready for Dr. Kev.

With Dr. Kev here, she struggled with some embarrassment.

"Thanks for coming over. It was good of you."

"I wanted to be here for you." Changing the mood, Dr. Kevin said, "I love the look of this home. The front view of your aunt's house is fantastic. Will I get a tour of the main floor and grounds?"

"I've always been proud of Aunt Jenny's house."

I appreciate the change of discussion. "I'd like to show it to you. This front foyer is quite grand with its stained glass. There're 17 rooms in total. My grandfather was an architect and my grandmother a decorator. Things may be a little dated, but I love it as it is."

Walking from the foyer, Selena showed Dr. Kev the living room, family room, library, kitchen and eating area, as well as a formal dining room and a den. All these rooms had excellent oak woodwork, crown molding, features like bevelled windows, cherry wood flooring, good carpeting and exceptionally fine furniture. There was also a spectacular main floor bathroom and a main floor laundry room which they skipped thankfully as Selena realized it was an untidy area. Caylie had settled down in her little kitty bed in the kitchen. They stepped out the garden door at the back to the patio, at which point Rufus brushed past Dr. Kev, slipping outside.

"Ruff, ruff."

"Oh right. Rufus wants a walk. He's already had one today. He'll be fine with that when he realizes I don't even have his leash." The wag, wag ended with a little "Ruff", and he was off exploring the perimeter of the garden.

"The grounds are superb. You've the park behind you. My father and mother live about ten blocks from here around the other side of this park. If you walk far enough into the woods, I bet you'd be able to see their home."

"Oh, I realized that. At your parents' home a few months ago, I looked out their back garden area. I thought that the woodlands joined the homes." Since Kevin gave her a confused look, she added, "That evening to say a farewell to Colleen on her last day at the Clinic. You were off at a conference."

"Yes, it was a conference that came up suddenly. I did have to miss the farewell. I felt very badly about that. To make it up to Colleen, I took her out to the restaurant called *Thymes*. Do you see her often? I knew you two were close friends. It was enormously disappointing to have her move to another Clinic."

"As I had said, she came over last night, along with Karen, to watch a movie. Colleen and I get together about once a month for lunch or drinks and a chat. Aunt Jenny liked her, too. I was quite disappointed that she left to go to that medical clinic near Overbrook. Of course, it's closer to the home that she bought last year."

Walking around the grounds with Rufus rushing toward them and then bounding off was a good distraction and enabled conversation pertaining to Rufus' antics.

"So, do you have any pets yourself?"

"No. My mother and father had a fantastic English Springer Spaniel when I was still living at home. She was extremely intelligent. We wouldn't even have to speak the commands to her after she became used to them." He smiled at the memories and continued with the explanation. "With our hand held straight up vertically, it meant 'Wait'. Finger beckoning 'Come'. Hand horizontally flat 'Lie Down'. One finger pointing up 'Sit'. If she was getting a treat and I had none left, I'd wipe my hands together. She'd look sad and give up asking."

Selena laughed and felt herself relax with Dr. Kev. "It was fortunate for us that she knew all these commands because she lost her hearing."

"That is sad, but very fortunate for all of you that she knew the commands."

They approached the garden area, and Dr. Kev spoke once again very enthusiastically about the yard. "This is extraordinary. How do you maintain all these shrubs and I imagine flowers each spring? Incredible. You must have a green thumb. I'm impressed."

She made a panicked face, laughed and said, "I couldn't possibly do it alone. Aunt Jenny has a gardener, Eric Brisbane, who comes and mows weekly doing most of the yardwork, the heavier gardening and pruning. I do the weeding, some pruning and all the vegetable gardening. I enjoy puttering with that. Well, let's set up that Chess game," offered Selena.

"And have some Cherry and Cream Soda," replied Dr. Kev.

"I haven't tried that flavour yet. Great."

As Selena and Dr. Kev turned and walked toward the patio, Rufus realized they were leaving him. He did several "Ruffs", wagging his tail hopefully. He must have realized the futility as he turned toward Selena and Kevin, and then he sniffed every single plant and rock on his way back.

Once inside, Selena escorted Kevin into the family room. "As you can see, I have Chess ready to go. You can be white."

Beginning with moving the pawns, knights and then the bishops forward with a little sacrificing and taking, Selena was ahead on pieces captured. Kevin was a skillful player, and he had his queen out advancing to Selena's end of the board quite quickly. Selena had enough pieces moved out of the way, so she safeguarded the king by castling. Kevin captured Selena's queen before she could move it back when she realized what he was preparing to do.

More pawns were taken for black and for white. Kevin's bishop fell to Selena.

"Oh hell!" Then he looked a little askance, mouthing 'sorry for swearing'.

Selena just shrugged like "no worries".

Both his queen and one of his castles were getting too close to Selena's king when she realized that her bishop could take his castle, giving her breathing room to get her other bishop in a position to take his queen. Proceeding to get much closer to Kevin's king with her bishop and one knight, Selena managed to get Kevin into check.

Kevin said, "That sucks big time. Ahh! Perfect! Here's my opening" as he moved a piece into her path, enabling him to get out of check. She moved a pawn, but her king was then also checked.

Selena groaned, "You're too good at this!"

She had to move her king and that race stopped when she was safe again, just in time to put him into check mate with the bishop and her knight.

As they played, there was discussion back and forth about the Clinic and the people that worked there. Selena talked about her Aunt Jenny and her books. She indicated places she would like to travel. Kevin listened intently, and he seemed interested in her aunt and her work.

"Do you think your Aunt Jenny's interest in history and geography have effected an interest in travel for you?"

"Definitely!"

When the Chess game was finished, Kevin said, "That was excellent. I think that we should have a rematch. What'd you think?"

"That would be terrific." This time though, Selena had more thoughts of her Aunt Jenny and less concentration on the Chess match. However, Kevin must have gotten a second wind as well because he checkmated Selena within 12 moves.

"We're evenly matched," Kevin said.

Selena, although sad, kept up good appearances. She was enjoying having Dr. Kev for company. "Would you like another soda? I'd like one. That was fun!"

After getting his soda, Kevin re-ignited the travel discussion, saying, "As a child growing up, I had a trip almost every summer. My family travelled much of Canada, the US, parts of Mexico, Great Britain, European countries – we had vacations over Christmas as well. I actually plan to stay put for a while as I have my practice to attend to."

Wow, that's a lot of travelling and now he's tired of it. I feel more familiar with him, and he seems very relaxed.

Selena stood to put the Chess pieces away as Kevin looked at his watch. He said, "I need to be going. Jeremy and I have arranged to meet with some friends. I'd like you to come with us tonight, Selena."

"No, not today. Jeremy seems someone who enjoys a good laugh, but I'd love to go with you another time. I appreciated your coming over today to keep me company. I enjoyed the chess games and your sodas."

"You know, I'll take you up on coming out with us again, and I'd love to play more chess. You're a particularly good opponent."

As she walked Dr. Kev to his new-model Passat, they said an awkward goodbye. They possibly even had a little connection, but Selena let it go. Today had been a pleasant distraction, but she was emotionally drained.

"I'll be at your aunt's funeral on Friday. Take care, Selena."

Watching him drive away, she smiled with real feeling for the first time since early yesterday.

Supper was left-over ham, sweet potatoes and roasted carrots, which she had cleared away while thinking of all her suppers with her Aunt Jenny and shedding countless tears.

It was later that Wednesday evening after Selena did her assignments for her Pharmacology class that she took time to think. As she was contemplating her hours with Dr. Kev, her cellphone rang with the song "*Hello*".

"Selena, oh I'm so sad for you. I got your message. I'm upset that I wasn't here to speak with you when you called, but I'd left my cellphone charging at home, forgetting it when I went out. I tried calling your aunt's land line and your cellphone this afternoon. There was no answer. You must be so distraught. I want to be there to be with you, but I've an early Friday morning class I'll stay here for. I'll come for the funeral. I know better than to ask how you're doing. Is there something I can do when I get to town? How lonely you must be. How is Rufus doing? Are you eating and sleeping enough?"

All this in almost one breath from my best friend since we were seven years old. Laura Waters is wanting to know if I'll be all right.

Selena fought the release of tears upon hearing from her friend. She could imagine Laura in her mind, standing with her phone in her hand, all 5'4", blonde, doe-like blue eyes, slender, toned from her passion for gym workouts and intent on finding out how she was doing.

I wish she were here. She always makes me feel better. Laura knows me so well.

Forcing herself to perk up, Selena said, "Whoa, Laura. Hi there. It's so good to hear your voice. I've been okay with Karen from next door, Colleen and the pets keeping me company. They're doing fine. I know that you've been busy. How's your love life?"

"Who? Me? What makes you think that I've time for a love life, for goodness sakes?"

Selena responded, "Well, last time I saw you, you blushed right down to your neck when I mentioned Theodore and Austin coming home at the same time you did."

"I did not."

"Well, you did. When I quizzed you, it was obvious it wasn't Austin that was giving you that blush. Being an observant friend, I knew there was something in your feelings for Theodore. I wondered if they were reciprocated."

"I knew you were fishing is all, and it embarrassed me." Silence for a moment or two.

"Are you still there? What's up?"

"Oh, well, heck. I'll tell you. We're dating. I'm not certain why we started this idea of keeping it a secret. I guess it was fun at first, keeping it to ourselves. We *are* still young, but we're feeling it's very serious. Actually, dear Selena, to tell you everything, we're unofficially engaged!"

"Oh wow. Congratulations, I think. Are you getting married soon or waiting until graduation? I'm surprised, is all – I'm happy for you both. After all these years of friendship, you know all my secrets, and now I know one more of yours."

Selena had an earnest thought. *Well, you don't know all my secrets and certainly not all Aunt Jenny's secrets. I don't know all Aunt Jenny's secrets.*

"Keep me in the loop if you can. That's terrific. Theodore is a good guy. He's a terrible tease. He'll make you very happy."

"Oh, he already has made me very happy. We have clicked since we were kids together at your Aunt Jenny's, but it's only since we went away to Toronto and were helping each other get used to the city, that it built into something more."

"Good for you both."

"We enjoy the same things, have the same values for the future and the same kind of temperament. I just want to say again I'm sorry for the passing of your Aunt Jenny. You must feel alone now more than usual."

"Sure. It's an empty house now. The pets are keeping me company. Karen and Colleen have been a blessing, popping over and helping to keep my mind occupied. I had a nice afternoon with Dr. Kevin Carey this afternoon. We played chess and walked in the woods."

"Wait! What? Holy Christmas, I didn't see that one coming. You were slow letting loose that information! He's so swole! When I've met you at your Clinic, I was impressed. What a hunk! So, you're dating him?"

"Swole, Laura? Fat? You think Dr. Kev is fat?"

"Oh, mercy sakes! No, swole, fit, ripped, muscular."

Giggling, "Agreed. Yeah, he is swole. But we aren't dating. That's not it. He wanted to help take my mind off Aunt Jenny – just like you do, just like Karen and Colleen are doing. He's been very helpful to me."

"Right, uh huh, yep. Helpful. That's it!" Laura said doubtfully and she chuckled.

After a little teasing and a little seriousness, they said they would continue their conversations when Laura came to town on Friday.

"Laura, then you can tell me how your nursing classes and part-time diagnostic imaging job are going."

"Take care, Selena. I'm giving you an over-the-telephone hug."

This entry was added to her diary:

> *"I'm alone tonight. I hear noises and I think I should be afraid someone else is in the house. But no one's here, I'm sure. Aunt Jenny isn't here. There's no one in her bedroom working on a story or reading.*
>
> *For sure, I feel more alone. It's been only a day since Aunt Jenny died, and her death doesn't feel possible.*
>
> *Aunt Jenny has passed away. Aunt Jenny is gone forever. I can't get her opinion about changing jobs; I can't ask her about that photo album and her locked closet door. When am I going to feel at ease about snooping?*
>
> *What a wonderful thing for Dr. Kev to keep me company this afternoon. Will this afternoon change anything between us at work? I think he's cute. I know I admire him, for sure. He told me that he took Colleen out to Thymes to make up for his missing her going away party. Hum, I wonder how many other times they got together. Colleen did tell me about going out for supper with Dr. Kev. I'll have to ask her more."*

12

Exploring

It was still dark out when Selena woke up. Barely a bird was chirping. Selena muttered, "No sleeping in for the wicked" with a wry smile. Remembering what a nice afternoon it had been with Dr. Kev, Selena was feeling quite good. She then registered in her mind a creak from somewhere in the home. Then the sudden and painful recollection of her Aunt Jenny no longer being in the house, her saddened thoughts came.

Even now, I hear the furnace starting which I didn't ever notice. It's heartbreaking to know Aunt Jenny would normally be still sleeping at this hour, but within an hour, she would've been busily researching and writing her newest book.

She threw the covers off, anger rising. "Damn it. I can't believe she is gone!" At that, Rufus and Caylie stirred near her. Selena saw in the dresser mirror how tired she looked, grabbed an elastic and wrapped it around her hair, pulling it up to a messy ponytail.

The last time we talked, she was very enthused at the progress she'd made and that she was very close to being done. I want to check on her computer to see where she was in her book.

"How could you die? I even thought I saw you yesterday. Out of the corner of my eye. I looked beside me, and no one was there. I miss you, Aunt Jenny. I didn't get to ask you about that photo album. Today, I'll find the key and get into that door. Okay?"

And no reply was heard. "It calms me to talk to you Aunt Jenny."

Selena looked forward to an early and refreshing walk with Rufus. *It's comforting to have these two pets to keep me company.*

As she left the house though, the walk was not refreshing, and Selena kept it short because the winds seemed to be blowing at her from every direction. Caylie Ceilidh had demonstrated to Selena that she liked her harness and leash, so after the morning walk when Rufus was in his dog run, Selena sat with Caylie while the kitty explored as far as her leash would let her, and then the pets caroused together in the yard. Today was not the day for sitting outside since the weather was doing a turn around. Spring had changed its mind today – the temperature was cooler, and the wind picked up again and threw last year's leaves every which way.

There's definitely a rain smell in the air. It'll be here today.

Once several twigs had landed near Caylie and she became too scared to chase them anymore, Selena took both the pets inside and dusted herself off. The weather was nasty, with the distant sky showing the navy-blue formidable clouds would be overhead soon enough.

It's a day to stay indoors. I'll do a little tidying because the cleaning lady doesn't come until next week. I can do some baking, preparing for Aunt Jenny's funeral tomorrow. With the lawyers' appointment this afternoon, I can keep myself busy. God knows that's important.

As Selena closed the garden door, she looked back outside. *There's a storm brewing, for sure.*

Through the window, it was evident that the winds had picked up even more and were making all the trees and shrubs dance in fury outside, and it certainly was not a dance of pleasure. Selena could see a few fallen branches strewn throughout the garden, the wind blowing them against the fences where they bounced around. Layered dark clouds formed across the sky, towing the thick navy-blue clouds behind.

A brief time later, coming out of the kitchen with the cloths she had used to wipe the counters and heading toward the laundry room, Selena heard the rain start with small drops and work their way into a frenzy of pouring rain.

It was mid-morning, the chores done for the day and finding herself on the second floor of the large and rambling house, Selena walked toward her aunt's bedroom. Knowing that she needed to pick out Aunt Jenny's funeral clothes, Selena went forward with that purpose in mind.

Aunt Jenny's door is always locked. Except for last Tuesday. Aunt Jenny was rushing to get to see Doctor Robertson, and he squeezed her in. She looked unwell when she returned. I was worried then but brushed it off. She's young, I thought.

Selena entered the bedroom. She knew this corner bedroom with beautiful windows was the largest of the bedrooms, and she had visited her aunt here on occasion. Selena felt surrounded by the emptiness and silence of the room. *How terribly I miss her.*

The wind was blowing the lace curtains askew. There was a slightly opened window, and she went immediately over to close and lock it. The beautiful outdoor scents had permeated the room, drawing her gaze outside.

This is going to be a stormy day, and this open window would have let the rain in. Good thing I was drawn to Aunt Jenny's room. Now, I must check through that closet.

Looking up at the ceiling toward the heavens, she whispered to her Aunt Jenny, "I know I said that I wouldn't go in until I had spoken with you. Everything has changed now. You know how I can't stand a mystery. Please forgive me, but it's driving me crazy. I have to see what's behind that door!"

How many places I've looked and not found that dratted key!

She looked high and low again. No key had been found yet. Having already checked the bedroom itself and then all the clothing pockets and on top of the door frames, she scooted down on the floor, felt along the tall, wide baseboards. Nothing. On the floor, along the far wall, Selena found a key.

A key! Did it fall here? Is it the key?

Then pushing the key into the lock, turning it – at stuck at first. Then, thankfully, the door opened.

Finally!

As she pushed the door forward, she paused and took a breath, then another.

Sorry, Aunt Jenny. I'm trespassing.

However, determinedly, she walked into a huge room, as big as her aunt's bedroom itself. In a house this large, Selena had not thought where rooms began and ended. There was a narrow window near the ceiling of this new room which let in a minimal amount of light.

Why is there an additional closet? Did Aunt Jenny come in this room often? The window is so high up. But I can certainly see the darkening sky. I hadn't seen this window from the outside.

Selena fumbled for a light switch and, locating it, pressed the switch quickly. Inside this new room, the nearest clothes rack was full of older-styled clothing, all of which had a strangeness about them. Selena realized that the clothes, although of older styles, were not at all worn out.

These are new looking. They don't appear to be costumes. What the hey!

Some must be ancient garments.

There were other racks of clothes farther back that were from different periods than the present. She walked closer, moving the clothing this way and that to get a better look at them.

There must be 200 articles of clothing, with shoes, bags, purses, some with head apparel!

Selena found peasant outfits; a suit of armour; an ancient priest's garment and a nun's habit; dresses of Russian styles with the corresponding men's clothing; a flowing gown which Selena thought to be Spanish; a medieval shopkeeper's apron; an ageless Chinese robe; English lady's gowns on the same rack as several other English styles; veils as if from a dancer's costume; dresses perhaps of South America; and period-matching men's clothing beside each outfit, and so many more.

Turning in a full circle, Selena noticed shelving with a large quantity of books, each book having pages marked with sticky notes of various colours. There were numbers printed on the sticky notes in each book. Selena's attention then riveted to the walls covered with maps, coloured pins stuck in each map, and each of the pins had one number on the end of the plastic tip.

Astonishing!

For over an hour, she was obsessed with the room's clothing, books and wall maps. Selena noted one of the pins in England had the same number as the suit of armour. When she looked through the books, she found the same number on a book section entitled, "*Knights of the Round Table*."

The number must be a year.

One of the pins stuck in Germany had the same number as the peasant dress. The dancer's veil had a number identical to one pin in the map of India. She was breathless with the mood that the room projected, feeling a thrill deep inside her. The sensation of excitement was electrifying.

She exclaimed, "This is crazy. What can all this mean?" Her mind raced with a multitude of questions.

Muttering to herself, "All these clothes. Any memories I have of Aunt Jenny, she didn't attend dress-up events – not costume events. Why men's clothes? My grandfather? Each garment looks new. Why would Aunt Jenny or my grandparents collect these clothes? Why in heaven's name is the door locked and why was Aunt Jenny so secretive about the closet? It's not that big a deal. It's a mystery, but not a colossal mystery like I'd hoped for. Locked doors. Missing key."

Disappointed, she now looked around the entire room. Selena's eyes fell on an amazingly oversized roll-top desk set off to the side of the room under that high window.

Did Aunt Jenny ever sit at this massive desk? It's made of steel!

There was a large key on top of the desk. Momentarily feeling as though in a fairytale, Selena slowly walked over to that key, picked it up and just held it in the palm of her hand, solemn and paralyzed.

Should I trespass even more into Aunt Jenny's room? Do I have the energy for this? So many emotions. I shouldn't be here. I could leave now and come back to the room and closets tomorrow.

"Not a chance!"

Mindlessly looking down at the desk, she noted the keyhole, placed the key that she held in her hand into the keyhole and turned the key. Selena slid the roll-top lid open slowly, as though she was afraid of what there would be inside. In her imagination, she thought *Something unknown could jump out at me. Boo!*

As she moved the lid, it lifted up, and inside was a peculiar sort of machine with a monitor. Selena stepped back, amazed.

A computer?

Whispering to herself, "An old computer. This is a very mysterious looking thing. There's a keyboard. It's so strange looking that I can't seriously consider it to be a computer. If it is, it's terribly outdated."

Gleefully, she continued muttering, "This odd-looking machine – possible computer – in Aunt Jenny's room – within another closet is more than interesting. Just consider everything else locked in here. Now these can be considered serious mysteries. That's more like it!"

At that moment, Selena noticed that the machine and equipment were molded to the desk, and it could not be moved.

This stuff forms part of the desk.

Scoffing, she muttered, "I doubt this thing has been used for decades. It probably doesn't even work. If it is a computer, it seems too old to have programs. No wonder Aunt Jenny hadn't mentioned this strange contraption. But, even if it's a useless old relic, why keep her closet doors locked?"

Curious, Selena searched for the power button.

"Now that's strange. Where's the darn power button? How do I turn this on?"

Searching the front, top and sides of the machine and molded desk, she was confounded.

There is no power switch. Where's the "on" button? It's plugged in on the back wall though.

Her fingers found a switch at the back of the machine.

There!

"It's a computer, isn't it? Holy man, this is crazy!" She flipped that switch, waiting for the screen to change. The screen remained black, but there was a faint *ping* and then another sound, growing louder: *Buzz, Buzz, Buzz.*

Now assuming it was going to start, waiting impatiently, she studied the unit. She gave the keyboard a gentle tap, then a much firmer tap.

Blank, black screen. What's taking so long? I could hammer this thing! How annoying can it be? THUMP! There, take that! The blank, black screen stared maddingly at her.

It's taunting me!

Buzz, Buzz, Buzz.

Tick, Tick!

"There, it's on! But this screen is odd."

The screen turned several whirling shades of colour, settling on a light blue hue. The screen changed to the words *Waiting in Queue*. Selena waited for directories to come on screen, but there was nothing listed. Still hoping for something useful besides *Waiting in Queue*, Selena was rewarded when the screen changed yet again to different wording.

TIME TRAVEL MACHINE. The one Directory was *TIMETRVL*.

"What the? This isn't possible. Time Travel. No Way, but that's what it says! Is it an ordinary old computer?"

When Selena brought the TIMETRVL directory forward to her screen, she found the command:

ENTER

My fingers are itching to press this. I know that one of Colleen's friends has a Virtual Reality set. There should be a headset, headphones, goggles, hand-controllers. Nothing here. Was this the "base station"? Perhaps this is virtual reality that joins to an app on a cellphone.

She had been looking for a name – *Google or Sony*, but whether it was one of those brands or not, there was no maker name on this machine.

None of this makes sense! Aunt Jenny doesn't even own a cellphone. This is ridiculously old looking, before Virtual Reality, I'd think. What would an obsolete version of that look like? Besides, VR has only been around for a decade.

She looked again at the TIMETRVL directory.

What! Why do I feel there must be a rabbit hole for me to slide down? Time Travel! That's crazy… Maybe it is a game of some sort.

Maybe Aunt Jenny was into role-playing games! Dungeons and Dragons in her day. The clothes would make sense if LARPing. Aunt Jenny doing Live Action Role Playing? I think I'll split a gut laughing! But what else could it be? She was a mystery after all.

Selena pressed ENTER. There were lists and lists of alphabetical places with numbers following. Each place then indicated a FROM YEAR and a TO YEAR and then the word RETURN.

From the recent lists going up in year, Selena read the words out loud.

"CURRENT, chronological TRAVEL DESTINATIONS – RETURN CHART"

What the blazes?

She continued reading the screens in their entirety, fascinated.

CURRENT, chronological TRAVEL DESTINATIONS - RETURN CHART

BY WHOM	City	FROM Year - & - TO Year / Return	Month
A&O	Ottawa	2007 to 1966 (To and return same day)	December
A&O	Ottawa	2008 to 1967 (To and NO RETURN SET)	April
JJ	Ottawa	2009 to 1968 (To and return same day)	December
JJ	Ottawa	2010 to 1969 (To and return same day)	April
A&O babyJJ	Ottawa	1969 to 2010 (To and return same day)	August
JJ	Ottawa	2010 to 1969 (To and return same day)	December
JJ	Ottawa	2011 to 1970 (To and return same day)	April
JJ	Ottawa	2011 to 1970 (To and return same day)	August

JJ	Ottawa	2012 to 1971 (To and return same day)	April
JJ	Ottawa	2012 to 1971 (To and return same day)	August
A&O babyEJ	Ottawa	1972/2013 (To and return same day)	August
JJ	Ottawa	2013 to 1972 (To and return same day)	December
JJ	Ottawa	2014 to 1973 (To and return same day)	April
JJ	Ottawa	2014 to 1973 (To and return same day)	August
JJ	Ottawa	2014 to 1973 (To and return same day)	December
JJ	Ottawa	2015 to 1974 (To and return same day)	April
JJ	Ottawa	2015 to 1974 (To and return same day)	August
JJ	Ottawa	2016 to 1975 (To and return same day)	April
JJ	Ottawa	2016 to 1975 (To and return same day)	August
~~JJ~~	~~Ottawa~~	~~2016 to 1975 CANCELLED~~	~~December~~
JJ	Ottawa	2017 to 1976 (To and return same day)	April
JJ	Ottawa	2017 to 1976 (To and return same day)	August
~~JJ~~	~~Ottawa~~	~~2017 to 1976 CANCELLED~~	~~December~~
A&O	Ottawa	1976 to 2017 (To and return same day)	December
~~JJ~~	~~Ottawa--~~	~~2018 to 1977 CANCELLED~~	~~April~~
JJ	Ottawa	2018 to 1977 (To and return same day)	August
JJ	Ottawa	2018 to 1977 CANCELLED	December

DUE/PENDING Pre-programmed To/Return			
JJ	Ottawa-	2019 to 1978 (To and return same day)	April
A&O	Ottawa	1978 to 2019 (To and return same day)	August

Selena's mind was jumbled, and her mouth formed a perfect "O". *Oh! What?* "This definitely can't be happening! It's ridiculous. I need to get a grip.

Is or isn't it virtual reality, tabletop role playing or a computer game? But look at that list! Travel Taken by: JJ and also A&O.... Virtual Reality Time Travel?

This might not be a game of any sort, or a game about time travel? JJ? Jenny Jenkins - Aunt Jenny?? Aunt Jenny playing a computer game, role playing?

And what if I consider that this isn't a game?

Could this be what it says it is? Time travel?

She said loudly, startling herself, "What's this machine and who were the people?" Quieter, even though there was no one else in the room, she said, "And the initials A and O.

"A&O travelled in 2007 and 2008? My grandparents, Arthur and Olive, died in 2008 – Arthur and Olive - my grandparents?? What kind of coincidence would that be if it were not them?? Am I imagining anything here makes sense? This had been my grandparents' home back in 2008 before they died - with Aunt Jenny still living here with them. Who else could be A&O?"

Selena paced around the room. Not a chance she could sit down. Rubbing at her face, frowning and scowling, she was thinking and analyzing.

"In 2008 – the SAME YEAR that my grandparents died, A&O didn't return from their supposed travels to the year 1967!!! They had died that year. They did die, didn't they? How absolutely crazy if any of this is true?? Of course, I must admit scientifically this points to what it says – Time Travel.

"I can see that those initials apparently used this machine again four more times after 1967 to come here?" She sniffed discursively. "Why does it appear they travelled FROM and TO Ottawa? Why Ottawa?"

Whispering, "Where did this thing come from? Who brought it here? I thought my grandparents were an architect and a decorator?? I thought Aunt Jenny was a history writer. Well, I wanted a mystery. Be careful what you wish for. This is far past being just a mystery!"

Checking the dimensions of the door, Selena told the room, "One thing I can see is that this molded desk and machine sure the heck didn't fit through these doorways! Look at the width of it!"

She laughed a giddy laugh, a lunatic laugh, shaking her head at herself.

I'm having a hard time comprehending the full impact of this. I think I believe what I see. But I don't believe what it appears to be.

"What happened?"

She just could not grasp the fact that her Aunt Jenny and her grandparents had indeed been involved in time travel! She was trying to comprehend the fact that the year her Grandmother Olive and Grandfather Arthur were "*gone*" as her aunt had phrased it, that they travelled to 1967 and did not return, but travelled FROM/TO Ottawa in 2009 and so on.

What about those years they travelled in time? I've more than a mystery. I have something that isn't possible to explain away.

With her breath stilted, heart pounding and still fervently examining the computer screen, Selena had an obsession to see what else there was.

Press a button, find another rabbit hole...

Then she used the cursor down to a different screen, and she noted these additional entries:

PRIOR LISTINGS, chronological TRAVEL DESTINATIONS - RETURN CHART

BY WHOM	City	FROM Year - & - TO Year / Return	Month
A&O	U.S.A.-New York	2005 to 1776 (To and return same day)	September
A&O	South Africa—Table Bay/ Cape Town	2006 to 1795 (To and return same day)	August
A&O	Rhine—Kaiserwerth/ Florence Nightingale	2006 to 1851 (To and return same day)	December
A&O	England—South of London	2007 to 1215 (To and return same day)	June

And on and on and on, dozens of lists showed travel for A&O back and forth in time, many times before 2007 – Not to Ottawa, but to many other places in history and other countries!!!!! Nowhere did these trips say JJ, her Aunt Jenny, travelled.

Behind the place names, a year and a month listed.

Selena's mind tumbled and raced. She remembered the books with the sets of numbers, so she ran to grab a book. The slips of paper in the books about the various countries also had the numbers. For example, one was China--1644 on it. She checked the screens.

Travels before that fateful year – 2007. It made her shiver. That was the year her parents had died as well as the year before A&O had stopped travelling away from Canada.

Did that mean anything?

Checking the "PRIOR" screen again, she confirmed the dates.

There were no travels to other countries after 2007 when A&O travelled to and returned from the trip marked as "England—South of London in June 1215 in 2007".

Again, she shivered and felt drips of perspiration on her brow and at the nape of her neck.

Before my parents died.

She marvelled, "You didn't travel to other countries after 2007, the year my mom and dad (your son and wife) died tragically in that car accident. No out of country travels by A&O after my parents died in 2007. You just stopped going away from Ottawa. No travels at all by JJ (Aunt Jenny?) anywhere at all before my grandparents, A&O, stopped going to other places.

"So, you stayed in the year 1967.

"And you, Aunt Jenny, started to travel to and from Ottawa?"

Selena looked again at the original screen to confirm dates.

BY WHOM	City	FROM Year - & - TO Year / Return	Month
A&O	Ottawa	2007 to 1966 (To and return same day)	December
A&O	Ottawa	2008 to 1967 (To and NO RETURN SET)	April
JJ	Ottawa	2009 to 1968 (To and return same day)	December
JJ	Ottawa	2010 to 1969 (To and return same day)	April
A&O babyJJ	Ottawa	1969 to 2010 (To and return same day)	August
JJ	Ottawa	2010 to 1969 (To and return same day)	December
JJ	Ottawa	2011 to 1970 (To and return same day)	April
JJ	Ottawa	2011 to 1970 (To and return same day)	August

JJ	Ottawa	2012 to 1971 (To and return same day)	April
JJ	Ottawa	2012 to 1971 (To and return same day)	August
A&O babyEJ	Ottawa	1972/2013 (To and return same day)	August
JJ	Ottawa	2013 to 1972 (To and return same day)	December
JJ	Ottawa	2014 to 1973 (To and return same day)	April
JJ	Ottawa	2014 to 1973 (To and return same day)	August
JJ	Ottawa	2014 to 1973 (To and return same day)	December
JJ	Ottawa	2015 to 1974 (To and return same day)	April
JJ	Ottawa	2015 to 1974 (To and return same day)	August
JJ	Ottawa	2016 to 1975 (To and return same day)	April
JJ	Ottawa	2016 to 1975 (To and return same day)	August
~~JJ~~	~~Ottawa~~	~~2016 to 1975 CANCELLED~~	~~December~~
JJ	Ottawa	2017 to 1976 (To and return same day)	April
JJ	Ottawa	2017 to 1976 (To and return same day)	August
~~JJ~~	~~Ottawa~~	~~2017 to 1976 CANCELLED~~	~~December~~

A&O	Ottawa	1976 to 2017 (To and return same day)	December
~~JJ~~	~~Ottawa~~	~~2018 to 1977 CANCELLED~~	~~April~~
JJ	Ottawa	2018 to 1977 (To and return same day)	August
~~JJ~~	~~Ottawa~~	~~2018 to 1977 CANCELLED~~	~~December~~

DUE/PENDING Pre-programmed To/Return

JJ	Ottawa	2019 to 1978 (To and return same day)	April
A&O	Ottawa	1978 to 2019 (To and return same day)	August

Deciding on and then rejecting the answer – that the computer could no longer traverse to another country because of a malfunction, Selena paced back and forth, sitting down and standing up. It was all so confusing.

In her diary later, she contemplated again:

> *"Unbelievable that I discovered a Time Travel machine in my Aunt Jenny's closet. After all that hunting, I found the key.*
>
> *I know – don't tell anyone because it sounds crazy to me even though I just examined all the 'facts'. Time travel, time gravel, time dabble, time babble. Now I do sound loony.*
>
> *Aunt Jenny would never say that her parents had actually died!! I guess she hadn't lied, but said, 'They were gone' and her famous words 'and that is all there is to it!'*
>
> *They left: Ottawa--2008 to 1967 in April*
>
> *Aunt Jenny wasn't interested in going anywhere besides back and forth in time to her own city of Ottawa as the lists indicated, no other country travel.*

A&O HAD RETURNED TO VISIT IN THE FOLLOWING YEARS – two times with a baby!! And a different baby at that.

In my scientific mind, I must accept that Arthur and Olive, my grandparents, had left and then had stayed in 1967 to live – but they came back here to visit. In the mystery photo album, they were the young couple with my Aunt Jenny (as the first baby) and my dad (as the second baby) visiting when I was younger, during those years listed.

Real mysteries. Not sleeping and all this going on is hard to handle. As if there's not enough to grasp with my only living relative having just died.

How could I possibly consider unravelling this when my own mind is so unravelled? I know that I'm always speculating there are mysteries. This IS real. This isn't my imagination!!! I'm tired, and I need to think about all of this. Wasn't there a sentence in some song or movie about there 'always being a tomorrow'?

Tomorrow is my aunt's funeral! I'll think tomorrow."

Selena slumped down into a nearby chair.

I just can't process this right now. My mind is going back and forth and back and forth.

I must get out of this room, close the door and pick out Aunt Jenny's clothes for her funeral tomorrow.

"Aunt Jenny's funeral."

Selena closed her eyes tightly and then pinched herself. She looked up and there was everything as it had been a minute before.

Selena told herself harshly, "Go get Aunt Jenny's clothes and take them to the funeral home." Shouting at herself, "Now!" She backed away as she had instructed herself, yet she hesitated. She then moved through the door and closed it with a firm "click". With precision, she locked the door with the key she had found. Before Selena picked out the clothing and accessories in her Aunt Jenny's regular closet, she stumbled to a waiting lounge chair and plunked herself down. Mind spinning, playing over what she had witnessed.

She shouted back toward the closet, "I could have a breakdown right now."

I've read "Outlander" books with a character travelling through time. Is this computer time travel possible?

Then, to Aunt Jenny, "What in heavens name have you been doing, Aunt Jenny? What have you been doing? Did you travel with that old time travel machine?"

What should I do now?

Selena felt so very adrift. Unprompted, one of her old poems slid into her mind:

You are travelling over the strange wide world,
Then comes a feeling of being suddenly hurled
From one cloud to a star in an unexplainable calm
As though God had taken you in his palm,
Making you feel safe as if you were asleep
With thoughts of peace while in a dream so deep.
Then, far from your most imaginative dreams,
Comes, so swiftly, such vivid scenes
Of beauty and splendor – more than you could ever seek,
So unthought of and, oh, so utterly unique.

Suddenly, she noted again the horrific rain pouring down outside, the wind howling.

Have I been totally oblivious while in Aunt Jenny's inner closet and the travel room? Why had I not heard the rain, the wind or the thunder? That's a nasty storm out there.

Standing and going toward the window, Selena felt faint. She again went to the lounge chair.

She softly mused aloud, "I can't worry about a storm. I'm just so overwhelmed and mentally tired. Aunt Jenny, I always wished we had spent more time together. I knew you could teach me so many things."

Quieter yet, pleading to her aunt: "I had no idea that what is in that room was something I could have learned from you. What am I supposed to do now? Why did you leave me? Why didn't you tell me about this stuff? It's all just too much for me."

Almost as if she was hearing her Aunt Jenny's voice, Selena thought:

"Dear child. You must wait! There can be nothing done today. You have too much to learn. Attend the funeral tomorrow. Then search for some more information. Think after that. There is plenty of time."

The thought was said a commanding tone that was meant to be respected. It was just as Aunt Jenny would say it, authoritative and decisive. Selena put her head back on the chaise lounge and, astonishingly, fell asleep with the calming release of those words in the familiar voice sounding like Aunt Jenny.

Nearly 20 minutes later, a clap of thunder vibrated throughout the room. Selena woke up feeling odd.

Why am I in my aunt's bedroom?

Was that a nightmare I just had?

Unusually, the dream did not melt away as dreams tended to do. Remembering what transpired prior to her fitful sleep, Selena started wide awake. Selena whispered, "That was no dream."

"How could I possibly have fallen asleep?"

With so much going on, her mind was in a whirl.

A time machine! Aunt Jenny and my grandparents travelled in time. Maybe I can travel in time. There's so much to do with the funeral, and I'm so tired.

The words from before she fell asleep resonated in her head.

"Dear child. You must wait! There can be nothing done today. You have too much to learn. Attend the funeral tomorrow. Then search for some more information. Think after that. There is plenty of time."

It seemed as though Aunt Jenny was telling her to just wait until tomorrow when she could think more clearly. She wondered if she should be angry or at least annoyed that all this had evidently been happening without her knowledge. However, Selena felt she did not have the ability to be upset with her aunt.

Selena stood, regained some composure and went to get the clothing and accessories for her dear Aunt Jenny's funeral. Suddenly, her aunt did seem much dearer. The voice she had thought or heard was welcome after these past days of isolation and missing her aunt, and her spirits lifted slightly. Gathering up what she believed was her aunt's favourite outfit, Selena chose a lovely pearl necklace with matching earrings and bracelet.

It's unsettling for me to do this because I know this will be the last thing I ever do for Aunt Jenny. The last thing.

"Rrr-ruufff". Rufus was getting drenched from the rain, and he looked accusingly at Selena as though she were holding the water hose on him.

"Why", he seemed to be saying, "Why are you tormenting me this way?"

"Please just go, Rufus." Off he unwillingly went, and he scurried back inside just as thunder rattled the house. He shook all the water from that "garden hose" onto Selena, and she grabbed his towel and rubbed him until he was decently dry.

"Good boy Rufus. There, now you completely look like a Curly Joe. Here is your doggy treat and bone."

"Rrrruuuuuufff" – "Wow, thanks Selena" Rufus seemed to say as he munched.

It was during the morning's pouring rain, wicked wind, deafening thunder and blinding lightning storm that Selena carefully backed her aunt's Ford Escape out of the garage.

It's a fitting time to be going to a funeral home.

Selena arrived with her aunt's clothing and accessories packed up to keep the rain from them. While shaking the rain from her pulled back caramel-coloured hair, she was led to a waiting room. Sitting in the waiting room, Selena thought over the conversations she wished she could have had with her aunt. No answers would be forthcoming, but it would clear her mind a little, perhaps giving Selena some peace.

A small, balding, weaselly-looking man interrupted her thoughts, introducing himself as Henry Holmden, the funeral director, greeted Selena and gently took the clothing and accessories from her, confirmed that Reverend Sherwood Badham had finalized all the arrangements for her Aunt Jenny's funeral, and said a few practiced kind words regarding the service tomorrow. Together, they confirmed the casket she would prefer for her Aunt Jenny. He also surprised her by informing her that the pearl necklace could be returned to her following the service as was custom.

Selena signed the funeral home documentation requested by the funeral director. She then sat for a little while longer with her Aunt Jenny. Selena cried.

I feel consoled by being here with you, Aunt Jenny.

It would be therapeutic to reveal my feelings to you in person. I believe, yet don't believe, and I can't possibly understand the 'how's and why's' of what I discovered in your "Time Travel Room". We needed to have so many talks while you were alive. Why would you leave this for me to find after you were gone? I miss you so much, and I need answers.

In the rain, Selena ran to the Escape from the funeral home as raindrops galloped on her head. Once Selena settled herself in her aunt's vehicle, she called Reverend Badham on her cell. He was a kind man, and he was able to encourage Selena to feel a little restored in spirit regarding her aunt's death. She and Reverend Badham conversed a little more about the service tomorrow. Selena was relieved that Reverend Badham had been able to talk with her today as he was such a good man. He had been a rock to her and her aunt when Selena's own parents had passed away, and he had spent a lot of time with her Aunt Jenny when Aunt Jenny's parents passed away or *were 'gone' away....*

Swirling winds had really mussed her hair, and she took the time to comb and straighten it out before proceeding to the Perrault Law Firm.

"What a day. Sidewalks are full of pedestrians with the wind causing their clothes to cling to them like tight plastic wrap. I'm glad I'm going to be in a parkade."

She liked a good rain, and Ottawa had plenty of that, but this one was a downpour, and Selena had to keep her wits about her to see all the highway and Ottawa street signs.

13

Long Live The King

At home again, she wandered through the living room and family room, feeling once more as abandoned as she had 12 years ago when her parents had died.

How sad I am for Aunt Jenny. But, oh how sad I am for myself.

Selena casually picked ornaments up and glanced here and there. "I never had a place of my own. This is a new feeling for me.

"Such terrible sad circumstances to have lost Aunt Jenny and to be alone. I'd sooner have Aunt Jenny here with me."

Selena picked up a large reddish coloured brass candle holder. Her aunt had said one day it was from the 1800s, and Selena again wondered where her grandparents or her aunt had obtained it. Since Aunt Jenny had lived in this house all her life with her parents, these items could have been here for dozens of years. On many occasions, Selena had tried to talk to her aunt about what certain articles were.

As was her private personality, she brushed me off and ignored my inquiries, not saying where these ornaments had come from.

One ornament that was evidently Chinese, in blue and red design with fish swimming amongst water grasses, and also a painting with what looked like it might be *Karmatskiy* signed on bottom especially intrigued her.

There's no rhyme nor reason for the things here – ornaments, paintings, sketches, coins and carvings and so forth. The provenance mystery is explained by the time travel adventures, at least. All the items in this house that I've tidied over the years without much sentiment. Now, they have much more meaning to me.

Selena felt her nerves were frayed because of what was happening inside the house and, as well, what was happening outside the house as the storm was worsening. The lightning and then thunderclaps were putting on a show, and the thunderclaps were like a standing ovation for a fantastic performer -- every few minutes getting more pronounced.

How I wish the concert were over!

Selena had foregone tea at the mall, and now realized that she was ravenous. She quickly made herself three eggs and toast.

Too jittery to make anything else.

Sitting cross-legged on the family room sofa a while later, sipping her cup of tea with Rufus studying her, she heard Caylie licking the bottom of her own empty bowl. She went to the kitchen and put some morsels in Caylie's bowl and looked around her house.

Oh my gracious. My home! And my mysteries. And I think I'll take a trip… from that closet today.

Her thoughts returned to the astounding events that had occurred that afternoon. Before she had left her Aunt Jenny's house, the shower Rufus had given her ensured she needed to change her clothing. She hooked a silver-plated pendant around her neck and had chosen her matching sky-blue rib-knit pant and pullover with a little more care considering the trendy neighbourhood where the law firm was.

The Perrault & Associates Law Office was in the expansive mall on Bayshore Drive, so Selena had taken Richmond Road and arrived at her destination. The mall was situated in a bustling region of Ottawa near Nepean with its exterior design not simply a painted stucco building.

Selena arrived 20 minutes early and checked her storm-ravaged hair once more. Giving it a brushing, she also added a thin layer of eye mascara to help disguise her tired eyes. As she often did without thought, her fingers went to and caressed the birthstone bracelet from Aunt Jenny. Checking in the mirror one more time, she felt composed enough to exit the vehicle and get to her appointment.

Look at this mall now. It's very modern since the update. I remember this mall had once been only two floors and the architects had added a top level. Aunt Jenny lamented the change in colour scheme to this green and tan marble design. Nor did she like the removal of the wrought-iron railings now replaced by glass panels.

Selena had thought at the time that her Aunt Jenny had appreciated the former architecture because of her own father's profession as an architect. Selena abruptly sniffed in exasperation at not understanding anything right now.

Was my grandfather the architect who built that travel room? How had that computer been put in the house?

When Selena drove into the parking garage, she realized just how busy the mall was. It took several minutes to get a parking space. As she walked through the throngs of people, she reminisced about her previous trips to the mall.

I love looking in Forever 21, The Gap, Victoria's Secret, Winners, Bath & Body Works and Made In Canada Gifts. Gently touching her bracelet, she said out loud, "Birks is where Aunt Jenny got my bracelet – this beautiful bracelet, a remembrance of a lovely birthday. I could stop for a cup of tea at *Real Fruit Bubble Tea*."

She took the elevator to the law firm. As it had been muddy outside when she left the funeral home, she checked her good shoes to ensure they were not mud-covered and entered the luxurious office space. Selena approached the receptionist.

"Hello, my name is Selena Jenkins, and I have a 1:30 appointment to see Mr. Perrault."

The professional looking, red-headed receptionist replied, "Good afternoon. Just one moment, please." She spoke through an inter-office telephone and then returned her attention to Selena.

"Mr. Perrault and Ms. O'Bryan will see you now, Miss Jenkins. Please come this way." Selena followed the young woman down a long hallway. She was ushered into the lawyer's office, where two people greeted her.

A distinguished, tall 60ish, well-groomed and well-dressed gentleman stood up and shook her hand as he introduced himself.

"Selena, I'm Gavin Perrault. I'm deeply sorry that your aunt passed away. I know that you'll miss her terribly. Please have a seat" indicating a chair placed between two other chairs. "May we offer you coffee?"

The accent is a well-educated French-Canadian man, not from France as it has an entirely different nasal tone.

"No. Thank you for asking, but I don't need anything."

Mr. Perrault was saying in his lovely Quebec accent, "Please meet Tessa O'Bryan. Your Aunt Jenny has met with Ms. O'Bryan several times over the past few months. Her specialty in law is Estates, as well as having a financial major. I want to advise you that Ms. O'Bryan is one of our most qualified estate lawyers. She will be handling this meeting pertaining to the procedures to settle your Aunt Jenny's estate."

"Please call me Tessa. I'm glad to meet you in person. Again, I am so sorry for your loss.

"Everything is all right, mais oui?" This from Mr. Perrault to ensure she was fine with Ms. O'Bryan handling the estate.

"Oui. Merci."

Mr. Perrault held her hand for a second and said, "I'm so sorry again for your loss. Jenny was a friend to me as well as a client. We had known each other since university days. I leave you with Ms. O'Bryan. You are in capable hands."

Selena managed a smile, forcing herself to speak to Mr. Perrault. Her voice came out almost in a murmur.

"Thank you very much, and it was a pleasure to meet you."

I'll be calmer if there is only myself and Ms. O'Bryan, less required of my frazzled mind.

After a short pause, Ms. O'Bryan spoke, "Your Aunt Jenny has been in three times over the past few months, ensuring that the documents and information we have is up to date. The estate is clear and simple as far as the Courts go. Your Aunt Jenny had no family other than you, and in her Last Will and Testament dated June 11th of 2018, she left everything to you, Selena."

Upon seeing Selena's taken aback look, she added gently, "Yes, Selena, you are Jenny Jenkins' sole beneficiary. Mr. Perrault and I are the Executors as per your aunt's Last Will and Testament. Your Aunt Jenny didn't want you encumbered with the management and distribution of the estate. Perrault & Associates will get the Last Will and Testament probated as soon as the Court system allows."

In a mild daze, Selena noted without emotion no accent from Ms. O'Bryan – *categorically not directly from Ireland*. Tessa was 35ish, black haired, dark eyed and nice looking, again tastefully and expensively dressed.

Selena felt overwhelmed, almost paralyzed, like riding a boat in rough water, hanging on to the sides of the boat for her own wellbeing. Even though Selena could be aware of each lawyers' clothing style, characteristics and listening to them speak, it was like a defense mechanism so that she did not have to experience her true, raw feelings.

With her eyes slammed shut and breathing a short breath, Selena stammered, "She was all I had left. I don't know what to say. My mind is boggled. I came to ensure Aunt Jenny's funeral instructions." Tears of shock and worry slid down her cheeks, "And I don't know how to organize Aunt Jenny's bills."

Tessa stepped again toward Selena, and gently confirmed what the funeral director had advised her. "The funeral arrangements are all taken care of. We confirmed that you signed the documentation this morning. As far as the bills, your aunt has the accountant, Julian Andrews, handling everything. *Julian Andrews Accounting* has been handling all your aunt's financial dealings for over two years now. Your Aunt Jenny made the arrangements when she felt she was not doing a good enough job of keeping track of her investments and finances."

Again, speaking as though to a child, Tessa continued, "*Julian Andrews Accounting* takes care of all invoices, taxes on the home, house insurance, electrical, power, water and all incoming invoices. As well, your Aunt Jenny didn't want you to stress over things like monthly bills that she could take care of ahead of time. Today, when you have signed some legal documents, I'll arrange with the accounting firm to have your aunt's vehicle, its license and your home insurance transferred into your name."

When Tessa handed Selena the Last Will and Testament, she reiterated that Selena was the sole beneficiary. Seeming to sense Selena's shocked state from the look on her face, Tessa said, "Would you like to take a copy of the Will home and come back another day to discuss it or would you be able to talk it through now?"

Upon looking at the Will, Selena internalized the fact that the house was hers. Selena felt she was barely keeping her emotions in check day to day.

Now this shock.

"I hadn't thought about where I'd live. I didn't think that far ahead. It's really been an emotionally exhausting time for me. I'd like to take the Will home. I'll sign whatever you have for me. May I make another appointment after Aunt Jenny's funeral to discuss it further with you?"

"Yes, we'll discuss every detail at your next appointment. Sit over here at this desk, and we'll make quick work of these two forms."

Having signed them, Selena stood. "Tessa, thank you for your time today – for ensuring that Aunt Jenny's estate will be handled. It was a pleasure to meet you."

Tessa said, "Take care of yourself, Selena."

With the Last Will and Testament of Jenny Louise Jenkins in her hand, Selena had drifted absently out of the offices of Perrault & Associates, feeling fragile and exhausted. She sat for quite a while in the car. She could not bring herself to look at the Will.

Aunt Jenny? Oh my gosh.

Selena then drove through the frenzied storm with all the concentration she could muster to get home to Aunt Jenny's house – her house, her refuge.

Now, home with the rain battering the windows, increasing in severity, she rose, let Rufus out again. He came in shaking water all over her once more. This time Caylie got in the water's path, meowed and scampered off. Selena gave Rufus, aka Curly Joe, another rubdown.

Now, I'm determined to settle my mind. So, I need to go back up to Aunt Jenny's bedroom.

I have a home. I don't know how I feel! Aunt Jenny wanted this for me. Aunt Jenny had planned for this eventuality.

But I think this house feels more settled at this moment if that's possible, and its loneliness has diminished in a small way. I belong to this house, and it has embraced me too. I'm sure I feel that.

Upstairs, Selena absently ran her hands over the dresses and outfits in her Aunt Jenny's travel room behind the main closet. It felt good in a way to be where Aunt Jenny had obviously spent part of her life.

What an adventure awaits me "if", no, when I decide to take a nosedive to see what would happen. I sense amazement behind every fiber in my body.

Selena could hear in her mind again the instructions she had heard to wait and be patient. However, she kept scanning the screen, seeing the places and the numbers. Country names filled up entire screens, with numbers following them. Selena moved back to the map. England had many pins on it, numbered from the year 1000 AD. The city of London alone had numerous pins in it and Selena wondered, if her thoughts were going in the right direction, this must mean that London would have over 20 different dates to choose from!

Clearly, here is the answer to so many mysteries. Of course, my grandparents brought back the beautiful, magnificent ornaments, coins, sketches, knickknacks from their A&O travels in that time machine.

Being in this room and thinking of that again required a sit down on the computer chair.

She moaned, "I need to see this all again. The photographs and what I found on the computer speak for themselves. All this must be true. I'm feeling excited about the possibility of travelling somewhere, somewhere to give me room to breathe and to gather my wits. A different place might help me move forward. To sense what Grandma Olive and Grandpa Arthur felt – perhaps exhilarated, perhaps in control. Control of something would be a great feeling."

Selena clicked the arrow key down to "England--1851". Selena searched and found the gown and accessories for England--1851 on the racks of clothing, a gown of the finest gold material flowing to the ground, with sleeves of spun lace.

Back at the screen, startled, she realized there were pictures on the screen, moving as though she were watching a television screen. At the bottom of the screen, information was flashing for her. There were commands she could enter when willing. She took a few minutes this time to note the information that the computer gave her and what was needed to continue its process. Since Selena had RETRIEVED a country and a year, there appeared to be information programmed into the computer, such as the date and GO-THERE: CONFIRM.

"These are the exact same Travel Machine choices used by my grandparents. Aunt Jenny also could've gone anywhere had she chosen to."

Her breath catching in her throat and rubbing her face, she whispered, "I could use any one of these choices – If I wanted to travel myself!"

Several lines down from this information, Selena noticed the words: "ENGAGE TIME MACHINE". Flashing on and off, over and over. The words rushed to her lips, "Engage Time Machine! This was so real and yet I feel it's not! The garments, maps, slips of paper in the books all related to the computer and travelling in time. I can become part of a time-travel excursion."

Her hand hovered over the keyboard, her thoughts rushing through her mind.

Engage Time Machine! Oh lord!

Selena's thoughts seemed to echo in her mind.

My grandparents had used this time travel machine repeatedly to travel far away. Quiet, reticent Aunt Jenny locked herself away in this room, travelling away from and to her own city after her own parents had "gone".

Still in a daze, Selena stood up and her hands reached tentatively, then eagerly, for another hanger with one of the gowns, again accompanied by all the accessories. She decided it looked much too inviting to just hang there or simply hold it up. Selena put on the gown and matching accessories, noting the gown had England--1215 imprinted inside the collar. She again moved to the computer, pressed the <RETRIEVE> screen and cursored down to "England--1215".

"Incredible!" she shouted. The screen showed her a photo of this exact dress. The information on the screen already programmed into this "Travel Plan" that her grandparents A&O had used showed:

TODAY'S DATE: current date/time

GO THERE: CONFIRM England--1215 No Yes

The information already programmed in was: England--1215 = 2:00 pm June 15, 1215

COSTUME NUMBER: The information already programmed in was England--1215
COME BACK DATE
(using current location) Time/Date/Year:
current date/time? Yes
choose different time to RETURN? No Yes
TIME AT DESTINATION Minutes/Hours/Days:
Minutes …..
Hours …..
Days …..
PLEASE CONFIRM Minutes/Hours/Days No Yes
+CHOOSE DIFFERENT LOCATION (CUSTOMIZE)+
ENGAGE TIME MACHINE: No Yes
PLEASE CONFIRM = ENGAGE TIME MACHINE: No Yes
Press ENTER

Selena saw the request:

COME BACK DATE (using current location) Time/Date/Year:

"Come back? Have I decided to go to 1215? Computers. Time travel – 1215 England. Yeah! I want to go very badly. I can program when I want to return."

Entered in her diary later, was the following:

"I was intent on going on a time travel adventure of my own. I needed to get it out of my system.

I could envision it because I knew history. There was the clothing. The computer was programmed.

I could just blend in with everyone. No one would notice me. I'd joked with Laura for years with both of us talking in a posh accent. Who would know? I felt I could set the time for just a few minutes and then pop back home! Who would give up the chance to have this thrill?

The excitement was intoxicating. I darn well could do it. Yet I hesitated.

Did I want to go? Oh, yeah. I need to go to see what is going on here in this room and live and experience this mystery!

There is power in feeling that I could go to any country, to any time and year I want to. I could witness historical events.

I was trying to put Aunt Jenny's words "to wait" out of my mind. Was it an order? Aunt Jenny might want me to try it at least one time. I can feel closer to Aunt Jenny in doing this. I know she said to wait...."

At the time travel machine, goosebumps were prickling up and down her arms and spine. Excitement invaded the entire room, saturating her every nerve ending. But – still she stalled.

What if I don't come back?

Hesitation crept up on her, twisting and grabbing at her heart. More thoughts, more time wondering. Selena realized she had been holding her breath for a few moments. She could no longer hold it and the breath rushed out of her lungs.

Selena shouted and she waved her arms in the air as though forcing the doubt away. "This worked for my Grandpa and Grandma Jenkins and Aunt Jenny time and time again."

Selena stated to anyone and everyone in a positive manner, "Yes, by goodness, I'll have my own adventures and see this mystery through." She pinned her hair up with nearby pins and set the accessory hat on her head. She was set.

After one more glance at the computer screen, Selena settled herself down on the computer chair, swiveling the chair into position as though planning to attack the computer and demand it do as she wished – and maybe she was. Barely pausing, Selena touched the keys.

The computer's cursor was still positioned at:

```
TODAY'S DATE: current date/time
GO THERE: CONFIRM England--1215 No Yes
```

The information already programmed in was: England--1215 = 2:00 pm June 15, 1215

`COSTUME NUMBER:` The information already programmed in was: England--1215

```
COME BACK DATE
(using current location) Time/Date/Year:
current date/time? Yes
choose different time to RETURN? No Yes
```

There were decisions to be made here – big decisions. *Think, think.* Selena chose to Come Back at the current time so she could come back to the same time that it was now.

Is that what it meant?

```
TIME AT DESTINATION Minutes/Hours/Days:
Minutes …..
Hours …..
Days …..
PLEASE CONFIRM Minutes/Hours/Days No Yes
+CHOOSE DIFFERENT LOCATION (CUSTOMIZE)+
```

This would mean the amount of time that I'd actually be there. I could be at my destination for any length of time. What will I find there? Would I be noticed? I am fully aware of what was happening in 1215.

I'm going!

Selena picked Minutes 30

30 minutes of absolute excitement! And control, right?

```
ENGAGE TIME MACHINE: No Yes
PLEASE CONFIRM = ENGAGE TIME MACHINE: No Yes
```

She pressed `Yes` Yes

Selena hesitated, thought of England in 1215, took a breath, and pressed
`ENTER`

◇◇◇

Wwww-Wwwww-whirl, Sssss-Sssss-spin, then blur!

◇◇◇

As she looked around, Selena found herself in a magnificent and beautifully treed forest. The sky was barely visible through the tall trees. She took a breath of wonderfully fresh pure, 1215 countryside English air. Her gown rustled as she changed position.

I'm certainly not imagining this! What a feeling of elation, exhilaration.

"I did it", she whispered triumphantly to herself. Robins were chirping, serenading her as they flitted from tree to tree. Selena watched a rabbit dart behind a shrub as though investigating her to see if she meant well or not. The area she had arrived in was beautiful. Under her sleeve, she still had her fitness watch on – 28 minutes left.

I feel relaxed with the surroundings bewitching me. Next time, I'll type in hours, not minutes. This is so easy, piece of cake. Oh my God, this is exciting. Now, I'm eager to find something to show me the year of 1215 England!

Walking several more steps, hearing something (*a wolf? a bear?*), she stopped and moved quickly, yet quietly, behind the closest large bush to see what the noise was before venturing out.

People! I hear feet stomping about, and now voices directly in front of me.

Regaining her composure, Selena could recognize that they were angry voices. Quietly, she stood, listening as several men's voices were commanding someone to do something, to persuade – no, to force, someone to sign a document.

I know what this is!

Creeping closer, she heard, "King John, you must sign here. Whereby you shall admit you all your errors and promise thus to respect the laws of England!"

"England", "England" everyone seemed to be shouting.

A frightened deer ran too near to Selena. She attempted to stifle a gasp of surprise; however, not stifled quite enough, for after a moment passed, someone behind her roughly grabbed her arm, dragging her to the men and their angry voices.

"Wench, why are you here spying on the signing of the Magna Carta? I demandeth, wench?" Not having time to form a response to this, Selena tried to regain her footing, at the same time, attempting to pull free of the fierce grip, only to be held more firmly and roughly. She was shaking in surprise and apprehensive as to what would happen to her, but her courage won out.

"Take your hands off me!" Selena demanded, hoping for the proper accent.

Another voice shouted, "Wait, Sir James. This is no wench! Who are you, your Ladyship? Your garments indicate that you have some standing in our society. What are you doing here, your Ladyship? Who sent you? What do you want? Who are you reporting to? What is your name? Where are you from?"

Since I am a Lady, I had best think how ladies would be acting and get the accent correct.

"Just wait one moment as I need to catch my breath. My horses have run away with the carriage. I am Lady Maggie Smith from Downton Abbey.

I know that's not a real place – Do they?

The well-groomed gentleman in fine clothing gave a slight bow of his head in acknowledgement.

"This may be a Lady, Sir Edmund, but she might still be here to spy, and we cannot have her witness this important event. Charles, here, take her to the waiting carriage. Watch over her there. We will come there in time and deal with her."

Selena feigned a gracious manner. She had a hard enough time managing a dignified walk in this heavy gown, which was huge and full of material. She gathered up the garment as best she could and followed the man named Charles to a carriage of some sort. When the man Charles helped her up into the carriage, he said he was sorry to have to treat her this way, and he hoped that in her report, she would speak well of him. There was silence as Selena did not reply. She tried to be ladylike and swiveled her head this way and that, looking disdainfully at the man called Charles.

"Where were you off to, My Lady?"

Where was I off to indeed! Hum. "I was off to London to visit the Queen," was the reply that formed in her mind from an old nursery rhyme, but she knew exactly who was on the throne. Her history knowledge was excellent – King Richard the Lionhearted had been king, but in 1215, his brother King John who had taken over the throne from King Richard, was being forced to sign the Magna Carta!

I cannot, of course, be certain what King John looked like; however, the man near the large stone and holding the documents was extremely well dressed and jewelled. He appeared to be guarded by other well-dressed men with weapons drawn.

She paused for as long as she felt he would tolerate, smiling in a mildly condescending way. "I am certain the ladies and chaperones that I was with will be looking for me now." She improvised. "Could you please call out that Lady Smith is with you, and they will come to get me. They will answer any questions you have regarding our destination."

There was more shouting from the men in the distance. Her captor, Charles, seemed to want to go off to where those men were. He looked back at her obviously wishing he could be gone.

"I am not to leave you."

Minutes later, there was rustling in the bush, and the other men were coming toward her holding scrolled papers. They were looking in her direction in a furious manner.

"You will tell us from whence you came and what your purpose is here" one man shouted, several armed men echoing his words. She was now surrounded by them. Inside the carriage, Selena, aka Lady Maggie Smith, was becoming concerned.

I'm not afraid. How shall I answer them?

At that instant ...

◇◇◇

Wwww-Wwwww-whirl, Sssss-Sssss-spin, then blur!

◇◇◇

(Back in 1215 England, an incredibly surprised group of landowners looked at what was now thin air in the carriage and then back again to the King of England).

Selena felt herself drop to the computer chair in her Aunt Jenny's secret room. She remained there, completely unhurt, nonetheless happy to be back. Aloud, she stated, "What a close call!"

Shakily, Selena removed the hat and exchanged the gown and shoes for her own clothing, having to sit down twice to catch her breath. Rufus was barking on the other side of her aunt's bedroom door.

Somehow, he must have sensed something amiss, or he did not want to be alone with the intense storm that must be raging.

As she was coming from the room, noticing lightning flashes through the curtains immediately followed by a thunderous *BOOM*, Selena opened the door and spoke in soothing tones to Rufus, "Rufus, it's fine. I'm here. Are you okay puppy?" Searching, she found Caylie hiding under her bed. Caylie was coaxed out and petted and that petting calmed Caylie Ceilidh and the resulting purring calmed Selena.

Also entered in her diary later, was the following:

> *"When I landed from my trip, again, I didn't hear the pounding rain, ferocious wind or thunder until I came out into Aunt Jenny's bedroom. How weird that I was so engrossed in the travel room that I hadn't noticed any sound.*
>
> *I had my own trip! And what a trip! I went through the time machine. I went to 1215 England, saw King John, almost saw signing of the Magna Carta!*
>
> *That was exhilarating. I'm so excited. Yet how odd I feel, exhausted, my legs are wobbly, my heart is racing.*
>
> *I can't believe I did that myself. I wasn't afraid. It was an amazing adventure. My body still feels shaky and I've a slight headache. That storm is crazy. Sleep, I need sleep."*

Selena still could not take Rufus for a walk even though they both needed it. The rain seemed to be coming down in solid masses.

I sense Rufus and Caylie are still nervous about the horrific wind and banging thunder. I'm starving! At least the power is still on.

She made her supper of shrimp and ramen noodles cooked in sesame oil with peas. Satisfied that her tummy was full and settled from everything today had thrown at her and, evidently, she had decided to throw at herself, she relaxed in the family room to watch, of course, the show, "Downton Abbey". There on screen was the real Lady Maggie Smith.

How appropriate!

Selena had to let Rufus out again in the storm, wiping him down as he looked at her accusingly – as though he did wonder why she kept doing this to him.

Getting to sleep that night was difficult with so many thoughts swirling through her brain and the storm exploding outside.

As the storm outside raged, branches slammed into her bedroom windows. It must have been after midnight when she fell asleep, mentally and emotionally drained from the day's meeting and her time travel.

The storm moved in. Brilliant and blinding flashes of lightning, accompanied by the distant, yet deafening claps of thunder, changed the entire atmosphere to one of violence. A roaring and powerful wind added to the wickedness of the storm. Figures, whether running or walking, were rushing to the safety of their homes. The hail poured down continuously in a steady stream of destruction. Still the lightning flashed and still the thunder crashed. Bending from the force of the wind were the trees, some smaller ones snapping in its strength. Fences shattered against the sidewalks. Gardens and flowers were soon hidden beneath the whiteness of the hailstones as they smashed against the earth. Signs of the storm were everywhere. Grain crops were demolished – months of work and patience destroyed. Glass lay about, broken from the hail. And then it was quiet. Suddenly it had left, having done its damage.

Selena woke up suddenly, perspiring and being aware that she had had another dream.

Jumbled on waking, she glanced at the clock – *5:00 a.m.* The storm was now subsiding, although it must have precipitated that dreadful dream. The trees were no longer banging into the windowpanes. Getting up and having a drink of water, then reading through a few pages of a book of poems, she settled down and fell asleep once again with a dream that she could not remember upon waking.

14

Good-Bye

H*e's looking at me very suspiciously. Bet he's looking for that blasted water hose that he thinks I turned on him yesterday!*

"It's okay, Rufus, honestly. No more rain today." The pets were fed, and Rufus was taken for a lovely long walk. Rufus walked with his tail down, and he seemed aware that today was a sad day. Selena stopped a couple of times to ruffle his fur and tell him it was okay, even though she herself was walking a slow, sluggish walk.

I know what alone really is. This is the day I'll say my final Good-Bye.

The wicked storm had blown past them, and today was turning out to be a beautiful spring day, no wind and the warmth of the sun was evident. Spring was here today anyway, and Selena could smell the fresh, clean smell after the rain and hear the birds happily chirping.

"I must get through today and see what tomorrow will bring. I can do this."

As Selena saw the debris and branches strewn around the yard and garden, she thought she would talk to Mr. Brisbane about clearing the worst of it away.

Maybe not today. It'd be good for me to work clearing the smaller debris left behind after that storm.

Once back from the walk, saddened and wanting to keep her mind occupied, Selena prepared for the group that would come over after the funeral. Her thoughts and the clothing she wore were dark.

Reverend Sherwood Badham, standing staunchly at the front, spoke. "We meet here today to honour and pay tribute to the life of JENNY LOUISE JENKINS." This was the beginning of a beautiful good-bye to her Aunt Jenny.

He then read out a poem that a good friend of his had written some years before.

"In my world there is no day.
There's only night,
But in this world of darkness
I see a tiny golden light.
And even if it's only by
This dimming light I see,
I see there's only one good hope
That's left in here for me.
And then, silently, I try
To kneel and pray
For the coming of a
Shining bright new day.
And then, slowly, by the
Growing light I see,
That God, my last hope,
Has come to comfort me."

That poem is so touching. She had not heard it prior to Reverend Badham suggesting it, and it really struck a poignant chord with her. Tears came easily at that point, and Karen, sitting next to her, touched her hand.

"It's all right to cry." Karen sat on one side of her and Bud on the other. Theodore gave her a kind smile from where he was sitting beside his father. Austin was sitting on the other side of his mother and reached to squeeze her shoulder, bringing intense memories to Selena of other touches from him in times past.

Not now.

Selena was very aware that her Aunt Jenny was in the casket at the front of the church – a beautiful hardwood oak with end and side designs. She was listening to the words of the Eulogy that she had written for Reverend Badham to say. He mentioned Jenny's work on writing the history books, her love of reading, the pets that she had acquired and her taking in Selena after Selena's parents had passed away. The hymns were easy to choose as Aunt Jenny hummed these particular hymns. "*Abide With Me*", "*How Great Thou Art*" and "*The Old Rugged Cross*" were the three Selena chose for her aunt. Tributes were said by two of Aunt Jenny's friends and one of her peers.

Earlier, Karen and Bud had driven Selena to her aunt's funeral. Both their sons, Austin and Theodore, had come home for the funeral. After all, they had known her aunt since they were small children. They had always been welcomed in her home when visiting with Selena.

Selena had said a friendly hello to both Austin and Theodore. Austin gave her a firm hug and Theo gave her a wink which may have meant that Laura had told him she had confided in Selena about their dating and engagement. Each said how sorry they were about her aunt passing away. Austin said, "I'd ask ya ta ride with me, but I guess you're gonna go early with mom and dad." As he touched her shoulder, he added, "I'll see ya there, Selena."

"For sure. See you both there."

He talks differently.

While Karen and Bud sat discreetly at the back of the church, Selena had been escorted to the front by the funeral director. She talked to her Aunt Jenny and said her final goodbye, barely in control, and these minutes of solitude with her aunt were enormously important to her.

Karen and Bud had then joined Selena in the front pew of the church as she had preferred not to be in the family room as was usual for family prior to the funeral.

I am the only family.

As she glanced back, she felt grateful to see several of the staff from The Caring Medical Clinic were in attendance. Dr. Kev and Elizabeth nodded to her. Bethany and Penelope each gave a slight smile. Then Colleen and Laura came to give her a quick hug.

"I'm going to be in town this whole weekend," Laura whispered. Fiercely hugging Selena, she added. "I'll see you after the funeral."

"Could you both please come sit in this row with me? Laura you can sit beside Theodore." Laura and Selena exchanged a knowing glance at each other.

Mr. Eric Brisbane, the gardener, attended, as well as Mr. Perrault and Ms. O'Bryan, Dr. Robertson, neighbours, many parishioners and several people that Selena did not know. Selena had telephoned some people and neighbours with the sad news of her aunt's death. With the Reverend's help, Selena had prepared and sent the obituary to both Ottawa papers. The church had emailed their parishioners of her aunt's passing and advising details of the funeral.

Everyone was invited back to Aunt Jenny's for a social after the graveside service. Along with a scrumptious buffet prepared by the church ladies' auxilliary, Selena had made punch and lemonade before the service. The ladies served tea and coffee. Selena had also provided tiny individual poppy seed cakes that had been her Aunt Jenny's favourite.

The mourners mingled, chatting about their relationship with her Aunt Jenny, and several came to speak to Selena for a few moments.

Smiling at last, Selena was content that so many people had been at the funeral and were now here conversing about her aunt. Mr. Brisbane confided that he had known her Aunt Jenny for more than 35 years. They had gone to school together and had maintained a friendship since university. Selena was surprised at that. She quizzed him about how long he had been doing her aunt's yard work.

"For longer than you have lived with your Aunt Jenny, my dear." For one second, Selena, even in her misery at her aunt's funeral social, re-lived her thoughts regarding the mystery of the other one-time gardener.

Pulling herself from that thought, she addressed him before she remembered that this might not be the time. "Mr. Brisbane, I'm worried what the storm has done, and I wondered if you could come by in the next couple of days and handle the branches and destruction the storm did last night?" Mr. Brisbane assured Selena of his intention.

"I'll be bringing my nephew to do just that tomorrow, Selena. I'm glad that you're aware of what needs to be done. It shows you care about what happens to Jenny's place. If you wish, I'll also be starting the spring yard and garden cleanup next week."

"Oh, yes please do, Mr. Brisbane. I found out that Aunt Jenny left me the house. I'm still absorbing that fact so please continue everything that you have been doing. I'm so confident in you, and you genuinely seem to love the yard looking its best."

"I do very much Selena, more than you know. Take care, and perhaps I'll see you tomorrow."

A gentleman with long-style brown hair and slim physique, came over to introduce himself—Julian Andrews, the accountant. Selena thought he looked familiar. When she asked him if she had met him previously, he said that he also attended their church. Selena said she was glad to properly make his acquaintance, and they agreed to meet next week. He advised Selena that he was working with Perrault & Associates on the final numbers. He said Selena should call for an appointment because there would be decisions to make.

Selena entered the following into her diary later:

"Aunt Jenny,

There were many of your friends and associates at your funeral memorial today to pay their respects to you. I'm pleased with the number that cared to say farewell. You had friends, Aunt Jenny. You had friends."

Laura, Colleen, Austin, Theodore and Dr. Kev stayed on the pretense of helping her clean up. Since everyone else had met on previous occasions, Selena had only one introduction to make.

"Austin and Theodore, this is my one of my bosses and friend, Dr. Kevin Carey. Dr. Carey …"

"Please call me Kevin when we're not at work."

"Of course. Kevin, these two scoundrels are my next-door neighbours. I grew up with them since I was seven and they were eight. We've played hide and seek, climbed trees and ran around until we couldn't run any more. Lots of good times."

"Not to mention the good times of a couple of dates either!" declared Theodore. Austin turned sharply to face Theodore, and that statement also got Kevin's attention.

"Oh, what's that about dates? Theodore and you were an item?"

"Well, not Theodore. It was Austin that I went out with. Then he ran away to become a firefighter, and Theodore left to join the police academy. It was fun when they lived next door. They're identical twins as you might have guessed. They were both full of mischief. I was over in their yard often because it was so quiet at this house."

"Hum, pleased to meet both of you."

Austin came out with, "Pleased ta meet ya too, Kevin. Will we be seein' much of ya around here?"

"So," Selena interrupted, "if anyone is interested, there's left over lemonade and punch. I'll make more tea and coffee. I also have enough cold cuts, cheeses and buns to get us through two days."

Rufus had his tail wagging, hoping for a morsel. Caylie Ceilidh had curled up on her blanket on the sofa, hoping for some peace and quiet.

It's wonderful of Dr. Kev to stay to help out. It's fantastic to have my friends together. They said they weren't leaving me alone for the rest of the day.

"I'll go ta our place and scrounge up some beer and pretzels," Austin offered.

Selena was contemplating what board games she might have when Colleen spoke up.

"I brought a game I like just in case we stayed. It's called *Two Truths and a Lie*. Since not all of us know each other well or haven't seen each other for quite a while, this could be a very entertaining."

This was met with nodding. Noting the consensus, Laura said, "None of us has played it, and there would be countless facts we don't know for certain about each other."

"Yeah"

"Definitely"

"For sure"

"Perfect"

Austin and Theodore left and quickly returned with a bottle of wine and a six-pack of beer, along with the promised pretzels and three bags of chips.

When Colleen returned from her car, she read out part of the *Two Truths and a Lie* instructions:

> "Two Truths and a Lie is a classic get-to-know-you type of icebreaker game. Players tell two truths and one lie about themselves (in any order). The object of the game is for everyone else to determine which statement is actually the false one."

Thoughts of manipulating the game to her advantage came to mind.

Oooo, this could work for me to say something about time travel. Should I?

While absorbing her current situation, she wondered if she should share with them what her family had been doing over the past number of years. She had not been able to think how to bring it up.

Could I simply blurt this out?

"Well, I've had some surprises in the past few days. My quiet and reserved aunt has been travelling in time; my grandparents whom I believed had died in 2008, time-travelled dozens of times. They went back to live in the year 1967."

Possibly I can add: "I myself travelled to 1215 and met King John."

How long would it take them to decide I had been under too much stress and needed some alone time, in a different kind of home, wearing a white jacket?

So, here was an opportunity. Selena's plan formed that during her turn, she would say a "truth" that she had a time travel machine. How to go about this was going to take ingenuity.

Two stunning truths and one lie …

Colleen stopped Selena's musings when she instructed, "All right. You're all settled. But let's move the chairs around in a circle. No, brothers are not allowed to sit together. You'll cheat somehow. Here, I'll help. Selena, Austin, Laura, Theodore, myself and Kevin. There you go. That'll work.

"We'll go counterclockwise for a change-up. I'm really excited about this. I've got paper with me. Can everyone dig out a pen? Selena, do you have two for the ones that don't? Please print your name across the top. Give yourself Zero if you get the answer wrong. One point if you guess right."

Colleen continued. "I've played this game before. I can go first if that's no problem?" She proceeded before everyone could even respond.

"Good, well here goes:

1-I snore. 2-I have six toes on one foot. 3-I hate lemon pie.

"Okay guys and gals – don't chatter before you vote. No sharing answers. Remember, two are truths and one is the lie. Pick out which one of my statements is the lie."

"Who votes the first statement that I snore is the lie?"

"Who votes the second one that I have six toes is the lie?"

"Who votes the third statement that I hate lemon pie is the lie?"

Votes were taken, tallied and written down. Now the inevitable witty conversation ensued.

"Look at her shoes. Is one wider than the other?"

"A sloth!"

"The lie is," she paused for effect, "that I've six toes on one foot." Laughter and hilarity followed this reveal.

"You snore!" exclaimed Kevin, and then he looked embarrassed.

Colleen turned a little red from Kevin's comment, gathered herself and ordered, "All right, write down your score. Zero if you got it wrong. One point if you were correct." Smiling at the fact that her game seemed a success, she said with satisfaction, "Since we are going counterclockwise, Theodore, can you think of two truths and one lie?"

"Um, okay. No problem. I'm ready –

1-I once kissed a frog 2-I love roller coasters 3-I took Selena on a date"

There was one stern look from Austin, a warning. This was not lost on Kevin either. He thought to himself: *I'm getting a lot of information on how things are or once were.*

"No chattering before you vote."

So, the process repeated as Theodore said:

"Who votes #1-I once kissed a frog is the lie?"

"Who votes #2 that I love roller coasters is the lie?"

"Who votes the third that I took Selena on a date is the lie?"

Austin's face grew darker in countenance as he thought over his brother's choices. He knew there had to be two truths. He did not know if Theodore had kissed a frog. Votes were written down.

"The lie is 'I once kissed a frog.'"

Selena's countenance turned serious, and she was not laughing. Austin was definitely not laughing – rather he was scowling in a threatening manner. Seeing his brother's face, Theodore looked uneasy, no longer laughing.

"You didn't take me on a date, Theodore," Selena said shaking her head.

Now Theodore looked nervously toward Selena.

"What are you calling a date? I claim this point because you didn't take me on a date. What you said right now is the lie!"

Austin growled, "What ya talkin' about, Theo?"

Seeming both proud of his lie and embarrassed of what he was going to say, Theodore revealed, "Well, it's true. One day, Austin couldn't make your date as he'd forgotten about an extra class. He had to rush away to get to it. I was supposed to tell you that he couldn't make it. Instead, I put on his favourite shirt and then picked you up." Another nervous glance at his brother.

"We went for a walk in the woods, and I took Selena to what I knew to be her favourite ice cream shop. It was easy since we are identical, and I even knew from listening to Austin what her favourite ice cream was."

Austin was up and jumped across the floor and grabbed Theodore's arm. As both men were compact and of medium height, their muscular bodies from daily workouts were not obvious until you saw them close up. There was concern there would be a fight. Austin's face was red and slightly contorted. He looked truly angry. Selena jumped when Austin yelled.

"You jerk! Damn ya! Ya kept this a secret all this time. Ya didn't tell me what ya'd done? How could ya do that ta me?"

Rufus started to bark at that burst of activity. Selena gave Rufus a pat on the back to calm him, but she wanted to give Theodore a whack on his back.

Selena intervened, "Yeah, Theodore, that was a jerk thing to do. We were such good friends. I'm surprised at you – not pleased at all. I remember that time because I wondered if Austin was upset with me." Selena's voice cracked a little as she was reliving that past emotion. "He was acting differently that day. It's a good thing both your looks changed so it couldn't happen again." Then Selena walked two steps toward Theodore and asked accusingly, "Did it ever happen again?"

"No, honest. It was that I didn't want you to be upset that Austin stood you up. I didn't mean anything by it. The longer I didn't mention it and the more in the past it became, there didn't seem any reason to bring it up. We're all adults now, and I thought for a moment it would be funny to confess with *Two Truths and A Lie...*"

Selena grimaced and admitted, "I'm glad it's out in the open now."

Austin's face relaxed just a little, the redness leaving his countenance, "Yeah, well, it's a good thing ya stopped growin' taller, and got chunky so that we're no longer identical."

Theodore demanded, "What do you mean chunky? I'm 172 pounds and 5'11'. This is all muscle, pal – pure muscle."

"Oh, for goodness sakes, you juveniles," interjected Laura. "I actually do have to get back to my parents so that they can see me for a little while this evening. They dropped me off here and I had told them I could get a ride. I'll call a taxi."

Theodore jumped at this chance to spend a little more time with Laura. "I'll drive you, Laura. I think I should make a grand exit at this point anyway."

"Thanks, Theodore." She grinned and gave him a wink. "It would be amazing for you to drive me."

Hugging Selena in a tight, long hug, Laura spoke softly, "I'm so glad we had this time together. I'm sorry about your Aunt Jenny, but it's good that you have all of us here to give you some friendship time. I want to see you before I leave. I'll call or text."

"Thank you so much, Laura. I'll absolutely get in touch. Thanks so much for coming and for staying." They hugged and again Selena fought the tears.

"Good-bye everyone."

"It was nice seeing you again."

"Good-bye."

Austin gave Theodore a solid punch in the arm when he saw them to the door. Closing the door, Austin looked at Selena. "Well, I didn't know."

"The little brat! He did say he was trying to help, though." She gave Austin a shrug, and they went back into the living room.

Kevin, aware the two had dated, watched, and he was saw that no hugs were involved between Austin and Selena. Each of the remaining friends moved, re-positioning their chairs and they agreed that they would take a little break for some munchies and drinks.

Minutes later, laughing a little nervously at what had transpired, and eager to get to hear what other revelations might be made, they sat down chuckling.

Colleen began again, "All right, write down your score. Zero if you got it wrong. One point if you were correct." Still having the odd giggle, they complied.

"Laura didn't take her turn. Yeah, I wonder what her truths and a lie are?" questioned Austin aloud. "Could that be why she needed ta leave before her turn?"

Selena looked at him sharply, hoping he didn't know Laura's true relationship with Theodore and spoil it for the couple. "I'm sure it was nothing, nosey."

"My turn then. I'm not sure I can outdo my two-faced brother, but here goes:

1-I'm a ventriloquist 2-My favourite singer is Cher 3-I'm colour blind.

Colleen looked sternly as Kevin leaned to say something to Austin, "No chatting, you two."

"Who votes that I'm a ventriloquist is my lie?"

"Who votes that I my favourite singer is my lie?"

"Who votes that I'm colour blind is my lie?"

Votes were written down.

"My lie is," Austin announced, "that my favourite singer is Cher. It's definitely not." Discussion followed, as well as excited comments, though no one seemed interested who his favourite singer actually was at that moment.

"Can you really do ventriloquism?"

"Show us."

"Here, use this pen for a prop and give us a demonstration."

Austin, happy to be in the spotlight, took the "microphone" and showed off that he had some talent to perform as a ventriloquist.

"Hey, it got me a gig in the bar near the Fire Hall, so I made a few bucks for drinks."

It was a fun performance. Selena was also amused and a little amazed, "I think you did a fabulous job."

Colleen took over again, "All right now, write it down. Zero for a wrong guess. One point if you were right."

Selena's turn came up. She blanched. "I'd like a glass of wine, and then I'll be back from the washroom in a couple of minutes. Visit and decide your story, Kevin."

Stalling for time, she had a decision to make. While in the washroom, she muttered, "All right, am I going through with a reveal of the Time Travel Machine?"

Upon returning to the room, she gulped a mouthful of wine, thought while taking a couple of large breaths and said, "Okay, here we go:

1- I knocked out a teacher 2- And, oh … I was on TV once 3- My aunt has a Time Travel Machine in the … basement."

Incredulity and bewilderment broke out.

"You what…!!!!"

"Selena, when did…"

"Sorry to interrupt this titillating discussion, but no chatter until you put your vote down," ordered Colleen while laughing.

Selena hesitated, rubbing her eyebrow and pushing her hair away from her face, deliberating: *How am I getting out of this one? I've changed my mind. I think I can cover it though by fiddling with a truth.*

They were all looking extremely interested toward Selena. She supposed they were wondering why she was taking so long to respond and quite amazed at what she had suggested as her truths and a lie.

Inside she felt sure she could answer the questions even though she was shaking with wonder at herself.

Should I tell them?

Then she spoke.

"Who votes the lie is #1- I once knocked out a teacher?"

Her friends were laughing…

"Who votes the lie is #2-I was on TV once?

"Who votes that #3-My aunt has a Time Travel Machine in the … basement is a lie?"

Colleen gave Selena a questioning glance, and Austin winked at Selena. Everyone voted on their idea of what the lie was.

"Okay, the lie is…. (coughing) … that My aunt has a Time Travel Machine in the basement."

I just couldn't say it. I almost made an awfully bad decision, but I caught myself. Not very mature.

"Phew! Selena. A Time Machine?"

"Knocked out a teacher?"

"You knocked out a teacher? You? When?"

"I did – during a Tai class. It was an accident, and I was so embarrassed."

Austin grinned and said, "I knew that, Selena. Laura said it was great!"

"So, you were on TV?"

Again, thinking how to answer and deciding, "Aunt Jenny has an ancient TV in the basement. I sat on it when I was little!"

Colleen gave her a look and said, "Selena, that might be cheating! At first, I thought you had three lies, but it's brilliant. Should we allow it? All agreed? Good, but bad. It's in."

Guiltily, Selena let them mark down their scores.

Kevin shifted in his seat, took off his glasses and gave each lens a perfunctory rub. He then stood up.

"Well, well, going last might be that I've nothing as interesting left to expose. Here I go though:

1-I have never eaten pizza 2-I have a half sibling in Scotland 3-When I was 16, I planned to become a race car driver."

Selena said this time, "No talking until votes are in, remember?"

"Who votes the lie is 1-I have never eaten pizza?"

"Who votes the lie is 2-I have a half sibling in Scotland?"

"And who votes the lie is 3-When I was 16, I planned to become a race car driver?"

Kevin waited, smiling to himself. "Perfect, have you got your vote in? The truth is that I've never eaten pizza. Second truth I did want to become a race car driver. The lie is that I have a half-sibling in Scotland."

"You wanted to become a race car driver! How interesting."

"Are ya safe ta drive with?"

"You've *never* eaten pizza? I can't believe anyone has never, ever eaten pizza."

Looking like she understood something, Colleen laughed and then said, "That's why you didn't ever eat any pizza when anyone in the Clinic went out for lunch or supper together. A pizza place was not ever your choice for take-out either. You didn't tell me, I mean us, all those times."

Naturally, discussion followed as they tallied their scores and chatted about what was revealed and what fun it had been. Laura and Theodore, not surprisingly, did not win the total count, nor did Kevin. Colleen and Selena were tied at second highest, with Austin the winner.

"Okay, what's the prize?" inquired Austin. "Do I win anythin'?"

"Anyone want to chip in? Take Austin out for supper tonight, maybe for pizza?" laughed Colleen.

"Yeah, let's go to *Fiazza Fresh Fried* on Murray Street," said Austin.

"Perfect! I'm fine with that. I'll … even … order … lasagna!"

❖

After the evening was over, Selena was getting ready for sleep. She said her prayers for her Aunt Jenny, while wishing her aunt was sleeping in her own bedroom.

She added to her diary:

> *"I'm sorry Aunt Jenny. I almost goofed like a teenager with a secret, telling about the time machine to feel important. Bless you, Aunt Jenny."*

PART TWO

15

QUESTIONS

CONFUSION PULSED IN SELENA'S mind as she remembered with a small half smile and a half frown her conversations with Austin on their way back to her place last night. They had reminisced about their younger days, at first just skittering across the fact that they had dated during high school and the last year Austin was still home, taking prep classes.

Selena sat with the spoon suspended over her breakfast of Kashi cereal contemplating her day and evening yesterday. Last night had been a genuinely enjoyable time out for supper. Austin had driven Selena home. Kevin went home by himself as did Colleen.

I am so freaking shocked and perplexed!

Reminiscing about what she and Austin had discussed in her driveway, Selena rehashed their conversation in her mind. She vividly remembered these parts of the conversation from the evening before:

"I'm sorry for your Aunt Jenny's passin' away." Then, unexpectedly, "I miss ya, Selena."

"Oh, yeah. I miss those days too. We had so much fun."

The 'do you remembers' had added to their conversation.

"Do you remember when we still played hide and seek?"

"Do ya remember me pullin' ya out of the ditch when ya fell in?" added Austin, "I remember kissin' your elbow better cuz ya hurt it."

"Sure, I remember."

Austin had then looked a little more seriously at her. "Do ya remember all the kisses we shared before I went away ta school?"

"Yes, obviously." Selena was frantically trying not to become too emotional in the memories. She remembered emotionally thinking:

What's he trying to do here, hurt me more? Stop!!

"Selena, before I left for Torona, we agreed since I'd be goin' away ta school, we should take time off so I could get my education, and that we'd try ta date other people ta see what our feelings for each other really were."

He pronounced it Torona. "I remember it a little differently. You've been gone for two years, and we each have a lot of interests now. I'm loving my job, and I'm taking university classes to become a Biochemist. You'll be a full firefighter soon, working in Toronto."

Purposely pronouncing it the way it should be.

"I've my Recruit Trainin', Fire Prevention, Candidate Testin' Services, National levels and CPR-HCP Health Care Provider courses nearly completed. And, Selena, I've applied ta the Ottawa Fire Department. It has over six stations. I've tried ta date other girls, but I can't get interested in anyone else but ya. You're in my thoughts many times a day. We're older now, and maybe we could think about givin' it another try. I'm ready ta do that."

Then the bombshell: "I love ya."

My knees almost buckled. And my head was spinning. He says he's ready to do this.

"Austin, I'm quite confused. I've really missed you, but I tried to forget about any of that. We've seen each only a few times since you went away. During this past two years, you either ignored me or treated me just like just a casual friend! I figured you'd moved on. In fact, I'm currently thinking of dating Kevin that you met tonight. I really admire him, and I think he likes me."

"Selena, let's start datin' again. I need ya. Say ya'll think on it. Ya have my cell number. That's the only number ta reach me at. Call me any time, but make sure ta call my cellphone number. I'd like ta be back in your life."

"Austin, I missed you so much in the beginning, and I'll think further, I promise you. I've not had an actual date with Kevin yet. Wednesday afternoon we spent playing Chess and talking and walking in my aunt's garden."

Selena remembered back clearly that Austin had looked disturbed. Then she felt he put on a hurt look while smiling at her. "Oh, you've hurt my soul. Ya played Chess with him? How could ya do that ta me? That's the game that we played - together."

"Oh stop. Sure, you and I played Chess. You won a lot if I remember right."

I can't do this right now. It's late. In many ways.

Feeling uncomfortable with these emotions and breaking into perspiration at this conversation, Selena searched for another topic. Getting her emotions in order, she prattled, "On another subject, I found out from Aunt Jenny's lawyers that I'm to have the house. I didn't think to wonder where I'd be living."

Then continuing her memories from last night, she recalled Austin had remarked, "I thought your aunt would leave ya the house, but ya'll be alone in her big house. Have ya thought if ya'll stay there or find a different place that doesn't need upkeep, or even move ta Torona?"

"Gosh no. That is farthest from my mind. Right now, I'm pleased to be able to stay where I know. I've lived here since I was a child. There were times living here with Aunt Jenny that I thought I should have a place of my own, but this house is that place of my own. But I hadn't thought about upkeep. Have you noticed something that needs doing? Aunt Jenny was more of a bookish person than a maintenance person."

"I saw the last time I was here that the roof's in bad shape. Ya should have someone check it out. Has it leaked?"

"I haven't seen any leaks, but that doesn't mean that there aren't any. Aunt Jenny keeps some of the upper rooms locked up because no one has used them for a dozen years. I'll check into having someone come in. If you think of it, ask your parents who they used a couple of years ago for their roof."

At that point in the conversation, Austin had seemed to get restless. She noticed that he checked his watch. "Well, Selena. I'll let ya get inta the house. I gotta call ta make. Ya'll think about my confession of still really carin' for and missin' ya? I want ya in my life."

"Austin, that makes me feel very special. I've thought a lot of you, really, I have. It's just a shock that you've felt that way too. I've attempted to put feelings for you out of my mind. This will give me so much to think about."

Austin had sighed, "Yeah, well, ta get back ta the house topic, I'll say that I'm glad ya got the house … glad for ya."

Selena conferred with her diary that morning from what had transpired the prior night:

> *"Austin wants to get together with me. For sure I missed him. I had no idea that Austin really missed me. I had no idea.*
>
> *I'll tell you, dear diary, it was heart breaking.*
>
> *Last evening, he told me he loves me. Can I love him again? He was so sincere. So caring about this house.*
>
> *Then I dreamed the whole scene of us breaking up two years ago, two long years ago. I remember the day as though it just happened. The scene playing out before my eyes, my being transported back…*
>
> *We were sitting in his backyard. The sun was waning, but it was still warm. I was feeling mellow, my hand resting on his. I could feel my eyes shining with love for him. Two years we had been dating. He looked thoughtful. I wondered if he was getting ready to discuss our future together, maybe an engagement.*
>
> *Then, suddenly, this:*
>
> *Him: "We need to take a break from each other. I've*

put a lot of thought into this. I'm going away to classes, and I need to concentrate on my studies."

Me: "But we'll still see each other every weekend when you're home from Toronto."

Tossing and turning, almost moaning, her dream continued:

I looked at him. His face had become hard, determined. He withdrew his hand from under my hand.

Me: "Are you saying that we won't date anymore?"

Him: "Yeah, that's exactly what I'm saying. We'll take our own paths and see."

Me: "See what, Austin? I love you."

He quickly got up and walked away from me.

When I woke this morning, I had dried tears in the corners of my eyes and my pillow was still damp from my emotional dream, my real nightmare.

But he says he wants to get back with me now. I should be happily thinking of being back together with Austin, in his arms, his lips on mine, talking about our future together. I need time to think. Why the blazes is this happening now? I cried for months when he left me.

I did date a couple of guys from my university classes. Nothing panned out. I still loved Austin then. They couldn't compare with what I thought I had with him.

He didn't always have all the slang he mostly talks with now. Is it a firefighter thing? Is he trying to make himself sound tough?

I do have so much to think about. This is something to be thankful for. Then I won't be so alone. Aunt Jenny has only been gone a few days, and I have friends checking on me. But I'm tired of feeling alone. I need someone.

I'm conflicted about this, but hopeful that it could work out."

16

Austin—The Plan

At his parents' house that same morning, Austin asked them if they had noticed the condition of the roof on Jenny's house.

Bud replied, "I noticed the shingles after Thursday's storm. I knew I had to, um, tell Selena. Did you say something to her, or did she notice it?"

"Yeah, I told 'er they needed checkin' out."

Bud's response was, "You and I could go over and look."

Karen replied, "You guys checking it out is a good idea. You're both firefighters and Bud with experience on buildings." Karen thought about Bud with his large burly frame, strong arms and legs. He would definitely be a safe bet to go up there. She smiled as she realized that she still thought him strong and sexy.

"You have a collection of ladders yourself, Bud. Who did we get to replace our shingles three years ago? I think it was the company called *Ramon Silva Roofing*. I'll check right now."

In the meantime, Bud's sharp black eyes hadn't missed much this weekend. "So, son, you've an interest again in Selena? I've seen you looking in the direction of her aunt's house many times since yesterday. When you broke it off, um, I wondered if that was the end of it."

"Well, if ya have ta know, I didn't intend ta break it off. Maybe I wanted ta postpone it ta see if we each felt the same. Now, I'm so certain I wanna start again, but Selena seems ta be interested in a doctor in 'er clinic."

Karen came back into the room with a business card. "I was right. *Ramon Silva Roofing.* But, just now, I heard that you were saying Selena is interested in dating a doctor in her clinic? Darn, I bet that was the young man I saw over there the other day. They were walking close together and looking as though having a delightful time."

"Yeah, well I hope I'm not too late. She said she likes him, and it seemed yesterday at her place after the funeral and last evenin' at supper, he also likes her. They sat close and chatted. Colleen Kirsch, another doctor, was on one side of him, and Selena on the other. I was beside Colleen. She's very pretty. I tried chattin' her up, but she seemed ta be interested in Kevin too. It seemed old Kevin spent more time chattin' with Selena. I don't know what they both see in that self-absorbed, pompous snob."

Karen quickly caught up to the gist of the conversation between Bud and Austin, saying, "Well, you can't push Selena right now. Just be there for her. You know how much your dad and I adore Selena, and we want her happiness like our own daughter." And then she added:

"You know, I've a feeling that Theodore isn't being forthright with us. There's just something going on with him, and he's not admitting to anything. He's coming home much less often and is on the telephone a lot when he's home."

In a conspiratorial manner, Austin leaned toward her, planning to cause some irritation. "Not ta tell tales out of school…, but I'll tell ya he asked me months ago what I thought a' Selena's friend, Laura Waters. If he has been distracted, then that's the one he's been distracted with."

"I hope you're both happy with your lives, but it's early to be getting really serious. And, also, as far as you're concerned Austin, I'd like to have a little mom-to-son talk with you. I feel you've been very edgy this time you're home. Is something going on? Theodore said that you had someone in Toronto you were serious about. Can we talk about that?"

"Austin, could you take this name and telephone number over to Selena? Um, she may as well have it right now" interrupted his father.

Karen spoke up. "Austin, do you know what Selena may have found out from the lawyer? Is the home going to be hers or I wonder if she'll have to move?"

"Yeah, well I'm sure Selena wouldn't mind me tellin' ya the lawyers told her she's her Aunt Jenny's heir. Isn't that great news?" Perhaps concerned he had revealed too much, he added: "I mean for her. I'm gonna run over there with this information."

Austin was thinking to himself: *Selena was getting her Aunt Jenny's house. Things are going to work out!*

Selena was preparing to take Rufus for his walk. Caylie seemed restless this morning, following Selena around from room to room, meowing. She apparently sensed Selena's mood, and she wanted a few pats and her chin and ears stroked.

"It was a sad, sad day yesterday. Yet I had a lovely time with my friends, Caylie. Aunt Jenny's funeral was a good tribute to her. Rufus, do you miss Aunt Jenny?" Rufus' ears perked up at this name. "I hope you're both doing all right. I had a fun time with Dr. – I mean Kevin – the other day. Goodness, I must remember not to call him Kevin at work. He's someone I've admired for awhile. I think he likes me.

"That's all I really need right now. Someone to like me. Right Caylie?"

Having Austin relay his ongoing feelings for me has perplexed me so much. I need to chat to Laura. Oh! But, really, I can't because she's involved with Theodore. Try as she will to be loyal to me, she may let something slip to Austin. Oh goodness.

I think I loved Austin since I was 13 years old. He and Theo teased me greatly, but it was Austin whose attention I wanted.

She summoned up glimpses of past experiences of herself at age 10.

Theodore yelling, "Hey, Selena, I have a gift for you!"

"Oh, Theodore, you horrible boy. Get that frog out of my face. Wait! Here, let me hold it. I'll chase Austin with it. He hates frogs. He says they're slimy to touch."

Another memory video in her mind, age 16:

Austin, outside, the sun and the heat of summer on my skin, leaning toward me at morning break in high school, saying, "Would you like to sit with me at lunch today?"

Selena snapped herself back with an emotional jolt.

I need time to adjust to everything happening. I haven't been myself long enough to belong to someone else!

Rubbing under Caylie's chin and hearing her responding purr, she thought about her home.

I own this house. Imagine Aunt Jenny arranging to have the regular bills and taxes paid. I miss her so much, her company, her understated manner. She really was a good aunt. But today, I need to get the keys from over the doorframes to get into the other upstairs rooms before I call a roofer. So many decisions. So many Mysteries. Possibly a new love life?

Realizing that Caylie was asleep on her own blanket beside her, Selena slipped from the room and went to take Rufus for his morning walk. Rufus, happy to be getting his walk, ran toward her so she could put the leash on him. The day was marvellous with a misting of clouds, the sun shining and only a warm breeze.

Changing her thought process while they were out having their walk, Selena inquired, "So, Rufus, if you could give advice, would you tell me to time travel?"

"Ruff!"

"I think that's a yes, Rufus. My Grandma Olive and Grandpa Arthur time travelled over and over. Aunt Jenny only travelled to and from Ottawa. Even though I've a wonderful life here, I feel so restless, and the mysteries are all calling to me. I should try the time travel machine again a couple more times. Rufus, do you think I will solve my mysteries?"

"Ruff, ruff!"

That evening she wrote in her diary:

Is there nothing that I believed five days ago that actually is what I thought? Should I start to keep a list of what I've discovered in recent days? Would it make me feel more or even less in control?

Well, here goes dear diary:

Aunt Jenny was gravely ill and hid it from me.

There has been time travel going on without my knowledge!

My grandparents hadn't died!

My grandparents left to live in 1967?!

Both grandparents and Aunt Jenny have been coming back and forth!

Did my parents know about this time travel business?

Obviously, Aunt Jenny knew, but when did she find out?

Why was Aunt Jenny told – unless my parents knew…

Laura and Theodore are secretly engaged!

And Mr. Brisbane, who has been caring for our yard, knew Aunt Jenny since childhood. I wonder what that means…

And Austin still cares deeply for me! He loves me. Austin loves me!"

Austin shouted to Selena just as she was coming back into the yard from her walk, Rufus by her heel.

"Selena, my mom found the name of the roofin' company that replaced our shingles so I brought the business card. Can I come with ya ta check the upstairs rooms, just in case there's somethin' that might have affected the roofin'?"

"I'd welcome you coming with me. Is now a good time?"

"This'll be fun, Selena… Like playin' hide and seek when we were young."

"I just hope that there are no more surprises hiding up in those rooms. I've had quite enough surprises for now." Selena was musing about the time machine.

Austin looked at her quizzically, wondering if the comment was about him; however, he thought it best not to say anything. *Let that go.*

Selena ran up the stairs. She assumed the keys were above the bedroom door frames, and she was right – each door frame had a key above it. She could barely reach. She was Aunt Jenny's height, but she managed to grasp them. Each key looked identical to the other, and Selena tried each key in each door to ensure they were the same and that she would not have to be concerned about mixing them up. They matched.

"I'll go into this first corner bedroom, and you can check out the bedroom right beside." Hesitantly opening the first bedroom door knowing Aunt Jenny did not want her in these rooms, she flipped on the light switch. The furniture was covered as her aunt had said it would be. However, before Selena went all the way into the bedroom, she froze, standing stock still just inside the doorway where she could observe that this only could have been her father's bedroom as he was growing up.

I feel instantly calmed. Mom and dad must have stayed in this room when we visited when I was little. Possibly I can smell mom's perfume, but it is as though my father is near me. I think it's a men's cologne. The scent remaining must be because the room has been locked up for years.

Surrendering to all the feelings that the room brought, she enjoyed the sensation for several moments, emotions running through her. Then reminding herself why she was here, she reluctantly checked for rain damage. She did a proper look around at the ceiling, walls and windows, relieved to know there was nothing leaking.

It's amazing that these scents could stay for so many years. Oh, I'm tearing up. I'll be back here today to sit on my own.

After Selena gently closed the door, leaving her father's old room and entered the other corner bedroom, she checked around, noticed a leak. She shouted to Austin. "I think there may be a problem in the ceiling in this bedroom." Austin quickly strode into that room.

"Yeah, I can even smell mould, so there's obviously some damp in here. Is that where ya found the leak, above ya?"

"You can see it's quite wet. Since this is an end bedroom, the water could have come in from this side. Heavens, this needs to be handled right away as the floor is slightly damp. I'll call the roofer your parents suggested, but let's check the other rooms up here. Did you see anything in that middle bedroom?"

After they had entered the middle bedroom, Austin commented, "Ya see, this room seems fine. The rain was comin' from the other direction for this storm anyway."

Nothing looked like a leak, but Selena felt surprised at the room itself.

Austin advised, "I opened the drapes when I came in. It belonged ta someone at one time. As far as leakage, there's nothin' visible here, nothin' in the ceilin', windows or below."

Selena observed, "The wallpaper is for a young woman. Wow, this must have been Aunt Jenny's room when she was younger. I wonder why they didn't remodel it."

Austin added, "There's a set of baby booties on the dresser that say 'Jennifer'. I don't think anyone has lived here for years."

Selena offered an explanation. "I don't remember who was in which bedroom when I was first brought here… after the, the… accident." Looking away, she continued, "I suppose Aunt Jenny moved into that larger and brighter corner master suite when she got older, after my grandparents were *gone*."

Gone! she reflected. "We'll close this room up until the contractor comes. I've been in Aunt Jenny's rooms, and I live in mine, so we can skip those. Let's just take a quick look in the bathrooms and storage areas. Then I'll telephone *Ramon Silva Roofing*. Thanks for bringing me that company name."

In doing a search of the remaining rooms upstairs, they found nothing obvious. Once on the main floor, Selena called *Ramon Silva Roofing*, and she was put through to Ramon himself. He said he was just finishing up a job, and he was only 30-35 minutes away. He would be right over.

"Oh, thanks so much. What a relief."

When leaving, Austin said in a determined voice, "I'll see ya later."

While Selena made herself a sandwich before the contractor arrived, she jotted down some items on her growing grocery list. Mental note: *Get groceries tomorrow*!

The front doorbell rang just as Selena was re-checking her grocery list. She eagerly greeted the contractor, a youngish man with hair partially hidden under a ball cap, dark eyes and thick eyebrows. She noticed that he was very tall and muscular.

"Hello, Ramon? I'm Selena."

Taking off his *Ramon Silva Roofing* ball cap, showing his neatly cut black hair, he answered, "I am Ramon Silva. Please to meet you, Selena. Tell me about your roof."

I love his Spanish accent.

"After the storm, my neighbours told me the shingles might not be sufficient. We checked out the upstairs just now, and there's one room for sure that has been leaking. I'd like you to check the roof to see what needs to be done."

"My last call end up not needing much work, so I am available for afternoon. I will check how much damage you have. Good news is no rain expect for nex' three days."

"Well, that's good news."

"As I walk up to your home and around house, I could see missing shingles and other shingles curl up from age. Roof may have been compromise. I'll check your inside now."

Nice way he speaks – so Spanish.

"Yes, in one of the bedrooms, we could definitely smell moisture and the carpet was wet."

As they were climbing up the stairs, Ramon asked, "How did you find my business name?" Selena informed him that Bud and Karen Semple next door had referred him this morning.

"Happy previous customers are ticket to successful business by way of referrals. I remember Karen and Bud."

Ramon examined each of the five bedrooms, the bathrooms and storage upstairs. Entering her aunt's bedroom, Selena escorted Ramon into the "first closet" and ensured that her Aunt Jenny's "travel room" door was securely locked and that Aunt Jenny's clothing in her closet hid the secret door.

"My aunt was a very private person. She has always asked that I not go into that room behind this closet. If you can check from the attic and by the roof outside, then I would prefer you did not enter this closed-door area. You can let me know."

"After I examine ress of upper floor, I would have been surprise if there had been any leaks here. I have made notes of issues inside. I will need to get to your attic to really see what is happening. If I thin I would need to go in there, I will let you know. I will need assistance with your inside house area, and I have a company I know and truss."

He seems very professional and knowledgeable. God, I hope he can get everything done without any more discussion on the travel room!!!

"I've a friend coming over in an hour so please go ahead to investigate and make your report. I'll be in our pottery studio. You can see the building through this window. Here's my cellphone number that you can call if I'm not back here when you are done."

"Ahh, you said 'our' pottery studio. I have been wonderin' if this was your home because, well, you are quite youn' to have this place. Is someone else I should discuss damage with?"

Selena suddenly realized his concern, and she replied, "No, my Aunt Jenny just passed away this week. I'm her sole beneficiary and, thus, the sole heir to all of the roof misfortune as well."

"I am sorry for your loss, Selena. All right, I check everything out, and let us hope it is not as bad as it seems from inside and on my look outside. I thin it is going to be expensive. We will discuss it when I am done."

I'll get some cakes ready for our tea because Elizabeth said 4:00 would work well for her. Discussing clay will take my mind off all the muddles in my life. Haha, I amuse myself – muddles, mud, clay.

Watching Elizabeth approach, Selena noted that keeping a regime of walking, lifting weights, pickleball sport, as well as throwing pottery on the wheel had a favourable effect on her stature and physique. Ever since Elizabeth had brought pottery pieces to work, it had prompted a strong desire in Selena to start her own projects.

Elizabeth was bending to see in the cupboards with her flowing black- gray hair falling forward, but not enough to mask the enthusiasm on her face.

"How exciting for you, Selena, to have your own studio. The equipment here is in decent shape, a proper electric wheel, the kiln a good model, a Skutt. You have all the shelving, stilts, sponges, brushes and glazes. In the beginning, there are bound to be learning curves. These glazes are fine – only add a few drops when they become any drier."

Elizabeth had brought three of what she described as her library of pottery books. "The important thing you need to note is that everything you make needs to be covered with plastic, loosening it as the clay dries, eventually uncovering pieces totally. That is the reason for these cracked pieces."

"Thanks for that information. I noticed a large tube with all the plastic wrapped around it, and the cut plastic pieces on this shelf. Dah! Live and learn."

They worked through some steps on hand building the clay. Cutting the slab with the wire cutter, giving it a few good whacks, rolling it out with the height guide bars, using the forms that were there to place the clay on. Importantly, Selena was shown how to always have plastic between the clay and the form that she would use to make the clay over or inside of. If not, it would stick to that form and ruin the pottery piece when she tried to get it off.

Having stopped for tea, Elizabeth now set the cup down, and said in her knowing manner, "You'll find that once you get into this, you'll never go into a hardware or kitchen store again without looking at fancy trays, utensils, piping, anything to see how you could implement it in your pottery ideas. Second-hand stores have low prices on embossed silver trays, bowls and fancy lace doilies that can be used. You'd place the doily onto your rolled-out clay and press with the rolling pin or even your fingers to imprint its design on your clay. I'm excited for you, Selena. I'd like you to text me photographs of your pieces."

Selena walked Elizabeth to her Ford Bronco as Ramon waved and said he would see her in a bit. Selena explained to Elizabeth what had happened. Once Elizabeth drove away, Selena went to see what Ramon had discovered.

"It appears there has been weakening of framework and ten dark patches of estains, some are absolute mould. I see shingles have been missing in all three places for several rains. Water foun' a pathway and is pool over one upper bedroom. When more rain or moisture come, will be additional damage inside home. I will have a report and quote to you by tomorrow morning. Could I have your email address?"

Selena gave him her email for the report. *Ramon Silva Roofing* email was on the business card he provided. "If you confirm hiring us, I will forward a contract that you sign and return, alon' with a $2,000.00 deposit we need before we estart. Deposit will be refun'ed if you change your min' before we purchase supplies. The report and estimate will have those particulars. Is anythin' I can answer?"

"No, I don't have any questions right now. Could I book you now for as early as you can come?"

"I call as soon as I get back to my office to confirm my eschedule. If you have any question, please call me. If you wish to discuss with Karen and Bud ness door, that is an option for you."

"I'll speak to Karen and Bud, and I'll check with my insurance broker. Thank you for all your time today. This is what you do for a living; however, for me, I'm so thankful that you could come as soon as you did."

17

Wanna Be Free

Selena rang Karen and Bud's doorbell, relieved to be able to discuss this situation with those that cared. Austin immediately answered the door with his cell phone in his hand, scarlet-faced, obviously still on a call as he said curtly into the phone, "Yeah, I do too. Bye." He pressed End and abruptly set the cell on the counter.

To Selena, he said, "I've been busy on my cell. I saw that Ramon from the roofing company was talking with you. Wait – I'll get mom and dad."

As soon as Karen and Bud entered the room, Karen rushed to Selena putting her arm around her. "Oh dear, I can see clearly that this isn't good news. Do you want to talk about it?"

Bud indicated Selena should come into their family room and she sat down heavily. "Oh boy, where to start!" Selena handed Karen and Bud the hand-written sheet that Ramon had left with her, together with the insurance company business card. The total affair was sinking in, along with the probable cost. Twisting the strands of her hair, she wondered how her Aunt Jenny would have handled this news.

That's it, though. Aunt Jenny would have just handled it. I must try harder.

Bud interjected, “You have insurance, so your cost will be the deductible -- between $1,000.00 and $2,000.00. That’s not insurmountable. Um, call your insurance company. They’ll be open on a Saturday. That way you can talk about it with them, and we’re here if you need us. You will need to secure his company with a contract and pay a down payment.”

“Yes, it’ll be emailed to me. I can arrange that.”

Karen made a cup of tea for each of them. Selena sighed with gratitude, “Thanks, Karen.” She grasped the cup of tea as though it were a lifesaver. Bud extracted the card from Selena and dialed the number. It seemed natural after spending so much time at their home years ago that he would take over when she seemed so lost. He handed the phone to Selena along with the paper with Ramon’s assessment on it. Selena discussed the whole predicament with her agent. The agent said an adjuster would come out first thing Monday morning. She reiterated that the insurance coverage had been signed over to Selena’s name already and suggested that Selena book the contractor.

“We’ll discuss the particulars Monday morning 8:30 a.m. I have your aunt, but now your policy, on my screen. The insurance is for full replacement cost, a great insurance plan I must say, less the $2,000.00. We will need to inspect the roofing before final payment will be made to *Ramon Silva Roofing.*”

Just clicking off from the insurance agent, Selena’s cellphone sounded with the *“Hello”* song while Karen smiled at the remembered ring tone. It was the receptionist from *Ramon Silva Roofing* confirming an appointment for 1:00 p.m. Monday afternoon.

“Miss Jenkins, I’ll email the contract to you before 8:30 a.m. Please print, sign and give the contract to the roofer tomorrow morning, along with your down payment cheque for $2,000.00, to be held in trust. Is there any difficultly doing that?”

Selena informed her, “I have an appointment at 1:00 p.m. and then another at 2:30, so I’ll be late getting home. I’ll print off the contract, sign it and leave it along with the deposit cheque on my kitchen table. I’ll leave the key with Karen and Bud next door.”

The receptionist confirmed that would work, and they left it at that.

Karen offered, "We are planning to order Chinese food for supper, and we would feel thrilled to have you stay."

Selena felt her world lighten a little more to have these friends in her life. With supper done, her tummy and her heart gratified, Selena offered to help with the little washing up.

"No, that's okay. How about Austin walks you home, and I finish putting this away?" Austin jumped up, offered his arm and opened the door for her.

"Well, that was quite a day. I need to take Rufus for his walk. Would you like to walk with us?"

"I would be charmed, I'm sure." Rufus was at her back door, so excited to see Selena. He nudged past Selena to get outside, wagging his tail. Austin bent down to Rufus' height. "How are you doin' fella?" Rufus ignored him and sniffed at the outside air. "Would ya like ta go for a walk with this lovely lady and myself?"

Boy, he's really trying hard.

Although Rufus ignored Austin, there was the familiar "Ruff, ruff" as he looked to Selena. She reached in for his collar and leash. Rufus was already over in his dog run and then almost galloping ahead. He came back to get his leash attached.

"Just like old times" remarked Austin. He studied Selena to see her reaction.

She said simply, "Just like old times. Let's admire the sky, just through those branches. It's glimmering in the twilight." She was aware of Austin beside her, and aware that she did not want to delve into what Austin had disclosed to her last night.

I need time. I feel we're walking on a path that twists through these woods, as we're journeying on a path that twists through our lives.

A rabbit darted in front of them, jumped over a large rock and kept running farther into the woods. Selena was trying awfully hard to feel the old attachment to Austin. With Rufus off leash, they stopped several times while Rufus sniffed and examined flowers, bushes, trees. He sprinted after a squirrel, then a wayward leaf. Once on the wooded path, they stopped to appreciate the spring weather.

"Selena, Rufus takes life as it comes, not worryin' about nothin'. I wish I could be like that."

"Sure, I do too. When I was young, being an adult meant freedom. Now, since Aunt Jenny's death, it seems like every day brings a new burden. I miss my aunt very much. I want to have less worries. There was a song probably 50 years ago I heard recently by some old group called "The Monkees". I watched them on an oldies station comedy television show. I think they re-played episodes because one of the singers had died this year. The song I'm thinking of is *I Wanna Be Free*. It was a catchy tune. Did you ever hear it?"

She softly sang, "'I want to be free, like the blue birds flying by me' … (I can't remember all the words) … Hum, hum … hum, hum, hum ... 'laughing in the sun, always having fun, doing all those things without anything to tie me down' … hum, hum, hum … 'I wanna be free …'" Then Selena laughed self-consciously. "Whoops, sorry. Got carried away. It just resonates I guess."

"Well, it's a tellin' song, isn't it, Selena? Ya wanna be laughin' in the sun and not be tied down, only being free? I loved ya two years ago more than I let on. I wanna be with ya, Selena… Okay, let's try laughin' in the sun. There's the sun. Ha hahaha hahaha."

Selena was aware of the dramatic inconsistency, noting Austin's laugh certainly did not reach to his eyes. He looked unable to hide some displeasure. Austin took her hand. "Can I have a kiss to seal our friendship?" After the kiss, Austin dropped her hand, looking frustrated.

When they got to the patio of Selena's house, Austin pronounced abruptly, "That was a good walk. I enjoyed being with ya as I truly still love ya. I've gotta make a telephone call, so I'll say goodbye now. Something came up this afternoon, and I decided ta leave in the mornin' for Torona. I'll call ya a couple of times this week so we can talk… and ta check how your insurance claim turned out. If I can get away ta come home next weekend, I'll come ta see ya. Take care, Selena." Then he was gone, hurrying across her garden, not looking back.

"Okay, Rufus, let's get inside and say hello to Caylie."

Selena, instead of going into the house, stomped with purpose to the pottery studio where she pounded the clay to get the air bubbles out and pounded it again just because she wanted to pound something. With finality, Selena covered the clay and left the pottery room, a little furrow creasing her eyebrows.

Talking to herself, "I must figure out exactly what my feelings are. But now, I want to get back to my father's old bedroom."

Later, Selena entered some jumbled thoughts into her diary:

"Austin kissed me today to seal a pact of friendship, different from a friendship kiss. I can't think clearly about that -- I have too many emotions in my heart and head.

After the kiss, he mentally left me. I wonder if he was perplexed that I didn't jump into his arms. Did he think I'd be swayed by his muscular toned body and his sculptured features. I guess I need time to assimilate how I feel.

He's different now. His speech. He seems so distracted. Then there's the tattoos of snakes and the bottom part of a skull peeking from under his shirt sleeve.

I'm also puzzled why Austin had to leave to suddenly when we were done our walk. He seemed edgy. Could he be baffled by feelings too? Don't know what's up with him, at all.

I'm frustrated. It's been quite a day! He left me once. Suddenly, he's back. What is with all this now? Why not months and months ago? What's changed?

I should be happy that we'll be seeing more of each other. I'm confused. It will all come out in the wash. Wow, my mom used to say that so many years ago when things got out of hand. It will all come out in the wash. Everything will work out all right given time.

That memory makes me so blessed happy."

18

DECEIT

IN THE MEANTIME, AUSTIN was feeling cheery because he felt that progress had been made with Selena. He knew it had been his demand that he and Selena break up two years ago.

God, I just wanted to be free to go to the big city of Torona and, to be honest, to see what other girls were out there and to have fun with them. Selena was fun two years ago, but there is much more out there.

I'll be done my courses in three months. It's necessary to return to the Ottawa region for Plan A to work. I've got my applications in for both the Ottawa Fire Services and the City of Toronto.

Austin was smiling to himself.

My Plan A includes gettin' Selena to fall in love with me again and to convince her to sell the house and use her money to purchase a nice place in Torona. She was so in love with me two years ago that it should be easy. Selena will have money, and I'll make a lot more money when I get a job in the big city.

It was good to have had a place in her heart two years ago, but it was sure fun times to date all those other gals. I'll miss my current girlfriend cuz she sure knows how to party like a big-city girl. But I need Selena and that inheritance.

At that moment, Selena was gingerly climbing the stairs to spend more time in that first bedroom.

I wish I had been more insistent to Aunt Jenny that I got to peek into these two rooms years before. Even now to be here in the room where my father had lived in as a young boy and a young man feels special.

She uncovered and sat in a comfortable armchair and surveyed the room, immediately popping up to see what was on the bookshelves. There were still copies of a couple of his books written by Judy Blume, *The Hardy Boys*, *The Prince of Tides* and the like.

Selena wanted to touch everything in the room. She marvelled at the headboard, the dresser – *all my father's* – and she stayed for a long while smelling the scent of her father and imagining a whiff of perfume in the closet. What was his life like prior to leaving for university and marrying her mother? She searched for anything of her mother's, but nothing was left in the room.

Upright in the closet, though, was a cot with a gorgeous blanket made of triangle-shaped pieces, hand sewn with the tiniest stitches. Curiously, she studied it. "That blanket looks familiar. Where's that memory coming from? The cot's so small. Who's it for? Who slept there?"

Suddenly, strong flashbacks strobed through her mind. She dissected the room, her eyes sweeping over everything again, the past calling to her. Her eyes snapped back to the cot.

"We stayed here. I slept in that cot! That's my baby blanket that I insisted on sleeping with. Oh lord, maybe we were here the night of their accident."

Selena felt blurring edges of a memory. They focused, and she remembered!

Flash: *Mom and dad dressing up and joking about the evening ahead. I was already here!*

Flash: *I was sleeping. A man at the door. I was looking down from the top of the stairs. Grandpa and Grandma sobbing. Grandma coming up the stairs, clutching me, moaning and sobbing.*

Time shifted, and she was back in the present. Her hands on her face, now weeping. Selena's heart was aching, breaking at those memories with accompanying emotions. Loss from long ago, emotions breaking her heart now.

What would life be like if I could see my mom and dad again?

19

Seek And Find

NEXT MORNING, SELENA WAS still mulling over her memories initiated by the cot.

I was already here the night my mother and father died. I was here with Grandma and Grandpa Jenkins. Not brought here after, was already here. I didn't remember.

That revelation had left her motionless. The memories settled on her. "Why hadn't I remembered this before? It took seeing the cot – my cot to shock a memory into me." It was a few minutes before Selena gathered her thoughts, stopped the ruminating, the sensations running away in so many different directions.

Speaking as though to her Aunt Jenny, she said softly, "All the things that you didn't tell me, Aunt Jenny. Why? I'll never find out more from you now to understand why I was kept in the dark about so many things. Everything! I was here. I remember my mother and father laughing, getting ready to leave for an evening out, Grandma and Grandpa sobbing."

In an exasperated mood, she had rushed down the stairs and out the door to the pottery studio – had to get out of the house. Once in the pottery studio, she decided to make a tray, cut and rolled the clay, used a press-on pattern for the clay and carefully placed it over the tray on the inside, using a damp sponge to smooth the edges.

I am still reflecting on that little cot and the memories it brought back. What else don't I remember, don't know about myself. What else can't I trust about my memory?

I'm bewildered about romance too. I like Dr. Kev, but I can't decide on what level. But when I think about Austin professing how he feels about me... That old romance re-kindles in me. I loved him for such a long time, a long time ago really. It's a revelation about his thinking of me all the time. It's wonderful.

Remembering her words to herself, "I haven't been myself long enough to belong to anyone else," she felt reassured that there was no need to make any decision. Laura's news of being in a committed relationship with Theo was weighing on her a little. They were so young.

I sound like an old fogie. The time isn't right for me to be as involved as Laura. Or is it the guys that aren't right?

She laughed at herself, but still felt she was correct. She adored her friend, Laura, but they were obviously different people.

With her mood lightened, Selena happily spun herself around, then glanced toward the shelving for glazes and brushes for her pottery art. She concocted a line for a poem.

"ART

What Defines Art? I ask you, I plead.

Can you tell me an answer or give me a lead?"

She danced around with a pottery glaze brush... and merrily hatched a plan for making a clay bowl with a poem written in it.

"Could it be a picture; beauty captured with a brush?

Or a dance so majestic performed in a rush?"

She continued with:

"Would you say music, dynamics and notes?"

Selena danced faster picking up speed. Thinking of Aunt Jenny, she added:

"Or words of wisdom extended through quotes?

Could it be defined as a prayer for your soul?

Or an itty bitty poem written in a bowl?"

Stopping when she realized that she would put those exact thoughts into a bowl at some point, she caught her breath.

"Yes! This is going in my diary, so I won't forget.

Selena took a photograph of the pottery piece made today and texted it to Elizabeth. She was delighted with the piece despite its imperfections and remembered to cover it with plastic.

Recorded in Selena's diary:

"ART
What Defines Art? I ask you, I plead.
Can you tell me an answer or give me a lead?
Could it be a picture? Beauty captured with a brush?
Or a dance so majestic performed in a rush?
Would you say music, dynamics and notes?
Or words of wisdom extended through quotes?
Could it be defined as a prayer for your soul?
Or an itty-bitty poem written in a bowl?"

Inside, after entering the poem in her diary and greeting Rufus and Caylie, she boiled the kettle, put the tea bags in and poured herself a very needed cup of soothing tea. Selena generously buttered a scone, subconsciously wish it was a Beaver Tail from Byward Market and added a dollop of honey to her scone.

"Well Aunt Jenny, it's time for me to get to your travel room and do what I've been stalling to do. I did it the first time without any proper information. I'll just do it again. But now, give me help for my search for information."

Selena had walked brusquely to her aunt's room, glanced into Aunt Jenny's room, feeling her aunt's absence.

Aunt Jenny didn't update me about "History in the Making" for a couple of days before she died. She had it almost finished. It will be wonderful and yet sad to read her book after I do this search today.

"I have been purposely putting off reading her book. Somehow, it seemed that once I looked at it, I would truly feel that she was deceased. I also know she would be terribly upset to have left it unfinished."

Setting down her cup of tea and scone beside the lounge chair, Selena went to the travel room and stroked the 1215 England attire. She gently and thoughtfully set them aside.

What a trip! I may have been lucky to get back unscathed since I had to do it at the time without any knowledge.

She muttered, "I'm certain there will be write-ups on how to's and what not to-do with this time travel business. Okay, I'm going to snoop through my aunt's bookshelves."

In the end, her search had been futile. Selena had fiddled with the books and pamphlets. Checking out a few, she said, "I'll just read this information, and that's all there is to it!"

Smiling to herself, she realized she sounded just like her Aunt Jenny. She leafed through *Computers for Dummies*, tossed aside a book on historic clothing, skimmed *Travelling in Time* and *Machines Made Easy*.

However, a small pamphlet entitled, *The Updated Time Travel Guidebook 2005* grabbed her attention. In her excitement, Selena's fingers could not seem to move fast enough. She fumbled through the pages. There were a few hints and some advice in this pamphlet, but Selena was still vastly disappointed.

Blast it all anyway! How could they use the time travel machine without knowing what they were doing? This pamphlet is not related to the travel machine at all. They had to have had instructions to do it safely. Who showed them how to use it? It's extremely frustrating that this search led to nothing.

Sitting once more on her Aunt Jenny's bed, Selena absently opened the nightstand drawer. Personal effects – these were no help to her.

It feels intrusive looking at personal items.

She opened the next drawer and then the bottom drawer. Still feeling that she was not going to stumble upon anything, Selena was closing the bottom drawer when she saw a lower drawer, very slim, under that third drawer. That drawer was locked.

Of course it's locked! But there must be a key.

Selena peeked in the drawers above, feeling under the drawers like she saw on TV. First drawer, inside and outside – no key. Likewise with the second drawer. *No key!* In that third drawer, taped to the inside, was a tiny key. Fitting the key into the slim bottom drawer, Selena held her breath. Turning the key, she felt something click inside. She slowly pulled the drawer open, reached in and grasped a booklet.

Great, this could be instructions at last!

Written on the booklet was a name: "OLIVE SELENA CHERNOFF (CHERNEY) – now JENKINS" (*the last written in a different pen*). She realized that this booklet was her grandmother's journal!

Holy Christmas! This was a find for sure. Will this Journal of my grandmother's be like my diary, started as a teen, full of innocent questions? Probably nothing about time travel. I'll find out about her young life – before she married my Grandfather Arthur – before she became a decorator – about her life in this house. I hardly remember them.

Fondly and gently touching the cover, Selena delved in, glancing through the pages. Without reading, Selena could see that her grandmother was brief and concise with words. The entries were simple short phrases.

Jotted down in a hurry? or she didn't believe in being verbose.

Reverently flipping the pages, Selena could see there was nothing most days. Weeks went by with a limited number of entries.

My heart's beating wildly. My dad's mother entered these words in her journal – in her own handwriting in concise, meticulous script.

Turning to the first page, Selena started reading. The inside first page read:

"OLIVE SELENA CHERNOFF (CHERNEY) –JENKINS"

"Born 1941, Luxembourg City, Luxembourg"

"Escaped to Marseilles, France 1941"

I had absolutely no idea that my grandmother was not born in Canada, but in Luxembourg under Nazi horrors! So how did she get to Canada?

"I was born with the last name Chernoff, but when papa became involved in politics and to get papers to travel to America, papa had our real name changed from our heritage to Americanized name.

What?!!!

Not family real name?

"Very hard to get all necessary travel papers"

"Mamma hinted we went over the mountains with resistance group – unconfirmed by papa or mamma, who were unwilling to discuss this"

"Papa tells me now that it all made his hair gray"

"Escaped to New York City, USA 1942"

This is appalling! Knowing history, Selena was shocked at what must be her grandmother's family history escaping her country to get to southern France, travelling in 1941 *as a baby!* to get to America to escape the Nazis!!

How horrifying.

Later Selena looked up the history of WWII Luxembourg and confirmed that she was right. She shuddered.

> ["From September 1940 to October 1941, approximately 3,000 Jews left Luxembourg, seeking refuge in France or Belgium. Some 700 were able to leave the German-controlled countries of Europe. By October 1941, most of the remaining Jews were old, poor or sick. In September 1940, the administration applied the Nuremberg Laws to Luxembourg and began to confiscate Jewish property. In July 1941, the Jews of Luxembourg were ordered to wear a yellow armband on their left arm and in October 1941 the Jewish badge. Many were placed in a ghetto-like camp, which soon became the assembly point in Luxembourg for deportations to the east. That same month, the deportations began; on 16 October, 322 Jews were sent to the ghetto of Litzmannstadt (Łódź). Overall, 662 Jews were deported in seven transports, the last of which left in June 1943. Only 45 are known to have survived. Many were sent directly to extermination camps (Auschwitz) or passed through Theresienstadt. Of the 3,900 Jews who lived in Luxembourg before the war, 1,200 perished."]

She continued to read her grandmother's journal.

> "Mama gave me this Journal when I was 15"
> "I hide it so Norah can't read it"

I don't even know if Norah is my aunt's name. Aunt Jenny strikes again!

The next entries were not enlightening because there were many years with nothing noted.

So she was born in 1941. Diary started at age 15, the same age that Aunt Jenny gave me my diary.

1956:

"Papa would not let me have a visit with my new friend Marta today"

"Papa and Mama think I am a baby"

"Noisy and smelly in this city"

"I have many chores to do on Saturdays"

Selena found the entries were not really dated. Occasionally, a year was at the top of entries. The next entries appeared and there was a space between the last entry and the next, indicating time had passed.

"Louise is having an after-school party next Friday. I am allowed to go with Norah accompanying me. I must go with my sister! They think I need a chaperone."

"The party was boring. Girls were all tittering about the boys"

"Norah also titters and preens"

"The boys were immature"

"Mama said I could cut my hair"

"This journal is so futile. I have nothing of interest to write"

More spaces between the entries.

"I am planning to go to university after I finish"

"I have applied six different times. My theory is that they do not like girls"

"I am continuing my studies at night"

"Finally, a school that will take females. I will show them"

1960

"I enrolled New York University – Polytechnic School of Engineering"

"I am content to be at this university"

"I will be a great Engineer!"

She what? What!!! School of Engineering ... an Engineer !! What the hey?!! Aunt Jenny, you withheld that too!

"Some professors are imbeciles"

"I know more than some of these professors"

Many spaces. She has not written in here for a while, I can see that.

"This school is good. Professor Kinsey at least knows something"

"Not all the students are here to study. Some think to party is better"

"I spend too many of my evenings studying. I should be invited out, but the girls and boys are insipid"

"I study harder than many"

1961

"Too busy to write in this silly journal"

1962

"I am learning much more"

"The professors take me quite seriously now"

"I have the respect of students"

"These male students know I am as qualified as they are"

After seeing many scribbles, crossing out of some entries and complete sentences obliterated, I can't tell what my grandmother had written.

Then there appeared:

"Arthur Rodney Jenkins – remember that name"

Oh, here we go. Even underlined. My grandfather enters my grandmother's life.

Checking the entries, Selena examined when this was. Her grandmother would have been 21.

Schooling had consumed her. I'm right not to make any decisions about serious commitment.

Selena expected lots of entries outlining her grandmother's boyfriend. However, stilted amounts of writing still ensued.

> "Assisted Arthur Jenkins to write Building
> Code for New York City regarding fire protection;
> soundproofing; pre-stressed and pre-cast concrete"

Wait a minute. "Assisted Arthur Jenkins to write Building Code for New York City regarding fire protection; soundproofing; pre-stressed and pre-cast concrete"

(Ping!) Soundproofing. That will require investigating.

"Not a decorator, not an architect. My Grandparents were both Engineers! Why hide those facts? Aunt Jenny, why didn't you tell me these things? Darn it!"

> "He says his ancestors also had their last name
> changed two generations ago"
> "Does anyone know who they really are?"

Exactly, does anyone know who they really are? Particularly me. I know that many names were changed when families arrived from other countries. Then my grandmother's family purposely changed theirs to be able to get documentation to leave.

> "Arthur is very intelligent"
> "I will be a better engineer"
> "I fought hard to pursue my goals in a male world"

"The first female Engineer only graduated in 1946, so I am still a pioneer"

"Arthur and I went to the Symphony at *New York Philharmonic*"

"Very good"

"I and Arthur became friends with a Montreal, Canada, Engineering student. She is one of the first female graduates in Engineering Physics."

"My life just got even more adventurous. Firstly, meeting Arthur, then the Building Code project – Now I plan to move to Canada. I must be careful in telling my parents. Arthur will follow me to Ottawa shortly"

1964

"We have now both moved to Ottawa in the Province of Ontario in Canada to do research at National Research Council"

"STEM Satellite technology 'space time' Government as Associate -Top Secret"

"I now call Arthur "Albert" and he calls me "Einstein" Perchance we are relatively right. I am so amusing."

If I was not already sitting, I would fall over. "space time" "Government" "Top Secret". What the hey!

"NOTE THIS IN FUTURE:

"Wormholes are not enough"

"Go at same time of day as arrive there to avoid effects of travel"

"Monitor waking hours and time exposure to daylight"

"Imperative to track bodily strain, heart rate and blood pressure when travelling"

"Directive to NRC staff has been applied. I am not allowed to have any notes regarding my work. I

> will hide this in a very safe location. Secrecy here is paramount"
>
> "Code will be TFT – Time For Travel machine. We will both be pioneers in (time) travel."

Selena had expected more information. Her grandmother must have kept to that secrecy directive. She sifted through pages trying to find where more entries should be. Looking closer, Selena found the most probable reason. She could see in the inside margin where several pages had been torn out close to the binding. *Darn! Darn! Darn! Where are those pages?* That thought kept reverberating.

The next entries were even more limited regarding their careers.

> "Married to love of my life"
>
> "Jennifer (Jenny) Louise Jenkins born, a lovely, red-brown haired, green-eyed baby girl"
>
> "So sweet"
>
> "A wonderful addition to our lives"
>
> "Madam Fontaine is a gentle babysitter. She has young daughter named Theresa. Madame will come day or night to help"
>
> "Work life is still a secret. Love our work. Love each other. Love our baby girl"
>
> "Work is a complex world involving things that no one can know about"
>
> "I wish I could write it down, but I cannot"
>
> "I am all done writing here until things are sorted out"

Selena was disturbed at what this all meant. She certainly knew now that this Journal did indeed involve the time travel machine. *Unbelievable!*

Thinking she might find the pages that had been torn from the

Journal, Selena again groped around in the drawer scratching her hand and arm in several places to get further inside and up. Then, under a secret panelling of the bottom of the drawer, (*I feel like a real spy)* she dug out a slim folder.

Oh, for the love of! What is this now?

"April, 2008

Dearest Jenny my love,

I wanted to write to you about what we have discussed with you.

We have sold our vehicle, and we have put that money into your bank account. We have transferred our house to you. We have everything we need. Our grief at losing our son, your dear brother, Elliott, and his lovely wife, Anne, is too intense. We know that this replica machine – Time For Travel – here at this house works. We have travelled many times as you are aware. You know we had travelled to 1966 to set everything up.

We will now return to the year 1967 before you were born.

We will visit you and Selena here as planned, and we have entered this into the Time Travel Machine.

We have now programmed the travel machine to get us to the point in time before you were born. We have used that hidden setting at the back of the travel machine "Choice of Arrival Age at Destination" so that we will arrive at our destination at the age we would have been during that time period. We will age in a normal manner after that point. We plan to live our life over from prior to your birth. Then we will be with you and Elliott when you each are born, all together again.

We have left you the "TFT" Machine, naturally -- What else to do with it? It will be our base, and we will pre-plan our trips and return from it. You know how it functions for when you wish to come to see us. We will be back only on rare occasions as indicated.

We want to watch Selena grow. We have pre-programmed our schedule into the travel machine. However, we know that this form of travel with this older technology – even with our updates – is extremely hard on the human body, and it is particularly hard on a baby.

We must start over from before this tragedy. Our dearest boy and his wife have been taken from us. We will see you in our visits to you, and you will see us when you come back in time.

You will be with us as a baby, and you will be able to come as yourself when you visit.

This is our choice. We will miss you as you are now, but all will be lived through again.

Please, Please Forgive Us, Darling Daughter.

Love from your Mother and Father."

Selena found herself sitting on the floor with the folder askew, tears streaming down her cheeks.

I have no words to even think right now.

Examining the folder to see what else it may contain, Selena found that there were letters from various people and agencies inquiring as to the disappearance of Arthur Jenkins and Olive Jenkins, newspaper articles and official documents investigating and, as some years went by, eventually indications that the investigation was closed and incomplete, whereabouts unknown and then at the bottom, dated many years after, two death certificates.

Selena felt so many emotions that her mind was clogged. Astonishment, shock, disbelief, devastation, hurt.

How could someone do that?

Just leave their child behind?

Well, sort of, behind.

Aunt Jenny inherited the Time Travel Machine from her parents.

Grandma and Grandpa built it? What!!!!!!

They didn't die. They just disappeared into their previous life.

Where did they go? Ottawa 1967 apparently?

Twelve years ago?

In today's time, the baby Aunt Jenny would now be about 11?

Father would have been born!

Obviously, they travelled to many other times before 2007 judging by the travel log.

Aunt Jenny had visited them?

Without her?

Why did Aunt Jenny not tell her all this?

"Oh – my Lord! My Grandfather and Grandmother must not know their daughter, Jenny, is now dead? The schedule on the travel computer showed that they'd be back here this year in August!! I'm sick of mysteries. I am livid at Aunt Jenny! But I can't be. I mean, she's dead. I can't be angry. But I have so many emotions: I am hurt, shocked, devastated."

There must be a proper explanation as to why I wouldn't have been told all this over the years, particularly as I got older.

Whimpering to herself, "I could have travelled with Aunt Jenny to see my Grandmother Olive and my Grandfather Arthur and seen my parents again!!!! This is so unfair."

In an injured and indignant state, Selena went to the "travel room" behind the closet. This time she searched thoroughly, not even being neat. The last time she had been in this room, it had been a limited search thinking any information would be easy to find because the door had been locked.

Dejectedly thinking about where her other search had ended with the nightstand drawers, she repeated her previous process. Selena found again, buried in a bottom drawer beneath what looked like the actual bottom drawer, a folder. In the folder, was a letter.

A letter. This is a letter to me!

Hoping that she was prepared, Selena began to read...

Dearest Selena,

If you have found this letter on your own, then I apologize. My plan was to tell you on your 20th birthday. I would have preferred to tell you all that has transpired over the past 12 years, as well as before that, personally. There would have been an enormous number of explanations and information for us to talk about then as I have plans that will affect you.

If I have not spoken to you, then you have discovered this room, and you will have discovered the Travel Machine that your grandparents planned out for the Government of Canada and replicated in this room that your Grandparents had built into this house.

"Holy mother of all creatures! Replicated the machine themselves!"

The walls to the travel room are pre-stressed and pre-cast to ensure maximum safety – all safety recommendations have been fulfilled. Check in a slim drawer beneath the bottom drawer of my nightstand, you will find a journal written by your Grandmother Olive, my wonderful mother. She was an engineer turned scientist for the Government. We had to keep it secret. I want to share the secret with you before I leave you. I do hope that upon your 20th birthday you and I will have had my longed-for conversation with you and that you and I or you alone can travel to see your grandparents and also your parents.

Selena rubbed away the streaming tears from her eyes.

At the least, I trust I will have had the time to teach you enough for you to travel safely. It is not something I would wish you to do until I taught you all the necessary procedures. I am not well, and I do not know how much longer I will be able to go on. The doctors wanted to put a pacemaker in my body, but I worried that with a pacemaker, I would not be able to continue to time travel. I need to make at least one last trip back.

Take care my dear. I am sorry if I have not had time to talk directly to you. I have kept you at a distance so that you would not be hurt, but I fear that you are a tender-hearted woman and that you will resent very much that I chose not to involve you in this.

I feel that you should not undertake the travel until you are 20 and that your body will have grown and be strong enough to withstand the effects. I had a bad heart to begin with, and my body has been through far too many trips, being woefully mistreated with time travel.

I love you, Selena. Keep well and safe.

From your Aunt Jenny.

PS You will now have to bear the burden of this time machine. There are times I wish I could blow it up.

Selena had so many thoughts rushing through her head.

Give me strength to not collapse. Colleen had said I was strong. I'd have to be strong not to have totally been done in by all of this. My head is spinning (again) with all that it has had to take in lately. I pinched myself, and I'm still awake. Have I been blind? How could ALL of this have been going on for all these years and I was oblivious?

Aunt Jenny wanted to tell me about this before she passed away. That was her plan anyway. At least I feel less confounded by that. She didn't plan to just leave me alone to find all this out as I did.

Staunchly said aloud, "I do want to travel to see my grandparents to talk to them about that travel machine. I want, need very much to see my mom and dad. God, so much."

Apparently, I need to be concerned how often I should travel – only do a few travels. Aunt Jenny says she had a bad heart to begin with.

"Well, what about RIGHT NOW?"

Wait…

She found the sentence that had struck her: "The walls to the travel room are pre-stressed and pre-cast to ensure maximum safety."

That was the ping I felt after reading Grandma Olive's sentence in the journal. Well, that mystery of not being able to hear the storm raging outside now makes sense.

Selena was certain she could do the replica trip that would take her to 1968 where her Aunt Jenny had visited her grandparents the year after they 'disappeared' and where she could see her grandparents and, at that same time, she would see the baby Jenny Jenkins.

That would be her first trip back to that Ottawa time frame, an important one. She needed to have a sit-down chat with Arthur and Olive Jenkins who had 'disappeared' around a year after her own parents had perished in that fatal car accident in 2007.

Muttering determinedly, "I'll be 20 in August. Just a few months away. I'm close enough to that magic age where I apparently am old enough to withstand the trauma of time travel. Then the next trip – to see my mother and father and to somehow say goodbye. Somehow say goodbye and then leave them. Those were emotions I'd have to truly manage.

Walking to the lounge chair – in shock, Selena gauged she should not change history, or she might vanish and not have existed.

"No matter how much I want them to be with me now." Her throat ached with sobs, and she just threw herself down on the bed.

I'll see my grandparents first, then my parents, that's all there is to it.

20

Olive And Arthur

ONCE SELENA HAD ALL emotions in check, she went into the back closet again. Searching the clothing racks, she stopped at Ottawa--1968 which was a business-like coral matching skirt and jacket, and a blouse patterned in tiny flowers.

These will fit nicely. I hadn't realized how close our height and proportions were.

Matching jewellery, purse with the correct money used and shoes hung on the hanger. With determination in her heart, Selena marched to the computer.

The information already programmed can be used since I will only mimic, not actual date of, Aunt Jenny's trip.

This "Travel Plan" that her aunt had used in 1968 was:

```
TODAY'S DATE: current date/time
GO THERE: CONFIRM Ottawa--1968 No Yes
The information already programmed in was Otta-
wa--1968
COSTUME NUMBER: The information already pro-
grammed in was again Ottawa--1968
COME BACK DATE
```

```
(using current location) Time/Date/Year:
current date/time? Yes
choose different time to RETURN? No Yes
TIME AT DESTINATION Minutes/Hours/Days:
Minutes ….
Hours 3.0
Days ….
PLEASE CONFIRM Minutes/Hours/Days No Yes
+CHOOSE DIFFERENT LOCATION (CUSTOMIZE)+
ENGAGE TIME MACHINE: No Yes
PLEASE CONFIRM = ENGAGE TIME MACHINE: No Yes
Press ENTER
```

Selena pressed ENTER

◇◇◇

Wwww-Wwwww-whirl, Sssss-Sssss-spin, then blur!

◇◇◇

She heard the whir sound and then looked at her surroundings. There was signage for a Convention.

Whoa, what am I doing at this Pierre Elliott Trudeau convention instead of Aunt Jenny's/Grandparents'/my house? Was this where Aunt Jenny came that day? Were my grandparents here?

I just assumed that the time travel plan was that when Aunt Jenny went back to 1968, it was to her own house. This isn't good. I can't let myself panic.

Selena looked around, searching for the people in Aunt Jenny's photo album – her grandparents.

They'd be young! For goodness sakes, they'd be in their late 20s, only some years older than I am! At least I know I'll leave here in three hours, and I'm in a safe enough place unless I yell 'VOTE FOR TOMMY DOUGLAS!' Then I might have to run.

Selena was feeling fine at this wrong turn.

I want to see my grandparents, but now what? I can always get a taxi because I certainly know the address.

Selena was a history buff. *I'd know Trudeau Senior on sight.* Selena saw him - he was working the crowd, shook her hand, and, when he looked into her eyes, he winked. She was surprised; however, she returned a smile at him. He had been decent looking at this age and had charisma, although not her style. The crowd milled as though to follow him when he walked to greet more potential voters. Selena could feel the temperament of the crowd though, and she was caught up in their excitement.

An announcer stood to recommend that everyone find seats and that in a few minutes Pierre Elliott Trudeau would speak with them on the state of the country and his plans for a brighter, more hopeful future. A few more minutes passed and suddenly, there was roar of excitement as Pierre Elliott Trudeau walked on stage and sat down at his assigned place. The crowd seemed to vibrate with enthusiasm.

Selena lost interest in Pierre Elliott Trudeau now as she would lose interest in his son less than 50 years later. Then Selena saw them – the couple that had come to visit Aunt Jenny and were in the photo album. *Wow!* Her grandparents, now turning away, walked toward the exit even though the event had not started yet. Her grandmother with bobbed light blonde hair; her grandfather, dark hair.

I must get their attention. How young they are! I obviously won't call out Grandma and Grandpa!

"Arthur! Olive!" They looked around and scanned the crowd. Each of their gazes landed on her as she was a person standing and almost everyone was sitting farther back in the auditorium. Her grandmother's blue eyes and her grandfather's dark eyes studied her.

I look like my grandmother. I think I've inherited her eyes and her hair colour.

And look at his eyes. Why do I feel I know my grandfather's eyes so well when I hardly remember them?

They walked toward her. When they were standing in front of Selena, her grandmother politely queried, "May we help you?" Then before Selena answered, she quickly smiled and said, "This cannot be possible! I am imagining someone else."

"Heavens! Yes, I might shock you, but I'm Selena, your granddaughter. I've been experimenting with the Time Travel Machine, and this is where Ottawa--1968 took me!"

"Selena, certainly! We came to visit and saw you only a few years ago! How unbelievable and yet so believable. It was hard to imagine who you would be in this setting and calling us "Arthur and Olive." I can tell so clearly now! Where is Jenny? Surely, she is not listening to the speeches. Did she not escort you? You are not 20 until August. The plan was that once you turned 20, Jenny would escort you to us or have come before you. You are crying! What has happened? Oh no, what has happened to my Jenny?" There were newly forming tears in her grandmother's eyes.

Her grandfather nodded with a woeful expression directed toward his wife, knowing her coming heartache. He took Selena's arm, steering her over to the empty hallway. Grandma Olive followed, not wanting to understand.

He hesitated before saying, "Our daughter has passed away, has she not?"

Selena simply nodded, sadly, silently confirming that her aunt had passed away.

Her grandfather, face ashen, continued softly, "Jenny has been dauncy for a few months. I apologize. That was a New York term meaning ill. She had taken too many trips with her bad heart and failing health, and she has cancelled a few. She did not confirm to us what was happening when she came to visit, but we know the signs. We advised her several times to take it slower and to come less often, but she loved us very much and wanted to be with us."

Selena had to lean closer to hear him.

Her grandmother relayed miserably, "We think that she would have chosen to stay here with us in this time period when she came this next time. It would have been possible."

Selena comprehended at this point that another reason her Aunt Jenny may have taken care of everything financially was because she had decided that Selena, at 20 years old, would be able to do without her and that she may have planned to be with her parents again, albeit in a different capacity. How peculiar that would be, yet less sad than what did happen.

Grandpa Arthur spoke with heartbreak in his voice, "Let us leave. We had planned to see this Trudeau once again, but we found that we just could not stay longer. Come, we will go to our home."

With her grandparents on either side of her, Selena was led to their older model Ford. There was no talking during the trip, but her grandmother sat with her arm around Selena in the back seat during the trip.

This has a familiar feel to it – my grandmother's arm around me.

"Come into the house. It will be very strange for you, but, indeed, it is the house that you live in now, only over 50 years newer or older, depending on how one looks at it."

As she was escorted into the family room, Selena took a little note of how the house looked different and yet the same, and it was touching to note what had not been altered. Some ornaments, pictures and sketches were the same; however, things like the cuckoo clock on the mantel, the fireplace which was not gas, the wallpaper and the carpet had been updated in her time.

The house looks newer. This is where the photos were taken.

Selena riveted her eyes back to her grandparents who were looking at her kindly, patiently.

"Tell us the events that happened please," said Grandpa Arthur. So, Selena told them everything that had happened in the past few days regarding Aunt Jenny, not bothering with her personal encounters. They talked about what Dr. Robertson had said and her visit to the law firm, how everything was taken care of by Aunt Jenny's planning for the future.

"A future that she didn't have!" Selena cried out that sentence in anguish.

Selena hung her head, confessing to her grandparents that she had noticed the door in the back of the closet; had been searching Aunt Jenny's bedroom after her aunt's death to find information on the strange computer; had seen the time travel computer screen; had found Grandmother Olive's Journal and figured out what had been going on.

"It has all been so mind boggling, and now, unbelievably, I'm here! I don't understand why Aunt Jenny and you both – when you came to visit – did not explain anything to me. Why was I not introduced to you?"

"That was a complex issue indeed. We discussed the situation with Jenny, and we all agreed that we would not explain anything to you until you were 20 years old. None of us knew the right answer."

"If Jenny travelled here to stay, then that would have been that. She would have explained everything to you had the time worked out, brought you for a visit at that time, and she would have stayed here in this time frame permanently. We, ourselves, decided not to do any more time travel to other countries, except to our old home once we were established here. It was not worth the burden on our health. We do a lot of travelling now, but it is in airplanes and buses in our current time frame to places that interest us."

There was a silence for several moments, a solid silence – each of them in their own thoughts of a different future, no future, with Jenny.

Her grandmother said softly, "Jenny would have been happy here."

Grandpa Arthur nodded mournfully in agreement, seeing it all come to an end now. Seeming to get hold of himself for Selena's sake, he said, "But you are here, and we are very happy to see you and to have this time together."

"I'm glad to have been able to come here, to meet you, hug you and be part of your lives for a little while. This time travel is exciting, but I just don't know if I'm cut out for it yet. I'll see how I feel when I return. I know that I want to travel within my own time.

"I'd love to see my father and my mother before I was born – about 1999 when they would have been just in love with no cares in the world."

Grandma Olive squeezed her hand. "If you decide to do that, Selena, we can talk about that now. We would love to see you again." At that point, Grandma Olive gave Selena a very warm hug and a kiss on the cheek. "You are very special to us, Selena, very special."

Some points were laid down about the "rules" of time travel. Her grandmother wanted Selena to pointedly understand that there can be no changing the past.

"What happened did happen in that time frame, you are not able to change it even if you wanted to."

"The fact is, we only took each of our children with us in time travel one time – the time you saw them. There are so many variables with the makeup of our bodies at different ages. Our own studies and experiences, along with those of peers, indicated that it would not be safe for a child in that older model. That is why Jenny, along with us, decided that you should be a full adult prior to your travelling with Jenny to us.

"We are aware that the time travel machine is now old technology, not on par with what would be modern government technology. It may be getting unstable as indicated by your not arriving at our home in 1968 when you should have been transported to our travel room."

Grandpa Arthur interrupted, "That clock cuckooing reminds me to ask how long you have set the return travel time for?"

"Three hours." They talked on and on about things relevant to them all, such as how was she coping, her Aunt Jenny, facts about her parents and themselves.

Her Grandmother and Grandfather sat on each side of her. Her Grandmother hugged Selena closely numerous times, and her Grandfather, more reserved, sometimes held her hand.

Grandpa Arthur said, "Oh, it is so good to see you again, here in the flesh, visiting us. Now when we meet through visits, Selly, you will know us."

Selena started to speak and then found she could not. That simple tone and his voice saying, "Selly" started an avalanche of memories. Suddenly, Selena was a little girl running toward this man, her grandfather, and he magically produced a quarter out of her hair – then a looney coin from her ear.

He had whispered conspiratorially, "Selly, now you have so much money, let us go buy ice cream." Blazing in her mind was the two of them walking down the street, his hand was holding hers. When they got to the ice cream shop, she proudly paid for her ice cream. She noticed that her grandfather paid more for his, but she was little, she had her ice cream, and it didn't really matter what grownups did with their money, did it?"

She reluctantly snapped out of her reverie of her past, and found she was smiling at this grandfather, staring at those familiar eyes, that now she knew she had loved, found she still loved. She turned further toward him to give him a solid hug. She couldn't let go.

Selena, with happy tears, whispered, "I remember the coins and going for ice cream now. I left so many memories behind, but some are coming back. I love you both."

"And we love you." From both, almost in unison. As she pulled away, her grandfather offered an explanation regarding her forgotten memories, "We felt that the emotional trauma of losing both of your parents that night removed events from you as a protection for your young mind. You went through a very emotional period. Thank goodness, you are remembering now that you are older."

"It feels good to have some pieces of my family life fall into place for me."

They all had much to discuss, such as how could they now be the age they are, and yet have all their memories of the "future"? Did her father and mother know of the time machine?

Grandpa Arthur addressed her, "They did not even know of the travel machine's existence. There was no reason. When we used to travel in time, we had not even mentioned it to Jenny prior to your parents passing away. After the horrible accident, we sat down and had the lengthy discussion about the entire process with Jenny."

"Ahh, so that is why there was no time travel for my parents! And Aunt Jenny did not ever travel before coming back and forth to see you! It makes sense now."

More discussions followed: How could her aunt be with them when they travelled and also be a baby? How to travel and arrive at a certain age? How this? And how that? Apparently, this was very possible.

Grandma Olive guided Selena through preliminary facts of the universe being four dimensions, three of space and one of time; that travelling back in time was like walking in a circle using a strong gravitational pull, bending space time; she explained a closed time-like curve. Selena realized she did not understand all of this, but that if her grandmother said it was possible, and that she herself were here to witness this in part, then so be it.

"Will you be coming to Ottawa in August as programmed into the computer?"

Grandpa Arthur advised, "That is a question that we will have to really ponder. We have kept track of you when we did visit, and we would love to see you again and again. We will have to discuss future visits." Exchanging a very loving and tender look with his wife, he nodded toward her.

"Well, a few more," Grandma Olive said, her eyes tearing up.

They inquired about her studies and what her plans would be now. Selena admitted that she had not thought of any plans. She would continue to live in her Aunt Jenny's home which was to come under her ownership; she would continue her studies to become a Biochemist. "Aside from that, my life is a blank."

"There is no young man in your life then? At one point you were dating your next-door neighbour, is that not so?"

"It's complicated. We went our separate ways as Austin wanted to concentrate on his studies in Toronto. We barely talked at all since he broke up with me. I think I've become interested in one of the doctors in the Clinic. He has been a good friend and he's such a nice man."

Selena relayed the extent of her relationships with both Austin and with Kevin, how she admired Dr. Kevin Carey very much and how she currently felt about Austin.

Grandpa Arthur said, "You have to take the time to think. He was a prat, I mean to say jerk, to you before. My New York upbringing is showing. There are too many other things currently in your life to contemplate that relationship right now. Perhaps overthinking is not the solution. Let time and more encounters lead you to the right decision."

"You're so right. That's my thinking also. I said I hadn't been myself long enough to belong to someone else."

Grandma Olive looking stern said quite emphatically, "You should never ever, ever *belong* to someone else – You only belong to yourself!"

"That is true. I'll make sure that doesn't happen. I gave my heart away to Austin. At 18 years old, he broke it. I'm not eager to give my heart away now that it's healed. Thank you, Grandma, for setting me straight. In reading your journal, I was extremely impressed how ahead of your time you were in every aspect as far as women's liberation and gender discrimination went in the 60s."

"As a matter of fact, she indeed was!!" confirmed her grandfather, looking proudly at her Grandma Olive.

As Selena produced her aunt's letter from her pocket, she said, "Here's the letter from Aunt Jenny to me."

After both her grandparents took time to read the letter, Grandpa Arthur said, "How sad, Selena. This does explain everything to you. It is a shame that you two did not get an opportunity to discuss this prior to our daughter passing."

"I was quite hurt before finding the letter. But then I was so relieved to be able to 'hear' the explanation in Aunt Jenny's words."

Her Grandmother rubbed Selena's shoulder.

When Selena told them of her trip to England--1215, they were horrified at first and laughed when it was revealed all ended well.

"As expected, these same types of things happened to us, but at least we travelled as a team. On one of the first occasions of our travels though, I went alone to USA--1692. I had thankfully programmed the time for only 30 minutes. I was so keen to see exactly what was going on then, that I had myself in a frightful mess. If you can believe it, I ended up being dragged in for the witch trials in Salem. I knew that this was the destination, but the magnitude of those poor people's fear and suffering was overwhelming. There was nothing I could do. They were going to judge me. When the time ran out, and I landed back at home, I swore I would be more careful what I wanted to see firsthand. Whirr, I was gone from them. You realize that then those horrible people would still believe in witches when I disappeared into thin air. I was very foolish."

Her three hours had almost flown by so quickly. Grandma Olive had brought in tea and poppy seed cake soon after they arrived.

"Poppy seed cake. Aunt Jenny's favourite. I realize that I'm famished."

Grandma Olive said, "My favourite as well. This being hungry is the way it always is. Do you have a headache when you travel?

"I do, and I feel so wobbly, too."

Encouraging Selena to also drink a glass of water, there were discussions about remedies to avoid some of the fatigue.

This is exactly what I needed, someone to confide in and relieve some of the pressure about the time travel machine, to reassure me, to educate me.

"Our time is up in fifteen minutes." Grandpa Arthur was jotting some notes down. As he handed the note to her, he reiterated, "We need to prepare you for your return trip. There will not be any warning. You will just disappear from us."

Giving a warm sigh, her grandmother added, "I guess you already know that from your King John encounter."

"I will get you Vitamins C, D, E, additional water and Calcium. You must be able to lie down and sleep when you arrive home. These supplements will help. You may have issues with balance, dizziness and nausea and, after many trips, be plagued with poor muscle mass. Just take it easy when you return. I will get you those in a moment. We will also tell you that… "

Suddenly, there was a knock on the door, and it was thrown open by a young girl who brought an energy into the room with her, along with a baby.

"Hello, I have brought Jenny back. We had agreed that she would nap at my mom and dad's house. Jenny just woke up. We have played and she has had a diaper change. I could see that your car was home. We had a fun time, did we not, Jenny? Oh, you have company. Look here, Jenny, come see your mommy and daddy and their friend. How are you? My name is Theresa, and, as you can see, I have been looking after Jenny while Mr. and Mrs. Jenkins have been to hear the new, young politician speak. How did he do? All my friends think he is so good looking."

This very vivacious young lady can certainly chatter.

And she was not done. "What is your name? As I said, I am Theresa. I live next door. How do you do?"

Selena was able to get a word in and introduced herself. "Hello, I'm a distant relative *(well, that was true – very distant in time)* of … Arthur and Olive. My name is Selena. Pleased to meet you."

Being so close to her recently deceased aunt as a baby made Selena quite emotional.

Oh, my lord, Aunt Jenny – a baby! Aunt Jenny, how sweet you look!

As Theresa held Jenny, Selena noticed Aunt Jenny was wrapped in a familiar beautiful blanket made from triangle pieces, hand sewn with the tiniest stitches.

My blanket! My baby blanket wrapped around Aunt Jenny as a baby? The blanket passed down to me from Aunt Jenny? To my father, then to me?

She reached for and took her Aunt Jenny from Theresa, gently holding her aunt in her arms. To hide her tears, Selena leaned over the baby, and said in the clearest voice she could manage, "How do you do, little Jenny?" Jenny was only a few months old, and obviously was not speaking. Jenny smiled and cooed at Selena, reaching for her hair, but, when Jenny saw her mommy, she started to cry out for her.

"Oh" Theresa said, "Jenny, your momma will nurse you and make everything better. It was nice to meet you, Selena. Have a nice visit. Oh, I will be available any time that you need me except for school or when I have music practice. You have the schedule for that. Mom sends her regards and will see you when you bring Jenny on Monday while at your work. Take care. Bye-bye."

Handing her Aunt Jenny to her Grandma Olive, Selena could not take her attention from her grandparents and her Aunt Jenny even to see Theresa leave. She was crying, but smiling, happy to be experiencing all of this, but terribly sad. Her emotions were raw.

◇◇◇

Wwww-Wwwww-whirl, Sssss-Sssss-spin, then blur!

◇◇◇

"Ruff"

"What?? Oh Rufus, I was away for a while and yet I wasn't. You'd only have noticed I was gone and then back immediately. That would have surprised you indeed. I'm here now.

"Oh, Rufus. I saw Aunt Jenny! I was with my grandparents! It's all so emotionally exhausting. There I go again with the headache coming on."

Once she was standing, she realized she had once again the feeling of being loose and wobbly in her legs and this time, she noticed in her arms as well.

I'm drained and really need a nap.

Selena slipped onto her own bed, grabbing her intricately hand-stitched baby blanket and snuggled under it, intertwining her fingers around the fabric.

I will keep this blanket that I found on my cot in dad's old room forever.

After a huge yawn, she said, "What a trip, Rufus! I'm exhausted, but exhilarated and awestruck! I did it! I did it! I could look at this scientifically and be proud and amazed." A huge yawn escaped her. "But I can't detach myself from sadness and loss. I just saw baby Aunt Jenny who was my only family, (yawn), and my grandparents. Alive! It's all so confoundingly wonderful..."

Selena cried; she laughed; and she felt woeful, yet relieved she had some answers to her many questions.

Half asleep, she continued, "And here I am home and alone." Reflecting about what to do about the portal she now had, she fell into another exhausted sleep, the blanket still clutched in her hand.

When Selena awoke, somewhat refreshed, but with the headache lingering, she remembered the note that Grandpa Arthur had slipped into her hand before Theresa's lively arrival. Searching her pockets, she found the note that read: "Before Travel, Vitamins C, D, E, additional water and Calcium." Selena also remembered that her grandfather started to say something about "We will also tell you that..."

Well, that can't be helped. I don't know what else he was going to say. I do sometimes take a vitamin. However, usually I forget to even buy them.

I must do my university assignments – final semester exams begin in a week. I'm glad to have time off work to do assignments and spend extra time studying. I've a great start for exams.

A distant, worrying thought was trying to organize itself in her mind. "There was something else I was supposed to do today. Oh well. It mustn't have been too important. I need to get to my assignments and do a little studying."

Selena had also taken advanced French language classes to ensure she could be hired in the French sector as well. It would give her a leg-up, and Selena believed that in the totally bilingual city of Ottawa, that was an asset.

I love living in Ottawa. I realize that I need to move on with my career. Another semester over!

There would be other choices to make regarding her classes, and Selena had to ensure that she spoke with a counsellor. Her interests had her heading toward the honours program with options regarding microbiology and immunology; microorganisms; role of the immune system; systems, cellular or molecular biology; physiology; genomics and bioinformatics.

Selena was impressed with her biology courses, and she knew she would now be checking into her cellular/molecular biology books with a different angle in mind: to see if there would be anything she could glean about the body and time travel.

Too much to expect, but I'll check, nevertheless.

At this point, I'm going to use Aunt Jenny's computer to do some research. I think I need a new place for this key to her bedroom though.

Selena placed it in a beautiful ceramic ornament that she would keep on top of her chiffoniere.

"I better get the vitamins and a headache capsule from Aunt Jenny's medicine cabinet as Grandpa Arthur instructed me."

There was no password required at her aunt's computer. "Look at all the document directories about *History in the Making,* reference documents and websites googled and saved. I'm interested in the progress of Aunt Jenny's book – tomorrow.

I can't allow myself to be drawn into this right now. My homework must be done.

Selena started a directory on the computer: SELENA. She made several sub-directories of her different subjects. Selena started the directory MICROORGANISMS. In the six directories she added, Selena proceeded to download some of the information and criteria from the internet that she would need. She transferred some documents from her cellphone directories.

Speaking as though to her Aunt Jenny, she said, "I'll purchase my own computer shortly. Aunt Jenny, my computer budget is at a good level. I'll then transfer everything I did tonight to my new computer. I want to pay for it myself as I had planned."

She had a class tomorrow morning to prepare for, and she spent two more hours on her assignments and extra time studying.

Before heading to her room for the night, Selena went to the pottery studio, peeked at her clay tray, and sighed happily. *It looks great to me – no cracking.* Selena looked through one of Elizabeth's clay books and found a simple creation that she planned to do next. She thought again of the bowl she would make with her *WHAT DEFINES ART* poem. Giving her pottery tray a little love tap, Selena left, brought Rufus in and went up to bed where Caylie Ceilidh was waiting for her. Caylie rolled over, stretched and purred. Selena gladly petted and chatted to Caylie and Rufus about her day.

Entry in her diary that day:

> *"I can't even begin to write any more of today's events. I have a file now of information bundled together underneath this diary.*
>
> - *Grandma Olive Chernoff's (Cherney) Jenkins Journal.*
> - *Letter from my grandparents to Aunt Jenny.*
> - *Letter from Aunt Jenny to me.*
> - *A copy of Aunt Jenny's Will leaving everything to me.*

I have time travelled today to see my wonderful grandparents. I spent three hours with them and then time with Aunt Jenny as a baby, all in 1968.

My parents didn't know about the time travel machine. Another mystery struck off.

I know so much more than I did.

You see how I couldn't begin to write everything down here, dear diary.

I must remember, I'm a strong person. All of this will make me stronger. It's time that I became a woman – not a girl anymore.

I'll make informed decisions for my own future.

21

Answers

Promptly at 8:30 a.m. the next morning, the insurance adjuster arrived. Selena explained that she had to leave for a 9:30 a.m. class, ensuring that the adjuster had her cell number. They arranged for a telephone call at 12:00 noon when Selena's class would be over.

The morning on microorganisms was very interesting to Selena. She could totally immerse herself in what the professor was saying and be involved in learning. Not a thought to any love life or problems involving the house (not remembering what she had meant to do), not even thinking of her Aunt Jenny or her grandparents and time travel. This was where she was right now, the only thing that mattered.

Then, the session disappointingly was over with some of her classmates looking at their watches, appearing relieved, and one almost ran from the room. Selena checked her cellphone, noting that the adjuster had not called. She needed to have some lunch before her 1:00 p.m. appointment with Tessa O'Bryan, then the 2:30 appointment with Julian Andrews.

Getting a wrap at the university café, Selena saw a magazine on the counter and inquired if she could read that while she had her wrap and tea. The magazine was about travel to the British Isles.

I'll subscribe to this travel magazine.

She put the subscription information into her cellphone, finishing just as it 'rang' *Hello.*

"Selena? It's Kate regarding your insurance. I'm done here. Everything is as the roofer reported. We'll get you an official report by tomorrow, but you should go ahead with your roofer. You mentioned this morning that he planned to start today. Your deductible, as I stated this morning, is $2,000.00, and we anticipate with all your angles on the roof that the entire job will come to approximately $20,000.00. Discuss this with *Ramon Silva Roofing.*"

Oh no! That's what I forgot. Son of a ...! I forgot to sign the contract or to leave Ramon his down payment!!! Now I'm not home and can't do it.

"Thanks, I'll be seeing Ramon Silva mid-afternoon when I'm done my appointments."

"Okay. We'll keep in touch. Got to run to another booking."

Selena called Ramon, "The insurance company got back to me. It's all a go as far as they're concerned. They'll inspect the roofing before they release the payment to you. I'm so sorry, Ramon. I apologize. I hadn't arranged the down payment before I left this morning, and I'm away from home. I've not signed the contract. I'm meeting with my lawyer and accountant this afternoon. I'll get back as soon as I can and make everything right with you."

He still seemed glad to hear from her, and that they would talk when she could get back to the house. He was enroute now. They discussed the invoice. He anticipated it would take his crew five days to complete. He had spoken to a company regarding the leaks in the bedroom. They could start today on the inside ceiling and structure.

"Selena, see you when you get home. I will be there."

As Selena manoeuvered through traffic to get to her lawyer's appointment, she said, "I wasn't planning well not to have left the signed contract and the down payment. I need to be on top of these things. From now on, I'll start an agenda and make notes and a timetable of what I need to be doing, especially business-wise."

I'll grow up!

Selena walked into the law firm and was immediately escorted to Tessa O'Bryan's office. Selena noticed things she had not noticed the first visit. She was aware of what fine woodwork and furnishings were in Tessa's office – *a lovely workspace indeed.* Tessa indicated Selena should take a seat on the plush beige leather sofa.

"Selena, how have you been coping?"

"I'm doing fine. However, there had been issues with the roof of the house. The insurance was taking care of about 90% of the costs. Other than that, things have been running smoothly. The house is quiet, but neighbours and friends have been stepping up and keeping me company."

"I'm sorry to hear of your troubles."

With that out of the way, Tessa said in her business-like tone, "Then if it's all right with you, we should get down to what's at hand here. I have several items to discuss with you. We can discuss the roofing issue as we go along.

"Your Aunt Jenny was going to transfer the home to you on your 20th birthday. Some of the paperwork had been drafted. I want to go over some current amounts that will be coming to you before your appointment with your accountant, Julian Andrews."

Tessa had the accounting documents set out, and they finalized the estate accounts. Tessa advised that last week the ownership and insurance of the Ford Escape had been changed, as had the house insurance. Credit cards for Jenny Jenkins had been cancelled, as well as her Social Insurance Number, passport and health insurance. Tessa presented Selena with the original documentation of Funeral Director's Proof of Death.

Twirling her hair between her fingers, Selena was following all this conversation, but the impact of her aunt's death kept overwhelming her as she listened to Tessa relaying facts. The home had been evaluated; the property already insured adequately. The home would be directly transferred to Selena as the named beneficiary. They would be filing the documents for probate. Tessa related that search of other assets had been completed; they had checked for any living relatives, children; notified Canada Revenue Agency of Jenny's death. The firm had obtained pension numbers, and the TFSA and life insurance would pass directly to Selena as named beneficiary. There would be an interim distribution at six months and the final distribution at the latest, one year after her aunt's death.

All of this was working its way through Selena's head. "I believe your aunt planned to speak with you before your 20th birthday. That was in our discussions. However, the eventuality of her advising you of these financial arrangements never happened. I'm sorry as this is a shock to you on so many levels. Selena, it isn't unusual for someone even two decades older than you to be astounded at all this information."

As each document was presented, Tessa explained what Selena was signing. Within the designated one-hour appointment, Selena had begun a new chapter in her life.

"There is indeed a lot of money you are inheriting over the next year, but we have also discussed the costs upcoming. I don't want to disparage your maturity; however, you are a young woman, and you have to be cautious this money is used carefully with an eye to anyone taking advantage of you. We advise our older clients the same."

I'm worth a ridiculous amount of money. My life is now different, and I can do different things. I know I'll still need Julian Andrews to advise me regarding future investments of my parents' and Aunt Jenny's money.

"I understand where you are coming from, Tessa. I'll use Julian Andrews as a sounding board. The fact is that Aunt Jenny instilled in me a good awareness of the use of money. As she was always careful with money, it has been my habit to also be careful. However, I'll be able to do things that I couldn't do a week ago. Thanks for all your professionalism and kindness during this."

Tessa added, "I will need to see you again as the probate continues. The firm will be sending out an interim account as well as a final billing to *Julian Andrews Accounting* with a copy to you once the probate is completed. There will be a couple of additional appointments to be scheduled in the future."

Selena had sat in the vehicle in the parkade at the mall for 20 minutes, attempting to grasp the information set out by Tessa O'Bryan.

She sat there, hands folded in her lap, shaking, re-hearing the conversations from Tessa. She had heard, but not entirely processed at the meeting, Tessa's comments that her Aunt Jenny's estate, including bank accounts, various savings plans, investments, as well as the house and land, would value $3,640,000.00. She had gasped as she let out her breath. "I understand everything you said, but that amount – it can't be."

Tessa had decided that a cup of tea would be just the thing to distract for a few minutes and give Selena more time to absorb what was happening. It turned out that some oatmeal cookies were also in the offering. Selena was surprised at how much she enjoyed that tea and cookies. She closed her eyes momentarily and sighed. It was a welcome comfort food. Brushing hair from her eyes and rubbing her cheeks, muttered, "I do understand everything."

Remembering the most astonishing part with Tessa advising, "I also want to remind you that in your parents' Last Will and Testaments, there is a considerable sum of trust, house, property sale money and insurance money in your name."

Seeing Selena's shocked expression, Tessa realized that Selena was not aware of her parents' estate.

"This has been in trust in a bank account for you through your parents' wishes. None of your parent's money went to your Aunt

Jenny at her request. She indicated it a privilege to have you in her home. With respect to your parents' trust, the entire amount in trust and accrued interest will be given to you on your 21st birthday. A rough estimate of your parents' estate, including insurance payout currently would be over $1,200,000.00."

Selena inhaled, almost in alarm.

"You understandably need to take time to adjust to your aunt's passing, and you certainly need time to absorb what I've told you today regarding your finances. Your Aunt Jenny was planning to ensure your finances were in order on your 20th birthday. I take it that your aunt hadn't shared any of this other information with you over the years?"

Holding back tears and slightly reddening with mixed emotions, Selena had said, "No, absolutely not. Aunt Jenny hadn't ever said a word to me about any money coming to me or that I'd inherit her estate. There also was no mention of my parents having an estate. I was so young then, so there was no need. But nothing has been said to me since either."

"Your Aunt Jenny confided in me that she always kept you with only a little money as she knew that you would inherit these large sums, and she wanted you to be aware of hard work being a reward in itself. Whether that was a good decision on her part, only time will tell.

Selena recalled all this, and she became aware that she was chilled sitting in the parkade without the car heater running. She quickly turned the key in the ignition.

I'm staggered by the amounts of money that Aunt Jenny has given me. It never even occurred to me to think my parents had Wills. On August 31st next year, when I turn 21, I'll inherit all that money as well. This can't change who I am. The feelings I have for Aunt Jenny and my parents are the most important thing to me.

She put the address into the GPS, listened to it bossily direct her out of downtown. Frowning with concentration at its toneless instructions, she headed to her appointment with *Julian Andrews Accounting.*

Selena appreciated that Julian Andrews was treating her like an adult. He went over the package and the draft tax return with Selena. All Aunt Jenny's information was set up on the computer, as well as the detailed documents he handed to her.

Together they made decisions that she felt were in her best interests. She had questions regarding tax returns, and Julian was able to give her all the information she required. Selena had seen all the documentation that had been faxed to the law firm when she was with Tessa.

Julian went over with Selena the places where she should sign. In closing his explanations, he said, "I'll have a cheque, along with the semi-final documents couriered to you within the next two days. Have *Ramon Silva Roofing* forward the roofing invoice to my firm. We'll deal with the insurance company as well."

Together with my meetings with Tessa and Julian, I have a good grasp on what's going on with the estate, but my head is spinning with the amounts mentioned.

It's all unbelievable! Aunt Jenny, am I doing okay?

As Selena drove up her street, she looked at the entire neighbourhood with a different attitude. Selena knew a little of the history of her neighbourhood in Rockcliffe Park. She could hear her Aunt Jenny proudly informing her:

"During World War II, Canada's own Bletchley Park, a code-breaking operation, ran as a branch of the National Research Council at a wireless intercept station at Rockcliffe."

This made her proud as well. Apparently, the "Examination Unit" fed a steady stream of intelligence-gathering equal to that of London and Washington, but in the fields of French and Japanese code breaking. Her aunt had also remarked that Lester B. Pearson (a then future Prime Minister of Canada), at that time working for the State of External Affairs worked with the day-to-day operations and staffing.

Rockcliffe Park was old, as old as the 1860s. It had been amalgamated about the year she was born. Her aunt had been enormously pleased with the area, and Aunt Jenny had told Selena that it had been designated a Heritage Conservation District in 1977, one of only a few 19th century communities thus designated in North America. The community was northeast of downtown Ottawa on the southern bank of the great Ottawa River surrounded by two small lakes, the McKay and the Sands Pits, and the Rockeries which were a rock garden and playing fields.

"I know this neighbourhood is part of me. I'm truly a part of it now that I own a Rockcliffe home! I love Ottawa, its river, canal, forests, lakes and the bustle of being the capital and government center of Canada. Toronto might be bigger, and Torontonians think they were the best in Canada, but I'm a true Ottawan!

"Gosh, I should have stopped to get groceries, but I'm mentally exhausted. Tomorrow I'll get the groceries to make my favourite lemon chicken recipe."

Upon arrival home, Selena could see shingles had been removed and hear the men shouting instructions. Ramon and Selena met to discuss the contract which Selena now readily signed. She quickly wrote out her cheque and gave Ramon the down payment. *I can trust Ramon Silva Roofing.*

"Oh, hi Laura. What's up?" Laura was already on her way over.

It'll be good to see Laura. She'll take my mind off so many things. I'll make iced tea.

"Selena, how good to see you. I took this as a long weekend so that I could discuss something with you. You look better than you did on Friday. These have been terrible days for you losing your Aunt Jenny, but I hope that all of us coming to keep you company was not too exhausting after the funeral and cheered you up a little?"

"Laura, it was appreciated. The game that Colleen came up with was a lot of fun and revealing." Selena went on to say that Kevin, Colleen, Austin and herself had gone out for supper. "It was a good evening too."

"Austin told Theodore that he's ready to get back together with you and that he loved and missed you. Theo and I discussed what I'm going to tell you."

Selena gave Laura an attentive look, waiting.

"Both Theodore and I are interfering, I know, but we think you shouldn't have Austin back in your life right now. They're twins, and Theo knows him better than anyone. You know that I saw Austin in Toronto with other girls and then there is the one that we believe he has been going out with for a year – just as recently as just two weeks ago."

"Oh, for the love of…! I'm totally sideswiped. Of course, it was okay for him to date because he broke it off with me. I couldn't manage a relationship myself because I did still love him. You say he has been with a steady girlfriend for a year – until even two weeks ago?"

Selena was looking at Laura who nodded in a tragic manner, her eyes sliding away.

"I should've said so. I thought 'why open wounds when you seem to be healing from his callous actions in breaking it off with you'. Selena, I didn't know he was going to come back suddenly and make a play for you – profess his love …"

All this while, Selena was fidgeting. She abruptly stood up and paced back and forth, mouthing words Laura could only guess about.

"So, what the blazes? Did he dump her that recently? Went out with her for a year! Does he love me? Did he love her? Was he using her? Is he using me? Who is this Austin?"

Laura came over, put her arms out, and Selena slipped into them and sobbed, "Maybe I would've loved him again. Is he just going to leave me again and get back with this other woman? I trusted him once. He hurt me. He broke me, Laura. Will he break me again?"

"Don't let him, Selena!"

Looking toward the wine cabinet, Laura said, "Do you have any good red wine? Only one glass cuz I'll be driving."

Settling down with a glass of wine each, Selena had pulled herself marginally together, she said, "We'll toast to not letting Austin hurt me again." Sighing she added, "I appreciate your telling me these things. I'm really confounded. You know full well that I really thought that I loved Austin and that I'd marry him. I was young, but young love is strong. You know that!"

"Let's just say you cool it with Austin – take your time with this new development as well. Have fun with Kevin. I liked the old Austin, but not the new Austin."

Selena mused, "This evening is exactly what I needed. I needed to know. I can't tolerate his dishonesty. I'll see what he has to say for himself."

Selena was so relieved to have had the conversation with Laura. She had disliked thinking she could not speak to Laura about Austin.

Here, even Theodore didn't think I should rush into anything with his own brother. Thank goodness Laura came over.

They enjoyed each other's company for another hour as Selena told Laura some of the information about the estate. Laura stood up, grabbing Selena by the arm, pulling her up to give her a long hug.

"My good and dear friend, I'm sad for you with your aunt passing away. I see you looking so much more determined and decisive within yourself about your future. Know that I am there for you, and I want you to call or text any time – I love and miss you. I need to get back to mom's place. I'll text you later so we can chat some more. Are you going to be okay?"

"Laura, I'm very glad you came. I understand why you were silent on Austin's antics in Toronto. Thanks for being frank with me about what you and Theodore think."

Later, Selena and Rufus walked and enjoyed the beautiful shining spring evening. *Now this was bliss.* Rufus was being Rufus the Goofus, running, rolling in the grass and chasing a squirrel to a tree, which proceeded to chatter at Rufus from high on a branch. Selena was simply living in the moment and pondering her options.

I feel today that this is my woodland as I'm on my own, not another living human around, just squirrels, birds and the occasional deer. I can handle being on my own. Being alone isn't so bad. I can trust myself!

To her diary, a short entry:

> *"Laura is a real friend. I've been considering not letting Austin into my life again, but having a good, solid friend to reinforce what I believe to be right is reassuring. But what an ass Austin is. Why is he even trying to get me back when he has (had) a girlfriend just two weeks ago? Did she dump him and I'm the rebound?*
>
> *I'll write more later. Just know, dear diary, that life throws punches."*

"Aunt Jenny, would you agree I'm handling all this well? Colleen may be right – I am strong. I won't let him break me again. I don't need Austin."

22

Just Supper

"Bless a dreamless night and a new day! I feel that yesterday's multiple appointments were difficult, but productive. At least I slept well."

Today she would stop at the Clinic to see all the staff and arrange to take the rest of the week off so she could oversee the work on the replacement of the roof and the work being done inside the upstairs bedroom.

"Dr. Kev already told me I could take as much time as I wanted and that I have holiday time as well. And that was before the roofing catastrophe."

I'll be able to prepare for those term finals. Honestly, I also need to search for new employment possibilities right away. Stop delaying the inevitable. Never mind the nagging thought that I like the Clinic.

Selena knew Ramon Silva was already at work. She could hear them pulling the shingles off and some of the power hammering. Once she went outside, she thought feisty Rufus was going to climb up the ladder, but he veered off to chase a rabbit which was faster than he was. Ramon came down from the roof when Selena appeared. According to Ramon, everything was going well and on a schedule for completion within five days.

Selena arrived at the Clinic a little before lunch break.

"Gosh Elizabeth, it's good to be here! Penelope, oh how good you look. Your dark eyes are as gleaming as your dark hair."

Penelope's response was the phrase, "Thanks, I try."

As Bethany walked into the reception area, she said, "Oh, we're doing slang, are we? Then, you are mirin' her looks. I get some slang. My brother uses slang on me just to confuse me. I don't get all of it. He says he does 'wildin' stuff that my parents don't know about. I guess that means wild and crazy. I told him I was too old for that new talk."

Elizabeth chimed in, "Me too." And they all laughed.

"Yeah," Penelope said. "We are boolin'!".

Selena, perplexed, said, "What cha talkin' about now?"

Penelope said, "You don't get to use slang much, do you, Selena?"

"Are you laughing at me, Penelope? I know the phrase 'You're right, you're right! I don't use it much. Aunt Jenny and I didn't chat that way. I may need to get with the program."

They all had another giggle at each other's expense.

Bethany said, "I made a reservation. Dr. Kev might come to lunch with us after you meet with Dr. Carey, Sr."

Elizabeth motioned Selena over to her desk, "Dr. Carey, Sr. is still with a walk-in patient who went in five minutes before you arrived."

"Oh, that's okay then. I'll just wait here." Selena stayed with Elizabeth at the front desk while the other two went to finish their work before coming to lunch with her.

Elizabeth said, "Mary is discussing the new bookkeeping system with our Dr. Kev. I'm sure he'll want to go for lunch with you. How is your pottery drying? The picture you texted looked great, definitely a keeper."

While they were discussing pottery, Selena heard Mary laughing. Then she heard Kevin, "My job takes so much of my time, but you know I would like to get married and have a couple of children. Hopefully, not too far in the future."

Elizabeth was inquiring something, and Selena had to pull her mind back to what they had been talking about.

"Umm. I'm still very keen on pottery. Honestly, there has been so much going on that I've only made the one item since you were there. Where does the time go?"

"Selena, you're hilarious. You, the spring chicken, asking me that. Where do the time and years go indeed?"

Kevin came in just then, looking startled, then pleased. "Perfect, I was just going to see if you were here. My dad is still with a patient. We can chat in my office about your time off." Leading her down the hall, he queried, "How've you been keeping since Friday? I enjoyed playing Chess as well as *Two Truths and a Lie* and going out for supper. It's good to see you today."

Getting to his office door, she managed to say, "Well, sure, it's good to see you, too. I've been doing well. Although there's been problems with leakages in my aunt's roof. I've had a roofer in.

"He says the damage is quite extensive, or, at least in my mind, $20,000.00 is extensive. That brings me to my request to take the rest of the week off. *Ramon Silva Roofing* will take until the weekend to complete the outside repair and the damage caused on the inside."

"That's terrible. You've been through a lot. My dad and I stand by our promise for you to take the time that you need. We're making do as the other staff are pitching in. We had my friend Daniel's wife in to help a couple of times. Marie is a nurse if you remember. Your job will be here when you return. Do you need me to do anything to help you? I'm free tonight, and I could come by to see how things are progressing?"

"No, that's fine. Everything is under control now. I'll simply be grateful to be there to see the day-to-day effects of their work. This extra time will also be helpful as my finals are coming up. Will you be coming to lunch with Penelope, Bethany and me?"

After he nodded, Selena advised she was taking her own car to leave directly from the restaurant.

He looked disappointed. After what I overheard him say to Mary,

I need some distance to gather myself during the drive.

Selena followed Kevin, Bethany and Penelope to the restaurant on Rideau Street to the girls' favourite authentic Mexican restaurant, *Si Senor Mexican Street Food*. When the order came, there were exclamations on how good all their food choices and presentations were. Chimichanga (Selena), Torta de Carnitas (Kevin), Quesadillas (Penelope), Burritos (Bethany), the best refried beans, guacamole and then Mexican flan. Yummm!

The conversations meandered around the usual subjects. They discussed work, their own families, holidays and sports. Penelope's current sport was racket ball, but she chatted about missing winter sports of skiing and hockey. Bethany mentioned how she was looking forward to her spring holiday to Greece and that she had been on a ten-day Contiki Tour to England, Belgium, Netherlands, Germany, Austria, Italy and France prior to starting employment at The Caring Medical Clinic.

With her dark eyes looking enigmatic, she added, "My next tour might be more reserved as I'm getting too old (haha) for all that partying!"

Penelope responded, "I've been to tournaments in other countries and particularly loved skiing in Aspen, Colorado. I wish that I could go to Switzerland or Austria as I've heard that there are fantastic ski hills 'everywhere'!"

Selena was kindheartedly asked how she was getting on after her aunt's passing. She conveyed that her neighbours had been very insistent in keeping her company and she had had friends over. She caught Dr. Kev's eye for a moment.

Not any reason to mention the days and evening with Kevin.

She also advised what was going on with her roof and interior of one of the upstairs bedrooms. Older homes were discussed, and Selena assured them that she was fine and was able to cover the costs associated with the roof with the help of her insurance policy.

Not discussing my aunt's estate.

Tummies full, it was time for the staff to head back to the office and for Selena to see what was happening with her roof. Kevin gave her a heartfelt wave.

He said, "Goodbye, Selena, see you next week when you return if not before!" Other goodbyes followed.

After that delicious lunch with entertaining friends, Selena stopped at the Farm Boy Grocers to purchase everything she would need to make her supper. She was a little distracted in her grocery shopping though as a result of what she had heard Kevin say to Mary.

I'm very annoyed at myself to realize I was wondering if Kevin was thinking about me when he said he was interested in getting married shortly.

Jolted into reality of what Kevin wanted from life right now, she realized even though she admired him and enjoyed his company, he was about 27 and apparently ready to settle down.

I'm absolutely not ready to settle down!

Selena was in a little bit of a fog, and she thought she had bought everything she had on her list. In her state of mind, it was understandable that she forgot to get the lemons that she would require to make lemon chicken.

She waved to Ramon Silva as she carried the bags into the house. Rufus and Caylie greeted her at the door. Attempting not to think about Kevin, Austin, the power hammering or staple gun noises, she unpacked all her groceries, put them away in the proper places, distractedly leaving out what she would need for her supper.

I always enjoy cooking as it gives me time to unwind from my workday or to contemplate my university classes.

When Selena had everything put away, she went out to see how Ramon was doing in the repair work. Ramon asked if Selena was pleased with what the inside repair company had accomplished.

"They barely made a mess, and they totally tidied up everything, leaving nothing behind. The ceiling looks fabulous."

Marching back into the house to have a much-needed chat with Laura to discuss the new development regarding Kevin, Selena pressed Laura's speed button before she even closed the back garden door.

"Laura, do you have a few minutes?" Not waiting for any confirmation, she rushed ahead. Smiling for a moment, she said, "Guess what! I found out today at the Clinic that Kevin wants to marry someone shortly and start having children. I heard him discussing it with Mary from the Clinic. I hope it wasn't me he was chatting about. I've been looking after Aunt Jenny in a way for years. I want my own life!"

"As you just said, it might not even be you he's thinking about!"

"Anyway, I'll wait to see where his head is. I just don't need anything else complicated going on. I wanted to update you. I'll take Rufus for his walk now and then start supper. Take care."

Once Selena returned from the walk with Rufus, she went to prepare the chicken for her supper. She started to arrange the ingredients and looked for the very necessary lemons.

"Oh no." She looked on her list to see if she had crossed them off, not believing that she had forgotten them. There at the very top of her list was "Lemons x3".

Just dandy! Turning toward Rufus, she said, "Rufus, I'm the Goofus," left him shaking his head and looking quite confused at her, and she rushed out to the vehicle to go back to the store.

Selena was in the fruit and vegetable section when she heard, "Hey Selena! What are you shopping for with such a harried expression on your face?"

Turning toward the voice, she waved and said, "Oh, hello there,

Jeremy. I've already bought $150.00 worth of groceries this afternoon, got home and realized that I had forgotten to get the lemons I need to make lemon chicken for my supper. What are you looking for?"

"Lemon chicken! My aunt used to make that when we visited. It's one of my unconditional favourites. Awesome. Well, I'm here to purchase the delectable, pre-cooked roast chicken from the Deli right behind the fruit and vegetables. That and a container of potato salad which will be my lonely supper tonight."

What a character!

Selena had met Jeremy numerous times at the Clinic, and she had found him very entertaining as he loved to joke and get a laugh out of everyone. She knew he was a genuinely nice fellow. Just then the loudspeaker announced a sale in aisle 6 for store-brand pastas.

Replaying in Selena's mind was the scene of Jeremy inviting some of the staff at the Clinic out for lunch. "Well, if you're paying, I'll be ordering caviar and champagne," Selena quipped one day. Jeremy laughed and jovially said, "Then you can stay behind and work."

Smiling to herself, she paused her memory and got involved in their current conversation. Making a spur-of-the-moment decision, she said, "Sorry, I was distracted for a moment by the announcement. I feel badly that I'm going to make this lemon chicken and eat it all myself and you're going to eat pre-cooked, not very delectable, cold by the time you get home, chicken. Would you like to come have supper at my aunt's house? Sadly, my aunt passed away last week, so it's just me there, along with my dog and cat."

"I'm so sorry for you about your Aunt Jenny. She must have been so young. Kevin did tell me. Wait, right before you can change your mind, I'm saying yes I'd come have lemon chicken!"

"No worries. Well, then, buy your items if you wish. We could eat your potato salad, along with my rice and asparagus. I'll go pay for my lemons."

"Selena, this is awesome. I *can* actually cook. I've a small kitchenette in my basement suite. Let me at least buy your lemons.

I'll follow you to your place. I think that I know generally where it is."

Jeremy paid for the grocery items, and they both walked a little self-consciously to their respective vehicles. Selena backed out and drove ahead in her Ford Escape, while Jeremy followed her in his Mazda Miata. They curved along the roads, winding into her neighbourhood, and pulled into the massive driveway out of the way of the two *Ramon Silva Roofing* trucks. Selena got out of her vehicle and went over to Jeremy's Miata.

"Oh wow, that must be my favourite sports car! You picked a great vehicle."

"I know. I really treated myself at the time my computer store took off last year. Although it's a couple of years older than it looks, it's also a good investment. I wrote part of it off as a company car. This type of vehicle won't lose a lot of value. I'll take you for a ride this evening if you'd like. What's going on with the workers here? I'm a handyman, and I wonder if they'd mind if I went up and took a peek."

Selena explained her roofing issues to Jeremy and then advised him that she needed to get a start on supper. He was taking the grocery bag in, but, at the door, he was practically bowled over by an eager Rufus. Jeremy petted Rufus as Rufus ran out to his dog run, circled around and came back into the house to wag his tail and say a proper hello to Jeremy.

"Well, that was exciting! Come here, fella. What a magnificent dog. I want a dog, but that'll have to wait." Jeremy stopped petting and talking to Rufus long enough to spy the cat curled on her own blanket, giving him the eye. He went over to Caylie, gave her an ear rub, chatted to her, then turned and offered to help Selena. Selena took the bag from him.

Selena gave Jeremy a sly smile and said, "I know you want to see the roof project. Come back once you've checked that out. Then you can set the table."

Gratefully, he departed, and Selena could hear him flagging down Ramon, presumably asking if he could come up. There was silence and he did not return, so she concluded he had been summoned up the ladder. Rufus looked longingly at her, and she shrugged and said, "We'll walk again later, okay Rufus?"

"Ruff!"

A perfectly timed 40 minutes had passed, and Jeremy stepped inside the door.

"Oh my, that smells fantastic! I can't wait, but I'll help now. Ramon Silva seems a knowledgeable guy. I learned a lot from my father and uncle who are tradesmen and have a company in Kanata. I always had to help out as a teenager and throughout university when I wasn't on a work term."

Jeremy washed his hands, took the dishes she directed him to, and grabbed the cutlery and glasses. He asked if he should pour water for her. After a few more minutes, he helped her serve their chicken, rice, asparagus and potato salad.

Jeremy took one mouthful. Then a second passed, and he said, "Goodness, Selena, don't ever tell my Aunt Aggie if you meet her, but I think, yes, I know, that your lemon chicken is every bit as good as her magic secret recipe!"

"Well, thank you. I took an interest in cooking and baking when I was 12. I get take-out when I'm in a hurry, but Aunt Jenny always wanted real food. I'm getting used to the idea that I'm on my own," she said, suddenly self-conscious that she may have revealed more than she should to him.

Jeremy looked unperturbed with the statement, and he added, "It'll take you many years to get over your aunt passing away and so young too. Have you lived with her a long time?"

I wonder how much he wants to know.

"You don't have to say anything; however, I always found it better to talk about these things. I'm very willing to hear your story, and I wish you'd confide in me."

So, Selena started at the beginning, slowly, to see how attentive he seemed. He interjected with just the right thing to say a few times; however, he mostly just listened as though he was genuinely absorbed in her life story. There was never a thought on her part of revealing the series of adventures upstairs in Aunt Jenny's travel room, so that remained unsaid.

I learned my lesson when I almost revealed it during the Two Truths and a Lie game.

Once Selena was at the end with what was happening about the roof, Jeremy again said, "I'm sorry for your loss, Selena. It's a good thing that you have such wonderful neighbours and friends though. Even your co-workers seem to be concerned about you. That's something special."

"For sure, I agree. In particular, having Karen and Bud right next door to help keep me company and to help with the decision on the roof was such a relief."

"You mentioned that they had sons your age?"

"There is Austin and Theodore who are both away at school this past two years. Austin is someone I used to date during high school and for one year after. He may be coming back to be a firefighter at one of the Ottawa Fire Departments. But ..."

"Ah, there was a 'but' and then a pause. You should know, Selena, I've always liked and admired you, so ... there that statement is out in the open. I love to listen. If there's something else that you want to share or need a second opinion on, please spill!"

"Well, tell me about yourself, Jeremy, before you get any more out of me."

"Ha, good sparring! Awesome. I'm 24 years old, and I've lived in the Ottawa area my whole life, and my parents are both living in Kanata. I've got one brother and two sisters – That's why I have the ability to listen – two sisters who love to talk. My brother, Daniel, is a doctor, a friend of Kevin's as you know. He's married with two children." He noted Selena's eyes casting downward after this sentence.

"My two sisters are Jane and Eva. My brother's wife, Marie, is a nurse. I'm interested in sports, art in most forms, travelling, great movies and live entertainment. I live with my brother in their walk-out basement suite which has its own entrance. With the money I earned on work terms, payment for my work for my family's construction business and minimal rent for my suite, I'm saving to purchase a house within the next year or so. As I said, I'm good at carpentry. I'm great with computers. And I'm a great live-in babysitter when needed. There, that should about cover it all. That's me in a nutshell."

"You just mentioned an interest in travel, Jeremy. That's something I want to do so much in the next few years."

Jeremy and Selena then chatted a long while about where they each would travel, becoming more comfortable with each other.

And then popped out, "Since you are a great live-in babysitter, how long would it be before you plan to have children of your own? Whoops, that came out intrusive."

At that point in their conversation, Selena noticed the hammering stop and then perceived the work crew exchanging muted banter. Jeremy continued in an amused voice, easing her embarrassment.

"It did seem a little forward, but we're sharing stories here. No, I really think that at 24, I'm just a tad too young to be interested in having my own children. What I really want to do is keep my business above water, take some trips, get to see the world, have my own place. It's Kevin who is so captivated with the idea of getting married and having children right away. I'm too young for a couple of years."

Selena tried to steer away from that topic, thinking furiously what she could say to change the subject without being too obvious.

Surmising from her demeanour that she did not want to pursue the topic of Kevin, he shot her a curious glance.

Perplexed at what to say next, Selena twirled her hair between her fingers. She hesitated, and finally muttered, "Well, I should do some homework tonight." Changing her mind and gaining momentum, she said, "But you said you're interested in art… Would you like to see my aunt's pottery studio?"

"A pottery studio? Awesome! Life can't get much better than lemon chicken and a pottery studio. My aunt that I mentioned lives in Saskatchewan and has a pottery studio in her basement, with a kiln in her garage. She just makes it for herself. Aunt Aggie loves making bird feeders, bird baths, little statues, as well as useful house pieces. I was keen on playing with clay from an early age."

By this time, the three of them, Selena, Rufus and Jeremy, in that order, were out the door with Rufus barking and sniffing and Selena and Jeremy amused by his antics. Jeremy started to run, and Rufus was off chasing him and running in front of Jeremy. Jeremy found a stick which he threw, and Rufus was delighted to have a friend to play with. Rufus brought the stick back, and so it went on and on until Rufus got distracted and left the stick in the distance.

Jeremy collapsed on a bench. "Take me to your pottery studio, anywhere Rufus can't find a stick!"

They walked through the yard to the pottery studio with Rufus sniffing right at Jeremy's heels.

"I'm amazed at this awesome studio. Look at the space you have here, as well as the supplies. Your aunt must have been an avid potter."

"No, she wasn't. She attempted it, then tired of it. She was going to donate all the equipment and supplies to the local high school. She realized I was interested and ordered me these boxes of clay, so I'm quite set up to go. I was having a lot of trouble," she said in an embarrassed tone. "I made things and then they cracked. I was an enthusiastic amateur who hadn't even read a book or looked anything up on-line. Our receptionist, Elizabeth, came over and set me on the right path."

Walking toward a shelf, she showed Jeremy her cracked pieces and then the one tray she had recently made. "This is after I discovered the magic of plastic to cover the clay." He glanced at her lips as they moved into a half smile.

"Hey, have you ever heard of pinch pots or working with coils?"

"I've now seen pictures in Elizabeth's pottery books, but I haven't done anything like that. In fact, with the roof, homework and appointments, I've only come back in here once since making this tray."

"Well, then, let me show you how simple this is. Our aunt always let us grab a clump of clay, little or big, depending on what size you want to end up with. I'll do a demonstration of creating a pinch pot. Then, if you're still interested, I can show a coil pot. Is that okay?"

"I can't wait."

Jeremy opened the clay and took off a three-inch square piece of clay, covering the clay up again in the bag. He used his hands to support the clay, rolled it to make a crude ball, and then put his thumb into the center of the little ball. Moving his fingers, he brought the sides of the ball upward, slowly making the base of the ball less in size and using that clay to make a little bowl. He bumped the "bowl" on the desk so that it had a flattened bottom.

"This is the easiest example, but you can spend time and made it a lot nicer. You can make pieces any size you want. Then you can use one of your tools and incise a design into the bowl."

"That is fantastic. Quick, show me coils."

He was excited to show off for Selena. He knew he was not an expert by any means, but this was awesome to be spending time with her looking on. Jeremy had liked Selena from the moment he met her, but he had realized later that Kevin may have set his sights on Selena. He was not getting in the middle of that with his good friend; however, this opportunity right now to spend time with Selena was not something he was willing to give up.

He took a small chunk of clay, rolled it with the rolling pin, flattening it into a three-inch piece which he used a round cookie cutter to make a circle. Selena watched as Jeremy then rolled several pieces of clay to make each look like a slim snake. Grabbing a kitchen-type bowl and a piece of plastic, he inserted the plastic into the bowl and put the clay circle inside at the bottom. Then he took the snake-like pieces and wrapped them around the circle previously cut, and which Selena realized was to be the bottom of something. Jeremy continued to add the snake-like pieces on top of each other, building the sides up taller, fussing with the clay to join the coils to the bottom and then to each other. After several layers of coils, he looked at a shelf and found a little sponge and a plastic bowl which he filled with water. As he used the sponge to wipe the clay, the bowl was taking shape.

"Ahh, I could've left the coils completely showing and that would've given it a rugged look. You'd still need to use the sponge or your fingers to ensure everything is joined together. If you ever wanted to use the piece of pottery in a functional manner, you'd want it to be joined properly. In this case, you can't see the coils on the inside, just the outside."

"I like it completed either way. This piece looks great. I can't even tell it had been made with coils from the inside view. You're a magician. I'll be doing these types of pottery for sure. Thanks. Do you miss doing clay at your aunt's? When was the last time you were able to visit and play with clay?"

"I haven't been in three years. Mom and dad have still made a trip every two years but setting up my business just has not given me a break. That's obviously good, but I do miss my aunt, her lemon chicken and the pottery room she has."

"Well, I guess you'll just have to come here and do pottery. This studio is large enough for four people to be doing clay."

What am I doing? I can't be starting another relationship. This is just for friendship. Nothing is going to happen here. Not on my watch!

"Selena, you don't have to let me use your pottery studio, but if you really mean it, um, occasionally, that would be awesome. It's such a stress reducer. Or at least it is if things are working out. I remember my aunt throwing some clay against the wall once, then laughing and saying, 'that really reduced my stress.'"

They covered Jeremy's creations with plastic, put them beside Selena's which gave them both an odd, contented feeling. Selena felt self-conscious, and Jeremy felt closer to her. They left their feelings in the pottery studio, let Rufus out so that he could take another run and a sniff.

"I need to go now but thanks for asking me to share supper with you. That was kind and unexpected. You're a good person, Selena."

"You're welcome. I do have one thing that I need to do upstairs, as well as an assignment to complete. Ramon and his crews are gone for the day, and I'm relieved since Austin next door got his parents to give me Ramon's name. It has been a God-send to have someone I can depend on."

"Yeah, it's good that you have Austin to depend on. Makes life easier."

"Ah, no. I can't depend on Austin. He broke up with me two years ago. He now wants to get back together with me, but… Well, he left me once so I can't really feel a total trust in him right now. He broke my young heart."

"I apologize. That was thoughtless of me to assume that you liked him now. You just seem friendly that I was taking advantage."

"It's okay. It's good for me to have someone to talk to. I'm in a very confused state right now. I've lost Aunt Jenny, my only living relative." Giving an embarrassed half laugh, she looked away from Jeremy.

"Hey, Selena. What are you thinking about?"

Taking a huge breath and sighing, she confessed her thoughts, "Austin seems to want to come back to Ottawa. Kevin, well, Kevin… I overheard him say to Mary at work the same thing you said – that he wants to get married and have children soon. Honestly, I just want to live my life. Kevin is considerate, kind and good to me, but that isn't where I am. I'm not ready to settle down." Selena, at that moment, became even more embarrassed.

Jeremy stopped himself from stepping closer to Selena.

She continued on in a rush of words, "Not that I really thought that he meant me when he was saying that to Mary. Goodness, I got absurd there for a moment…"

"Well, perhaps you really don't know how you feel yet, and everything will sort out. My grandma always said, 'Everything will come out in the wash.'"

Selena gasped at him, incredulous. "My mother used to say that. Isn't that remarkable? It's not a common saying, I don't think. How cute we both grew up with it."

There was a spark of eye contact that passed between them.

"That *is* a coincidence. Selena, this has been a lot of fun for me. We had some good laughs. Rufus is lots of fun. You mentioned you had homework, so I'll let you get to what you've planned for the rest of the evening, and I'll be off. Thanks so much for inviting me for supper. Good-bye Rufus."

Jeremy watched as Selena tucked a strand of her beautiful caramel hair behind her lovely ear.

Selena said, "Where's Rufus? Rufus, Rufus!!" Out he came, bounding towards them and instead of going to Selena, Rufus ran toward Jeremy and jumped up on him, knocking the unprepared Jeremy to the ground.

"Ha ha hahahahahaha! I should be sorry for laughing, Jeremy, but that was absolutely hilarious. Hahaha (snort)."

"Did you actually just snort?" said Jeremy as he was part way standing up but then bending over laughing. "Oh my gosh, that is priceless. A very pretty lady snorting?"

"Certainly, I didn't snort. Well, maybe – a little snort." Selena and Jeremy continued to laugh like two school children instead of two adults.

"Oh, Jeremy. This evening was just what I needed. I want to laugh a lot."

Still laughing himself, Jeremy said, "Well, I'm fine. Don't worry about me with my broken ribs and concussion from your unruly dog!"

Selena noted that with his toned, very athletic body, he probably was not hurt at all! *Indeed, he is swole, fit, muscular, ripped – all of that.*

"Tonight didn't work for me to take you for the drive, but the invitation's open. Also, to give you the sales pitch, if you're still interested in a computer, laptop, tablet, gaming device, new smart phone, speakers, going for supper …, give me a call. I have a business card here that I'll give you with my cell phone number. Seriously, I won't steer you wrong, and I'm full of information."

"You're full of it all right! Thanks, Jeremy. It was a pleasant surprise to have your company, and I'll need to call you about the computer.

My aunt has an older laptop, but I really need to take the plunge and get a nice compact laptop that I can take back and forth to class. I think how modern I'd feel to be able to have my very own laptop."

"We'll get you fixed up into the modern age. Give me a call, and I'd love to have you come into the store to see what I have or can get you. In fact, you certainly don't need to call. Just pop in."

Selena said she would be calling or coming in within the next couple of days. She walked Jeremy to his car, admired the vehicle again, and they said their goodbyes.

"I hope to see you real soon, but I'll sneak off before Rufus wants to wrestle again."

"Good-bye, Jeremy."

Rufus the Goofus was looking forlornly at Jeremy and then back to Selena while Selena was also looking forlornly at Jeremy and then back to Rufus.

Nope, not going there. Just a friend.

Selena thought how Jeremy's well-tailored dark blue shirt, fitting snug against his muscles, matched the colour of his eyes, and she started to compose a poem in her mind.

"Someone, someone with your big dark eyes..."

Out in his car, Jeremy was feeling elated, and he knew that he better watch his step as one of his best friends may get hurt or he himself may get hurt, and he certainly would not want Selena to get hurt.

Wow, she's as wonderful as I thought when I first met her.

A delightful feeling of companionship swept over Selena. She felt a sensation of having found someone she could talk with like a friend, like someone who understood, like family.

Noting the word "family", she ran upstairs to complete her mission.

23

New Year's

"I ABSOLUTELY HAVE TO MAKE the trip." A trip to see her mother and father back in the day when everything was happy times was the only thing that would settle her mind. Running up the stairs, Selena unlocked the doors and closed them behind her. She looked at the clothing on the racks, picked out an appropriate outfit. She dressed and rushed to the computer.

Haste makes waste, she admonished herself. Still, she went quickly to the controls.

```
TODAY'S DATE: current date/time
GO THERE: CONFIRM Ottawa--1999 No Yes
```

The information already programmed in was: Ottawa--1999

I can add December 31, 9:30 p.m. Alter program date: Yes

COSTUME NUMBER: The information already programmed in was Canada-1999

Selena replaced the clothing pre-programmed with a party outfit she found.

```
COME BACK DATE
(using current location) Time/Date/Year:
current date/time? Yes
choose different time to RETURN? No Yes
```

```
TIME AT DESTINATION Minutes/Hours/Days:
Minutes ….
Hours 3.0
Days ….
PLEASE CONFIRM Minutes/Hours/Days No Yes
+CHOOSE DIFFERENT LOCATION (CUSTOMIZE)+
ENGAGE TIME MACHINE: No Yes
PLEASE CONFIRM = ENGAGE TIME MACHINE: No Yes
Press ENTER
```

Selena pressed ENTER

◇◇

Wwww-Wwwww-whirl, Sssss-Sssss-spin, then blur!

◇◇

Selena noted that she was still in the travel room upstairs.

But what year? At least I am in the correct place this time. Did I arrive in 1999 Ottawa on New Year's Eve?

She looked in her aunt's mirror now and saw that she was wearing her chosen face mask and long black dress. Yet the room set up was differently.

I was so excited to come here that I came without a plan. I'm fortunate that I assumed correctly. A New Year's Eve party is happening. I can hear the music and the people talking.

In her reflection, she felt that her outfit looked like a sleek well-dressed New Year's Eve costume should look. As Selena opened the door to leave the bedroom, she hoped with all her heart that this was the evening that she could be part of her parents' life for a little while.

While descending the stairs, she stopped for a few moments, giving her heart a chance to calm down. She surveyed the scene, she noticed trays of snacks, appetizers, desserts, coffee, tea and several other choices of drinks, a few bottles of champagne, glasses and plates – everything was in place for a great evening with their friends.

Selena drifted down the rest of the stairs. She hoped she was anonymous in the crowd. It was obvious a lot of entertaining had already happened as she observed plates in the sink, used glasses and napkins strewn here and there. She noticed a couple of people tidying the kitchen area.

Her primary focus was on the couple on the couch. Selena saw the picture-perfect couple sitting side by side, arms around each other and whispering. Standing transfixed, fascinated, emotional – she wanted to run to them.

There they were only ten steps away, a short distance, yet an eternity, close, yet so far from her – *Mom and dad – My mom and dad* – Anne and Elliott. Her face went white, her heart stood still. She calmed her shaking and attempted to hold back the tears that threatened to stream down her cheeks.

That is the mom and dad I remember. I remember them laughing. I remember them hugging me. I remember them – alive. Oh lord!

Inside her mind and body, she reached out to them.

Her father stood and her mother then rose beside him. Her father took her mother's hand in his, brought it to his lips and kissed it gently. They each had a New Year's Eve mask pushed back over their head and were nicely dressed in simple attire.

"Excuse us, please. We have an incredibly special announcement to make," he began. "This is not an absolute definite revelation, but we have been trying to get pregnant for a year and a half, and tonight we announce that we quite possibly, hopefully, are pregnant." Cheers and congratulations were yelled, drinks held high, claps to the back and hugs to her mother.

"To Anne and Elliott." Selena had a drink pressed into her hand, and she also held her drink high, tears now in her eyes. Quickly calculating, she knew that this was just over seven months before her own birth. It was her they were hoping they were pregnant with! Her mask was holding in some tears, but she could feel a few running down her cheeks. If she were to come back to see them at any time, this was the "consummate", no pun intended, time. Not realizing what she was doing, Selena took a step toward her parents. An arm restrained her.

"Selena, it is Grandma Olive," the voice behind the mask whispered. "You cannot let them know it is you. You were going to go to them. Do it when everyone else is around and hugging. Remember, you cannot attempt to change history. You cannot let them know who you are."

"Thank you for stopping me. I really didn't realize what I was doing. I'd have walked up to them and given the biggest most loving hug and probably clung to them, not letting go." She sighed in anguish and reigned in her impulse to run across the room.

"It's so hard not to do, but yes, I know I can't let them know I'm here. I can't take my eyes off them."

Elliott and Anne milled through the crowd, getting hugs and congratulations. They came within inches of Selena, and she leaned forward and gave each a quick, non-personal (to them) hug. Her body and mind rushed to cling to them, but she resisted. Her mother and then her father gave her eyes behind the mask a searching look, and each of them hugged her back.

Did I imagine it? Was there was a current that passed between each of them and I? I felt it.

Later, her mother and father did again make eye contact with her through her mask. As her eyes followed their every move, drinking in their faces and demeanour, noting their loving looks to each other, Selena watched as they ensured everyone had food and drinks. She noticed that her mother did not drink probably since she was being careful in the hopeful event that she was pregnant.

Arthur and Olive kept close to Selena most of the evening as she watched her mother and her father, in love and happy. Sad and empty in one way, Selena also felt such divine love and satisfaction in being with them and watching them love each other. They were so delighted to be pregnant with her.

And then:

Oh my gosh. There's Aunt Jenny at what, about 29! She was a looker. How heartbreakingly marvellous to be able to see her as well.

Tears flowed, and, once again, she knew that, no, she could not approach her aunt. It was like watching a movie that you were involved in as a bit part player that had no lines. Then, surprisingly, there was a man with her aunt, holding her hand and her looking up at him.

Familiar???

"Grandma, who is with Aunt Jenny?"

"Oh, that is Eric Brisbane. At this point in time, they still see each other for something like this, but Eric is just her friend."

Selena started to ask more about this, but instead her attention again reverted to her parents. Guests chatted; glasses clinked; plates were filled and emptied. The evening wore on. Selena barely noticed any of the ongoing party.

"I am transfixed by my mother and father. Look how dad holds mom's hand. Now his hand is on her back as though he cannot get enough of her. He needs to be in contact with her. She looks glowingly at him."

Her grandmother gave Selena a smile, understanding Selena's need to see their every move, to be totally immersed in this evening's events. A movement to the side caught Selena's attention. Eric Brisbane stooped to whisper in Aunt Jenny's ear. Her Aunt Jenny smiled at him in the friendliest way.

"Grandma, Aunt Jenny and Eric Brisbane seem very close."

Her grandfather interjected at this in a sad voice, "Eric knows that Jenny feels she cannot marry him. It is an unfortunate story, but she is not in love with Eric, and she refuses to marry him."

Her grandmother again leaned toward her, resignedly stating, "He lives close by, and, as you know, in your time, he comes to do her yard work. They always visited on the patio, and they walk in the garden, but it never came to anything on her part." Her grandmother sighed.

Selena mingled a little with the crowd, but she kept close to her grandparents. Enough alcohol might have been consumed or the friends of her parents were just naturally accepting because no one questioned her reason for being here.

As midnight approached, Selena watched her parents with devouring eyes, knowing her time was running out. They were obviously in tune with each other, laughing, gazing at the other's eyes, in love. Friends came up to them and chatted and congratulations were the topic of many conversations Selena heard.

Midnight arrived and, with it, some tall, handsome guy gave her a cursory smooch on his way around the room kissing all the girls. She hugged her Aunt Jenny at the New Year's Eve midnight frenzy, a sob almost escaping her at the contact.

Oh, my lord, Aunt Jenny. Can I take you back to your home?

Selena managed to give another longer hug to her mother and father at the same moment that her grandparents moved in to say "Happy New Year" to them.

"Darling Anne and Elliott, we are so happy for your possible pregnancy. We have no doubt it is a fact. You will have a beautiful, healthy child", her grandmother said giving Selena a glance as she spoke.

Selena's mother did give her another sweet, searching look, smiling at her, but no words were spoken, except to say, "I'm so glad you could come" which was what she was saying to many attendees. Selena wondered if her mother simply was too polite to ask who she was, or if she assumed Selena was a friend of her in-laws. She knew her grandparents would cover for her if asked about her.

I'm relieved to wearing a party mask since I look a lot like Grandma, and it's best to be masked to disguise that from my parents' inquisitive glances. The closeness to them is overpowering. My mind, entire soul and emotions are reaching out to them. In minutes I must travel back. I have to walk away from them – walk away – for the last time.

Selena now stood back and watched them all: her grandparents; her aunt; her parents. She yearned to be closer to her mother and father, her heart hurting for what she could not have. Seeing the happiness and love between them was profoundly rewarding. Love poured out of her heart to them. Her heart ached again.

However, watching her parents, her grandparents and her Aunt Jenny, a switch clicked in Selena. It was too hard to try to be with them and yet not be with them. She silently groaned with that knowledge. A weight hung on her heart.

I don't think that I can live my current life to the fullest by doing what Grandma and Grandpa and Aunt Jenny have done. Time travel is not real life. As much as I yearn to be with mom and dad, Aunt Jenny and Grandpa and Grandma, visits to the past might not be my path. But I don't have to make that choice right now.

Her grandparents, Arthur and Olive, talked with her. Selena told them about her ponderings.

"You will know where you need to be, Selena – as time goes on," her grandmother said. "It was always going to be hard for you to travel as we did. We built it, knowing that we would time travel. We were each older when we made our choices, and we had reasons for returning to our past – even if Jenny did not fulfil her dream of doing so.

"You have a real life to live. You are a different person than we were. We are all where we need to be in time, and you must go live your life. Your grandfather and I love you. You have a full and wonderful life ahead of you. If you change your mind, the time travel machine is there for you."

"I'll think about time travel. Any decision I make isn't irreversible."

Grandpa Arthur said, "We may come to see you in August, my love."

They discussed the time and walked Selena up the stairs. Selena hugged them so tightly and they held onto her for a moment. Her grandmother caressed Selena's cheek. Her grandfather took her hand

and whispered, "So long, Selly." Her very soul burst with love.

As she lovingly glanced with longing back at her so very happy mother and father who were joyfully anticipating her birth, with tears gathering on her cheeks, she whispered, "Good-bye Mom and Dad. I love you so much. I miss you more than I can stand. I want to stay. I need to go."

◇◇

Wwww-Wwwww-whirl, Sssss-Sssss-spin, then blur!

◇◇

Arriving back in the time travel room in her own "time", Selena was again exhausted and had a blistering headache pounding at her temples. She had forgotten to take the vitamins, and quickly went to her aunt's medicine cabinet to grab them and two Advil. Selena wobbled, touching onto the wall to get to her own bedroom with Rufus right at her heels. She crawled under the covers with Caylie meowing because she had to move over a little on her blanket.

Her diary lay on the bed. She reached for it and wrote:

"I saw my mother and father tonight. I love them. I need them. I'm so sorry for myself. Most people still have their parents at my age. I hear my friends and co-workers chatting, laughing about their parents doing such and such. I never have anything to add. I'm not jealous of them. I'm envious in that I want what they have. Good events, annoying events, family squabbles, making up, hugs, telephone calls invading my privacy asking what I'm doing and who I'm doing it with, me borrowing lipstick when my mother isn't looking, crying on my mother or father's shoulders, asking questions, getting answers. I don't have any of that."

She welcomed sleep.

24

Progress

Selena contemplated Colleen's lunch and housewarming invitations from earlier this morning.

I'd been in the process of messaging Colleen so I could invite her over for a visit after her work today when the cell rang "Hello" while in my hand – Colleen's telephone number.

"How goes everything with you? Kevin says that you had quite a roof leak – right into your upstairs bedroom."

Selena had quickly relayed to her everything that had been going on with the roof, beginning with the fact that it had *not* leaked into her bedroom, but into one of the closed off rooms upstairs and ended with how good a job *Ramon Silva Roofing* and his inside workers were doing.

"They should be done the entire project within two more days if all goes according to their plan."

Colleen introduced another topic. "I've most of my own renovations done. I'm calling to invite you to my housewarming. Tell me you're free tomorrow night. I want you to come so badly. I called the Clinic to see if tomorrow would work. Everyone's available if you can imagine! Please say you can come."

"That would be fantastical! What can I bring?"

"Selena, come 5:30ish. Bring whatever beverage you want.

It's impossible to have everything that every person would want. I'll purchase some beer, red and white wines. I've inexpensive champagnes to celebrate with. Thank goodness you can come.

Selena thought about how Colleen had lived closer to the Clinic until last year. Then, after having watched real estate listings daily for months and months, a fantastic old house had been listed, and she snapped it up almost immediately.

"And Selena, I called for two reasons. I wanted to call you early this morning to say I'm free for lunch today. I hoped we could we get together, just the two of us? I can meet you for lunch between my office and your house…"

"I'd love that." They chatted about where and exact time. Selena heard a chime in the background.

Colleen announced, "My staff line is ringing. See you later."

I've seen various stages of her renovations, and it'll be neat to see the final reno.

Selena followed Springfield Road at the edge of the Lindenlea neighbourhood as she drove to lunch, noting that it was a gorgeous day – cloudless, sunny, warm and no wind.

The sky seems to sparkle like hoar frost in the winter. It's great weather to have the roof vent open.

She easily found a parking place. Not spotting Colleen's Austin Mini, she waited for a beat or two before deciding to get out of her Escape. Colleen had recommended the *Fraser Café*, and Selena was game for a new experience.

"Welcome to the *Fraser Café*."

"There's a reservation for two under the name Colleen Kirsch."

"Would you prefer to sit inside or on the patio?"

"Oh, the patio, for sure."

Colleen won't mind sitting outside. A robin's singing -- it'll be nice hearing nature while we eat lunch.

After being led through a very cozy restaurant with a casual décor, out to the lovely setting of the patio, she was content checking out the lunch menu and waiting for Colleen while sunlight filtered from above onto the table.

The delicious smells of food being prepared is intoxicating. I haven't been here before, can't wait to taste this food.

Colleen arrived, a little flushed. "I apologize. The last patient took several extra minutes of my time. Poor guy. He'll feel much better after the medication I prescribed. He also needed a little push for him to lose some weight so his acid reflux will lessen."

While Colleen scanned the menu, Selena pretended to mock her. "Ah, so you're ascribing to Dr. Carey Sr's philosophy of giving helpful information to avoid the patient having to be on mega medication for a problem he could improve himself?"

A very friendly waiter arrived, smiling as she asked for their order. They stopped their kibitzing with each other and gave their orders, receiving a 'We'll get that right out to you", along with another big smile. Collecting the menus, she left.

Colleen acknowledged Selena's teasing, "It was a terrific experience working at the Clinic for those three years. I might be a little more diplomatic when I offer my advice to patients than Dr. Brent Carey is."

When Selena advised had she had inherited her aunt's home, Colleen inquired if there were changes that Selena would make. They discussed the costs of the new roof and interior restoration. Selena said she had not spent any time wondering what she would change in the house as she was so content to have a home and not have to worry about moving anywhere.

"If you've any thoughts of renovating, I recommend my brother and his friends. They've been moonlighting with my renos. Also doing other projects for the past year."

Their garden salads arrived with another smile. As they were eating their salads, one with Thousand Island and the other with oil and lemon, Selena relayed her relief about obtaining a roofing contractor, "I'm so happy that Austin and his parents were able to get me the name of who did their roof three years ago and give me some good support."

Colleen frowned, rolled her eyes and pointedly said, "Foo-fah, Austin huh? He's back in your life? That's a mental image I don't want to imagine! Tell me no! He'd ignored you for two years. It'd shock me if you started up with him again!

A plane flew overhead. Colleen paused before she continued, "He's a fool! I've confided with you about the jerk that I went out with and almost married. That was prior to my starting at The Clinic."

"I know. I remember very well your stories about "the jerk". You were smart to get away. I don't know about Austin, or rather I think I do know, but he seems to feel we can start back where we were two years ago."

"Yeah, but I don't want you to end up blindsided by Austin again. You realized you needed to get on with your life. We're alike in that respect. Is there anyone else?"

Selena hesitated. Colleen gave her an inquisitive look, prodding Selena to continue by saying, "Hum?" A different waiter arrived with their Korean Chicken. Selena took the first taste, "This is fantastical."

"Yeah, I agree. It's delicious but give me the 'Tea'".

"We didn't order tea."

Laughing, Colleen admitted, "I got that from a teenage patient today. She said, 'give me the tea' and then had to explain to me. 'Tea' meant 'spill the beans' – come on now! Your expression tells me there's tea I should know."

"It'd be nice to have a boyfriend. But I overheard Dr. Kev conferring with Mary – To defend myself, I was at Elizabeth's desk, not trying to hear. He said he wanted to settle down and have children. Well, not that I was intending on him being my boyfriend, but that lets me out. I want to live a full, carefree life, for quite a while yet.

"Aunt Jenny was my dear aunt, a lovely person, and I miss her terribly, certainly I'll continue to miss her. I wish she were still with me. I've come to realize though, since Aunt Jenny isn't here, I want to be just me."

"Wow! That's clear then. To be honest, which I usually am, I thought Kevin wanted to date you. I understand that you had an afternoon together at your place. At the evening of our social after your aunt's funeral, he seemed quite interested in you – to be blunt."

"I know you well enough, like a big sis, to respect that you like to be up-front, so I don't mind you asking me. I think Dr. Kev is a wonderful man and a friend. But I couldn't see myself with him when I thought about it properly. Goodness, I'm only going to be 20 years old in August, and he's, what 27?"

"If you're certain – then I've a story to tell you. I said that I usually am honest. On this one instance I wasn't – But only by omission."

At that moment, they were interrupted by the waiter again, re-filling their glasses and asking if there was anything else that he could get for them.

"Thank you so very much. We're both fine here. Everything was delicious." As he walked farther way, Selena looked at Colleen, waiting for her response.

"Now, you give me the tea!"

Laughing, Colleen replied with a bemused expression, "For a long time, I didn't realize that you didn't know. Kevin and I had been dating for 18 months prior to you coming to work at the Clinic." Selena sat back in her chair – mouth slightly open.

"I said I didn't know you didn't know." Colleen gave Selena a look questioning her feelings. "But lately, he's baffled me. He's taken me out for supper and lunches a few times. I can tell he enjoys each time. I don't know if he wants to date you or me. I moved medical practices to be closer to my new house. I still feel very strongly about him. Are you interested in dating him? I really need to know your true feelings."

"No. I've had a few things happen in my life since Aunt Jenny passed away. I feel as though I've matured significantly, and yet I still want to be that free as a bird young woman who can do what I want. There always have been mysteries regarding Aunt Jenny and the house, and now I have some mysteries answered."

At Colleen's sharp look as if waiting for relevant information regarding the mysteries, Selena barged forward, "I'm no longer unsure what I want out of life. But just think, Kevin may still love you. You may be his 'settle down and have children' person. I'll find a way to let him know it's *not* me."

Colleen responded, "Oh, you're funny. Yeah, maybe neither one of us is his life's dream. I do know that Kevin is the one I love. At one point I'd say he loved me. My party is tomorrow night. He'll be there. I'm so happy we had this conversation."

"Colleen, I need to let you get back to work. Thanks for inviting me for lunch today. I'll see you tomorrow night."

Selena, still sitting in the parking lot of *Fraser Café*, decided to look on her cellphone Maps App for Jeremy's computer business using the address from his business card. She sternly told herself, "I'm not planning anything here. I'll just go look at devices." Sighing, she admitted, "Okay, I have feelings for this guy. But I'm not getting involved."

JM Computer & Consulting was a little drive out of her way home, but she was happy she had made this decision.

I need my own computer or laptop. Maybe they can help me set it up and transfer my files from Aunt Jenny's computer.

Selena made her way through all the traffic over to the #44. Then as she wound her way through the neighbourhoods, noticed the Byward Market and thought she needed to stop on her way back home to get a delicious, deep-fried Beaver Tail. Somehow, it had become so famous that, years ago, the then USA President Obama had eaten one from that market. Continuing on, Selena noted that she was getting closer to Jeremy's computer business. She drove past Confederation Park and the Ottawa City Hall.

She was muttering to herself as seemed to be the norm, "Here we are, the street number is working its way down. JM, for Jeremy McGregor (I would suppose) Computer & Consulting is right here."

Stepping into the glass-front store, Selena realized she hadn't been prepared for the vast number of employees, customers and array of stock there would be inside a computer business. Doing a slow walk around the large store, Selena paused at the laptops. There were several customers studying the devices and entering the checkout line to pay. Other customers were testing gaming devices.

This is a popular store. Whoops, here comes an employee, and I don't know exactly what I want or need.

"Hello, welcome to *JM Computers & Consulting*. May I assist you with something?"

"Well, I've come to find out the type of laptop or tablet I'd need."

They started to discuss what purpose she may be needing the laptop for when a familiar voice called, "Selena, you're here. Thanks, Ben for helping this nice young woman. I'll take over now if you'd help the gentleman in the yellow jacket in aisle 12."

As the tall Jeremy McGregor with his longer-style hair and dark eyes came toward Selena, she took a breath in.

He's gorgeous.

She said hastily, "You didn't have to interrupt a potential sale to assist me. I don't even know what I need yet."

"Oh yeah, I did, Selena. It's awesome to see you here, and I want to help you personally. Come, sit with me for a moment while I show you sales catalogues on the store computer. Do you mainly want the laptop or tablet for your homework, your personal correspondence, and perhaps your travel plans? You'll need apps installed as well. When you start to do your own financial planning, this type of program will help." He pointed to some accounting packages.

"This information is helpful, for sure. I want the device for those reasons, so you're right there."

Jeremy advised Selena of the price ranges, dependent on additional apps and packages she may want. He encouraged Selena to use the store computer.

"After you've had a look at the ones on the computer and the pamphlets, just walk around this area. Check the mid-price range first. Check out each feature on the different computers. You don't need to decide today as I want you to make a good personal choice."

"I've time to browse around. Just go and sell somebody something really expensive. I'll find you if I've any more questions or if I make up my mind."

"Awesome, that works for me. I'll be back to check on you soon. I won't take it personally if you don't buy anything. I'll just stalk you in the local supermarket."

Tilting her head and laughing at the memory, she said, "I'll know where to find you, too. You'll be drooling over the delicatessen chickens. Seriously though, these info screens are helpful, Jeremy." She was peering at the pages. He waved goodbye, indicated he would be back and sauntered off down the aisle to see whom he could help. Taking her time, Selena was intrigued at all the choices.

I want something very portable to take back and forth to classes and my job. These sites are helpful.

Selena then walked around the computer area, searching for what she needed. The third time Jeremy came to see how she was doing, Selena was perusing portable laptops.

"Jeremy, I've made a choice. What do you think of the ASUS VivoBook one on this shelf? I liked what it said on your computer information. It has an incredible touchscreen and is a 2-in-1 Laptop. I don't know, nor care what some of this RAM stuff means, but the fact that it's so portable and flexible is exactly what I want. The reviews are good when I checked the ratings on my cell."

"Good for you. It's not what I originally thought you'd want, but that's a terrific choice. Portability's a plus. Let's get one from a box, and you can scope it out." He asked Selena to follow him. They plugged it in to have a look at it.

"You'll like the pen stylus for school. The webcam would allow you to video conference and record videos."

Selena was overjoyed, with little tremors running through her because this was really happening. At least that is what she told herself the tremors were from as she glanced at Jeremy. They checked out the tablet thoroughly.

I've saved up enough for this treat, and I'm not yet wanting to touch my inherited funds. I just know that I made a good choice cuz I'm thrilled with what this ASUS can do.

"Will you or an employee be able to come to the house to help set it up? I mean, there's the manual, but I might be a little overwhelmed."

"Selena, that's what this store does. We help with set up. I'll be available during the day tomorrow or even tomorrow night to help you, and there's no cost for set up."

"I've nothing on during the day tomorrow, but tomorrow night, Colleen is having …" Pausing, Selena studied Jeremy. *He is Kevin's best friend, after all.*

"What's up?" Jeremy was now studying her.

"Did you know Colleen apparently dated Kevin for a year and a half? I just found out from Colleen at lunch today..."

"Selena, I didn't realize you didn't know. At any rate, sure, they were involved, but they simply stopped dating a while ago. They still have lunches and suppers sometimes." Prompting Selena to continue, he said, "Go on. You started to say something about tomorrow night and Colleen."

Selena quickly started her explanation. "She's having a housewarming tomorrow night. It'd be awkward for me to invite you when she said it was for our old Clinic staff. Can you come over tomorrow afternoon to help set up? I'll have to get ready for Colleen's housewarming, so I'll kick you out at 4:30. That sounds embarrassing about kicking you out so I can go off to a party."

"That's fine. The timing will work, so let's arrange for me to come to your place about 1:00. Set-up will take longer than you think. Let me mark that down in my agenda app. I've nothing on that I can't change."

They discussed what applications Selena would want on the tablet. "You should take the manual home to read."

"I'd no idea that there were that many computer choices, but, hey, I'm pleased with what I've decided. I'll see you tomorrow afternoon. Here's my cell number so you can text or call if anything changes."

Selena paid with her credit card and, with her manual in hand, she sailed out of the store happy and content.

After finding a parking spot at Byward Market, she walked through to get Beaver Tails. She did not even wait to get back to her car. One she munched on as she walked, and a second one she intended to eat right after supper.

Diet, what diet!

The roofing crew was hard at work when she arrived home. Selena stopped below the ladder as Ramon called out to her.

"We should be done by Friday. If we need to work overtime, we will be here on Saturday, but I thin' everything is eshaping up. I hope you are happy with the work."

"Oh, absolutely. With your having done Karen and Bud's roofing repairs and your work ethic, I've nothing to concern myself with. Thank goodness your roofing and interior teams were available to me. Thank you."

The next day, Jeremy arrived at Selena's door just prior to 1:00 p.m. She happily answered the door to let him in, and Rufus happily licked Jeremy's hands as Jeremy came into the house. Jeremy put the computer boxes down as Selena closed the front door behind him.

"Hi there, Selena, and hello to you too, Rufus." Jeremy bent down to give Rufus a good ear rub and to pat him on the back. "No more knocking me over, okay buddy?"

Replying, Rufus said, "Ruff, Ruff." Jeremy continued, "Is Rufus part cocker spaniel and part miniature poodle?" After Selena's nod, "Awesome, I love his tri-colouring." He gave Rufus another pat. "Well, let's start."

They carried the boxes as Selena headed into the dining room. "I'm relieved you're doing this set up. Gosh, I pored over the manual after I'd done my studying, but I'm relieved not to set it up myself. I had downloaded several documents onto my aunt's laptop computer upstairs that I want on this tablet. Do you want me to bring the computer down here or should you bring this up to her computer?"

"I'd say let's bring your aunt's laptop down, but we'll do that after I go through this tablet with you. Selena, I took the time to load the applications that you wanted already. Once we delve into your tablet, there may be other programs and apps you want. You can follow along with the manual, and then I'll let you have your tablet yourself."

Jeremy and Selena spent an hour initially going through care and security in a cursory manner, then onto the home screen, keyboard settings, apps and the internet connections. Since they were sitting side by side, their hands occasionally touched. Selena felt the heat rush to her.

Selena abruptly announced she needed a break, "Right now – my brain is like melting cheese." Jeremy laughed at her, and they had a snack of cheese, pepperoni and crackers with orange juice.

Rufus demanded to be let out, so out they went. Jeremy seemed to drink in the sunshine, raising his face toward the sky as Selena watched him, enjoying his pleasure at the outdoors.

He likes the outdoors as well. Fantastic.

"It's my dream to have my store and be able to help people with choosing their first or next purchase. But afternoons like this, enjoying time with someone whose company I want to be in – those are particularly special."

Jeremy caught her gaze, gave her an enigmatic smile and pronounced, "Tomorrow, I'm hoping that you'll come up with some questions that you need me to come over to answer...."

"Oh, I'll have questions for you. We're almost out of time. It's 4:20 now. Come back tomorrow. I've something on my mind, and I need to discuss this with a couple of people to settle what I should do. I want to ask you something."

Looking a trifle hopeful at what she might want from him, Jeremy asked Selena what she had on her mind.

"The problem is that I don't know whom to ask. I probably should make an appointment with my counsellor." Now, Jeremy did not look hopeful. He looked quite concerned.

"You have a counsellor? Is something wrong? How can I help?"

"Not that kind of counsellor, Jeremy!" She chuckled. "Oh, I should've led you on, told you I had all sorts of terrible anxiety issues, that I'm a changeling and that I see demons on every corner. Darn, that would be funny – a missed opportunity for sure.

"However, much less exciting, I meant I've a university counsellor, and I need to confirm that I should be changing jobs from *The Caring Medical Clinic* to something more advanced so that it fits in with my upcoming university semester." Jeremy visibly relaxed. "I know that you have a Bachelor of Science degree, and I wanted to know how you handled your work terms. I need to move on with my career, however hard it is."

After having a belly laugh at his misinterpretation of counsellor, and not the least bit embarrassed at his mistake, Jeremy admitted that he was not the person that Selena needed to talk to. She should see her university counsellor because his BSc objectives had been different from hers. However, they discussed her actual duties at the Clinic, what she thought she needed that was not at the Clinic and what other types of employment she felt she required.

"I need to advance to some place where I can immerse myself in doing actual analysis, research ideas and even be doing experiments in scientific data. I just don't know. My priority now that this semester is almost over should be to go on to something much more challenging. I can't let my joy in being at the Clinic overshadow my need to get much more out of my chosen career."

"You just said it exactly. You're having trouble making the decision because you like what you're doing as well as the people you're working with, maybe too much. When I had work terms, I enjoyed the places I worked and the people, but that was just a stop gap to my real desire in a career. Possibly, when you go to the housewarming tonight, it's Colleen who could steer you in the right direction."

"See, Jeremy! I knew you'd be able to help me. You're right. She, as a doctor, could be the person to ask. I really must decide because it's not fair to Doctors Carey and Doctor Kothare for me not to be able to give them notice of my intention. I'll check out Colleen's ideas and then, since I probably will change employment, I'll have to tell them when I'm back there next week that I'll be searching for a new job. I need to give them proper notice."

"At any rate, Selena, I do need to get out of your hair so that you can get to your hair. You look marvellous, honest. You have beautiful hair, but you could do with a comb through after we were outside, and you've also been running your hands through it constantly while talking!"

"Jeremy, you are insufferable! Guys are supposed to say I look nice, not that I look terrible." Scoffing at him, Selena laughed right out loud. "You need lessons."

"If you go back over the conversation, I said you looked marvellous first, and then I qualified that statement with the rest of it. Honesty is the best policy and all that."

"I'll walk you to the door and don't let it hit you in the butt on your way out." She laughed at her own joke. "You're quite the man, but I'll let you get away with it since I'm in a rush and I don't have time to smack you." Looking in the hall mirror, she added, "Yeah, it's a mess. Thanks for all your time today."

"You're welcome, and we'll transfer the documents from your aunt's computer tomorrow."

"Oh right. I'll see you tomorrow."

25

The Résumé

Selena had been up early, exhilarated with her plans for the day. Since there was still a morning chill in the air, Rufus hesitated at the door when Selena opened it. He came back in a little more hurried, which was fine with Selena on her quest to get going. Caylie was still asleep upstairs. Selena prepared their dishes of food and water and practically ran to her new tablet to do some research on the National Research Council, NRC as it was so well known in Canada, especially in Ontario.

Selena spent an invigorating two hours looking into the National Research Council on-line.

Cool! This could be a fantastic future, and I can't believe how this would be a good fit for me!

Reading the following from different web pages, Selena selected one she was particularly excited about. Almost shaking, she re-read:

> NRC works with Canadian and international clients to develop biologics (large molecule medicines) to treat cancer as well as infectious, inflammatory and autoimmune diseases. With its collaborators, NRC is accelerating biologics development and manufacturing up to early clinical trials, reducing risk and adding value for each product.

And a Collaborator's response:

> NRC has the diverse set of capabilities necessary to test and develop therapeutic proteins. They also have a very knowledgeable and professional staff. This combination makes them an ideal partner to complement our computational protein engineering capabilities.

Another hour had passed, and Selena checked out the web pages where she could apply as an intern or assistant, or whatever positions were posted.

She found articles about projects the National Research Council was working on: Therapeutic, diagnostic and carrier antibodies against cancer; infectious diseases; central nervous system et cetera. Heart pounding, she updated her résumé adding current classes and work experience. The NRC information starting to blur before her eyes.

"This is the cat's meow, Caylie!"

By speaking her plan to seek other employment aloud to her friends, it had strengthened her resolve.

This is exactly what direction I want my life to take, but I'd be leaving behind a fabulous work experience and co-workers I adore. It's time for me to progress to the next stage. I will be starting a whole new future, a new career.

Selena had eaten her spinach cashew salad lunch while completing her résumé to the VP of Human Resources. Selena found the email address and her résumé was ready to press "send".

Yep, I'll proudly show this to Jeremy before I send it.

Caylie had curled up on her blanket on the family room sofa after eating her own breakfast. Selena sat down beside her and rubbed Caylie for the comfort of hearing the purring, relaxing her own heart.

"Meow, purrrrrrrrrr".

Playing from her cellphone was "*Hello*".

"Jeremy here. On my way. I just wanted to make sure that this was still a good time for you."

"Good timing. Did you eat lunch yet? I can make you a salad and a sandwich."

"Nope, I brought lunch to work today. My timing is as we planned. See you in 15?"

"That'll give me time to do something to my hair, so you have no reason to comment!" said Selena, laughing.

"Phew, I was hoping not to have to look at that again today!" came the lighthearted reply. "See you soon."

As Selena finished getting herself ready to go out with Jeremy, her thoughts became immersed in what happened at Colleen's housewarming last night.

Interesting turn of events, for sure.

Selena had arrived at Colleen's doorstep ready for the party in an above-the-knee, rust coloured Wrap-like Ruffle dress that was Made in Canada. She had brought a bottle of Argentine Malbec wine for the housewarming. Colleen answered the door dressed in a gorgeous slit to mid-thigh dress. The red colours brought out the auburn in her hair. With a smile, Colleen took the wine from Selena, indicating that she had not tried that wine before.

"Hey, it looks like I'm the first to arrive. What can I help you with?"

"You can get the trays from the fridge. I've plates and everything else on the side table. You can help me serve coffee and tea later. What'd you think of the granite on all the counters?"

"Colleen, your guys did a splendid job. I can't even tell if there are joins in the stonework, and I hadn't seen your choice of backsplash either. They complement each other amazingly."

Elizabeth, Mary and their husbands, Rod and Len, had arrived next, then Dr. Brent Carey and Mrs. Eileen Carey. Kevin came in at the same time as Penelope and Bethany. Colleen and Selena gave each other a look, both wondering if the two girls had come with Kevin.

Who knows!

Colleen received compliments about her kitchen immediately upon the guests being ushered into the huge space. Drinks were offered and received. Colleen was a great hostess. With drinks in hand, Colleen walked them toward the bathroom, which was unanimously declared to be a masterful job.

Discussions, as usual, originally were about work. The conversation then turned to the *Two Truths and a Lie* game Kevin, Colleen and Selena had played the week before. Definite interest arose from that, particularly between Bethany and Penelope.

"We'll be playing that game with friends!" declared Penelope.

As trays of hors d'oeuvres, chips, vegetable and fruit trays were served, along with more wine, conversations were started among those sitting closest to each other. Kevin chose to talk with Colleen which was great for Selena. In Selena's chat with Bethany and Penelope she mentioned she had just purchased her first tablet.

"Where did you get it?" asked Bethany. Selena proceeded to discuss *JM Computer & Consulting*, telling them what good service she had had and how easy it was to make up her mind on the tablet considering that she knew little about home computers when she arrived at the computer store.

After a short time, Kevin approached Selena and said, "I heard you say that you purchased a tablet from Jeremy's shop. I understood that you were happy with the service." She explained that she certainly was and that the store also provided home set-up service, and that Jeremy had been kind enough to come to her home and go through all the steps setting up her apps and contacts.

Selena may have been a little too enthusiastic for Kevin because he appeared to scowl a little. *Although it could be just a little indigestion,* she thought as she remembered Colleen's patient discussed during yesterday's lunch.

Kevin said, "You must have had exemplary service then" to which Selena replied, "I'll be recommending the company to anyone in need of a computer or computer service." Kevin did concede enthusiastically that Jeremy's business was a particularly good one.

Colleen seemed carefree of thoughts of Kevin as she chatted with her former co-workers. Kevin asked Selena, "How are you feeling now with the funeral behind you?"

"It's not easy. There are so many emotions – grief, guilt, anger, regret. I will miss Aunt Jenny forever."

"I'm sorry, Selena."

Spontaneously, she decided tell Kevin that she was in a quandary and that she needed to speak to someone or a counsellor about her future employment requirements to advance in her career. Kevin took that information in his stride. He advised, "You should do whatever you think is best for your career."

"I haven't even checked into career opportunities. I hoped that you could give me advice on that topic when I return to work."

Kevin offered, "I could speak to you this weekend if you thought that would work. We could have a chat over supper."

Dodging any date aspect, Selena said, "Oh, I can't do that as final exams are coming up."

Lame excuse.

Stuffing his glasses into his front pocket and clearing his throat, "Could I see you on a personal level?"

Not taking a moment to think and having that comment as an opening, Selena replied, "While I was visiting with Elizabeth at the front desk, I accidently overheard you telling Mary something."

Kevin appeared to pick up on her tone, his expression becoming embarrassed and alarmed.

"Well, ah… it was that you were ready to settle down and have children. I'm happy for you that you know what you want from life, but it's not the direction I want for myself right now. I'll be waiting a few years to take that step."

The statement filled the air between them, settling – thick and heavy – a lead balloon that had dropped anchor.

That was a conversation stopper.

Undeniably Kevin looked surprised, showing the tiniest frown. Then he appeared to relax slowly, purposefully as Selena quickly changed the subject, rattling on for another minute about Rufus and Caylie until Selena hailed Colleen over and said that she needed to chat with Elizabeth and Mary. She looked back a moment later and saw Kevin and Colleen talking amicably.

About 10:00 p.m., the party began to wind down and guests said they needed to leave as tomorrow was a workday. Kevin gave Selena a look of regret as he was leaving with both Penelope and Bethany as he had arrived. Selena wondered if the look he had cast back was because she might be changing employment or her comment on not being ready to settle down. A short time passed, and Colleen came to say that Kevin, as usual, had been very friendly toward her when they were chatting.

Colleen confided, "I'm weighing another invite to Kev for supper soon."

Selena disclosed that she had told Kevin she was not interested in settling down to have children yet. "It just rolled off the tip of my tongue without me realizing I was saying it to him."

"Oh lord, Selena. You'll be relieved that's done." Colleen told Selena about one of the doctors at her new clinic who was a nice guy, rather good looking, a real gentleman – and he was an excellent doctor.

"He's not Kevin, but I like him. Thank goodness he's not like 'the Jerk' from before I dated Kevin either." Colleen added, "Loving Kevin or not, I haven't put my life on hold."

"Oh Colleen, aren't we are pair! No matter what, I just want everything to work out for you."

Selena turned the conversation around to discuss her employment situation and what Colleen might think Selena's next career move should be given in that she was entering her fourth semester. Colleen had some suggestions for her. Then she said, "What about the National Research Council?"

Selena's ears perked up and her heart beat faster. Selena relayed that she had discovered a journal of her grandmother's and that her grandparents had moved to Ottawa in the 60s to work at the National Research Council.

"Wow, Selena. That would be an amazing coincidence for you to land a job there. Check into it. I'll give you a reference from my time at the Clinic. I know that Doctors Carey will as well."

"Thank you, Colleen. Those suggestions are great! I'll look into the NRC website to see more of what they are involved with." She was exuberant about that prospect because from what she did know about the National Research Council, it might be ideal for her.

Selena said a heartfelt goodbye and reiterated that she loved Colleen's renovations. Once home, she let Rufus outside and thought over her prospects.

Happily, tomorrow will entail checking out the National Research Council. Then Jeremy will come over and help me more with the tablet. What a fantastic day it will be.

Into her diary that night:

> *"Well, that Jeremy is a nice, gentle, very good-looking man. I definitely could get used to having him around.*
>
> *Kevin is out of my love life – not that he was ever in it, I don't think… Austin. Gosh, there's Austin. I'll see him within a week when he's home. I could be thinking of our future together… But I'm not. I don't trust that man."*

Today though, opening the door to let Jeremy in, she was smiling a brilliant smile.

This is an uncomplicated relationship. He's what he seems to be, nothing fake here.

He smiled at her and said, "Wow, you do look great today."

"You do too, I reluctantly admit. But I've decided you've absolutely no sense of humour at all – you think everything is funny which equals no '*sense*' of humour. How was your morning?"

They chatted amicably about Jeremy's busy morning with customers doing some expensive purchases and that he had appointments set up with companies for two possible contracts.

"I'm satisfied with my business venture. It was a gamble to purchase this business from the previous owner. What've you been up to this morning? I see you look excited, almost bursting."

"I've had a very productive morning." Enthusiastically, Selena revealed her discussion with Colleen to try to get into the National Research Council, the part in her grandmother's journal about both her grandparents working there themselves starting in the 60s, and how Selena's research into the NRC had panned out with information intriguing to Selena.

"I have the résumé completed."

"That's a quick decision – fantastic! May I see it? It'll give me a chance to see your credentials and all the classes you've been taking."

After several minutes of carefully reading her résumé, he said, "I knew you were into biology and science stuff, and it is good planning for the NRC positions that you printed off. If you can get on with the NRC, then you'll be set with this work experience throughout the rest of your semesters. After your interim work with them, they might hire you full-time after university!"

"Yeah, that'd be great. Aunt Jenny always said, 'don't put the cart before the horse', so I'm trying to temper my enthusiasm."

Selena sent off the email and jumped happily around the room. "Yea, I have never been so excited! Now, I'd like to print off my research information and my fantastic résumé on my aunt's printer upstairs." Leading the way, she grabbed the key and unlocked the door with Jeremy giving her a curious look at the door being locked. After entering the room, Jeremy connected the device to the same network as her aunt's printer.

"This is wireless. When you're gainfully employed by the NRC, you could think about using your aunt's printer for bigger projects. You could use a small printer that you can set up downstairs in the library for your convenience."

After the transfer was done, Jeremy asked if there were any of her aunt's personal files that Selena wanted to transfer.

"No, that's okay."

No, that would be invading her privacy worse than I have. Boy, have I invaded her privacy…

Selena had earlier told Jeremy that her grandparents had the house built and that she thought they had put a lot of the second-floor construction effort in themselves. Selena let him wander with her following as he checked out the upstairs. Jeremy was interested in the architecture of the 1960's-era home and how it appeared solidly built. He barely entered her private domain, but he did mention how immense the house was, commenting on its two bedrooms with ensuites.

After Jeremy glanced around her Aunt Jenny's bedroom, he remarked, "I gauged from looking at your aunt's house that the other three bedrooms were smaller, and I can't get over the size of your aunt's bedroom and study and the enormous clothes closet."

I was aware he had an excellent eye for construction. Perhaps too good an eye for construction! He obviously had a good look at the exterior and roof.

Selena was totally trying to put Jeremy off track from his musings of the closet size by suggesting, "Would you like some iced tea? Do you need to get back to work?"

"Let's have a quick iced tea. Then in 45 minutes, I have a client coming in to discuss set-ups for 15 offices opening near Byward Market. Tomorrow, I hope that you'd like to have a good long tour in the Miata with me?"

"That sounds great! I'll pack a picnic lunch. How would 11:00 a.m. work for you?"

"That'll work. Next time, I'll do the lunch."

When Jeremy had left for his appointment, Selena wanted desperately to check more on the NRC, but managed to transfer her attention to her assignments and to study for two hours before supper and two more hours after supper.

She had delinquently left her cellphone upstairs. Retrieving it, she read Ramon Silva's text stating that he and his team had almost finished and that he had work at another small project early Saturday morning. He ended by saying that they would be back in the afternoon on Saturday and have everything completed before dark. She sent back a "great news" text.

Discussing plans with herself, she said, "I want to check out some travel sites. I've put a lot of time into studying, and I'm farther ahead than if I were working. I feel confident about my exams. Hope I'm not fooling myself. Another semester is almost over!"

As a reward for the hours she had spent studying, Selena looked up travel agencies, researched the reviews of several tour companies and her attention turned to *girltraveltours.com.*

"Here is what I've been looking for! Tours of Scotland and Ireland.

Girl Travel Tours.

She skimmed several of the tour destinations and dates, and she became more and more excited by the information on their website. Thinking of the timing of her university and exams finishing, she once again read the information and reviews regarding *Girl Travel Tours.*

What am I waiting for? This is clearly what I want – the dates and the destination jives. The itinerary is suited to me. Aunt Jenny, this will be my travel treat to myself.

Selena asked Rufus if he would like to go for a walk. Hardly had the words started out of her mouth, and Rufus was jumping at the garden door.

"Okay, okay. Here's your leash."

What a lovely evening. It's still light out.

Rufus proudly displayed his good manners, behaving like a gentleman out walking with a lady.

Maybe Lady Maggie Smith?

"Rufus, you're such a good dog. Are you a good dog, Rufus Goofus?" Rufus walked even more proudly, wagging his tail in appreciation of her comments.

For the luncheon with Jeremy next morning, Selena prepared in her mind the items to include.

I'm excited to be going for a tour of Ottawa with Jeremy in that vehicle! It's so cute and, even with its small size, it looked comfortable. Jeremy, what a nice name.

Muttering to herself, "Honest to goodness, I still have to sort out my feelings for Austin!! Who would've thought I'd have these questions? When Austin left me, I could barely function without him. I'd have taken him back in one split second – then. Now is an entirely different equation."

Opening the front door to peer out at the weather, she noted: *Sun. No wind. Warm. Such luck for our drive!*

Selena had finally looked at most of her Aunt Jenny's mail that morning during breakfast. It was obvious from the letters that had arrived that her Aunt Jenny was being queried when her book would be completed. The peers who had attended her aunt's funeral perhaps had not been certain how to initiate that subject while attending the funeral. There was another letter received a couple of days ago. It was addressed to Selena herself; however, on its arrival, she had not even noticed that it was in her name.

To me?

The letter offered condolences; apologized for intruding on her mourning for her aunt; inquired if Selena knew about the state of her aunt's book; offered to contact Selena regarding the contract that previously had been signed by Jenny Louise Jenkins. The letter explained they had purchased the right to publish and specified to Selena additional information on how the royalties would go through her aunt's law firm as usual and be paid to the beneficiary of her aunt's estate!

Re-reading the letter addressed to her, Selena said out loud, "It seems reasonably straight forward. Aunt Jenny has had several other books published by this publishing company and has already signed the contract with them. Obviously, they are a company that Aunt Jenny feels confident working with.

"I could contact Tessa's law firm on Monday morning, and then connect with the publisher. I have neglected looking at Aunt Jenny's latest book, *History in the Making*. Selena slowly ascended the stairs to her aunt's room and sat on her aunt's bed, glanced at her aunt's computer and made the decision to open up her aunt's latest book.

Sadly, her last, but I want to see my aunt's last words.

Once in the folder, though, she started to read where she had previously read to and enthusiastically read the chapters, recognizing again the subject was alluringly captivating. Aunt Jenny had such an interest in history. Selena appreciated the book title. Aunt Jenny's book was about history which was happening, literally 'while it was being made'.

The book started back in early Western European times (post-medieval, circa 1750 AD), and carried on to the pre-USA period and encompassed European, USA and Canadian histories. Selena read what all that history had meant for current times in each of these countries.

Fascinating. As she read, Selena was suddenly aware that her Aunt Jenny's book was complete! *History in the Making* appeared finished.

How fantastic that she completed it.

She muttered happily, "Not just appeared!! Sure, there still needs to be the usual 'About the Author.'" Glancing again at the computer, knowing "About the Author" would just be copied from past books authored by Jenny Louise Jenkins with current updates.

Congratulations Aunt Jenny. You must have been so proud.

Oh no! Had Aunt Jenny completed the book, gone downstairs for a cup of tea and decided to rest on the sofa and then departed this life? How awful!

"I must contact Aunt Jenny's editor about the book being completed. There may have been a letter on the front desk from the editor too that I neglected to open."

Aunt Jenny's book could be put out to the public. They love her books judging by reviews and the number of books sold. That would be something I can do for Aunt Jenny and make myself feel more worthy of the bequest of this wonderful home and her estate!

"It's emotional to be sitting here in Aunt Jenny's study where she spent months on *History in the Making*."

An hour or so later, while she sat at the computer looking at the references, the special Note from the Author and re-reading some of Aunt Jenny's book, Selena mulled over if she could do anything for her aunt. An idea formed in her mind.

With a feeling of satisfaction, she said, "In fact, I can donate a sizable percentage of the book proceeds to groups that Aunt Jenny held near to her heart! This is a fabulous idea. The decision to donate will be up to me as sole beneficiary. I'll think on this more, checking into the internet and researching possibilities."

After getting the lunch almost ready, Selena delved into her tablet to search for names of writing groups to make donations to. She looked at write ups regarding the organizations in Ontario, from the internet, including Wikipedia. Selena was confident she was on the right track. She printed out this, as well as the information from other groups. She saved some of the information in a folder marked 'Donations for Aunt Jenny – Writer's Groups'. She would study this further.

Canadian Authors' Association -- a membership-based organization for writers at all stages of their writing careers; aspiring, emerging and professional.

Writers' Union of Canada -- The Writers' Union of Canada (TWUC) is the national organization of professionally published writers. TWUC was founded in 1973 to work with governments, publishers, booksellers, and readers to improve the conditions of Canadian writers.

*Writers' Trust of Canada – i*s a charitable organization which provides financial support to Canadian writers.

Founded by Margaret Atwood, Pierre Berton, Graeme Gibson, Margaret Laurence, and David Young, and registered as a charitable organization on March 3, 1976, the Writers' Trust celebrates and rewards the talents and achievements of Canada's novelists, short story writers, poets, biographers, and other fiction and nonfiction writers.

I know that it'll be necessary to research these further. So many sounded worthy of contributions in Aunt Jenny's name. What a wonderful opportunity to give back this would be.

26

Where Is Caylie?

SELENA HURRIEDLY FINISHED UP her preparations for the picnic lunch, let Rufus out. When he bounded back in expectantly, she told him they would walk later, to which he replied, "Ruff, ruff" "Ruff, ruff" "Ruff, ruff" "Ruff" which to Selena seemed to imply, "Well, that sucks, but okay, leave me alone while you go out and have fun. Don't feel guilty. That's my lot in life."

At 5 minutes before 11:00 Saturday morning, Jeremy pulled up in his gleaming, cherry red 2017 Mazda Miata Roadster. Selena stepped out of the house carrying her leather jacket over her arm with a scarf tucked into the pocket and whistled her enthusiasm.

"That's a fantastic looking car! Going my way?"

Jeremy loved the attention to his pride and joy, his one extravagance in his life, especially when the attention was coming from this special source.

"I certainly am miss, whichever way you wish to go!" He jumped out of the car, met her at the door to carry the picnic lunch basket and the folded table. He added those to the two collapsed lawn chairs and blanket in the trunk. He opened the door for her to get in.

"Thanks Jeremy." She could see his sunglasses reflected her relaxed, happy smile, casually piled up hair tied with a clip, some falling from the clasp.

"I had a tour route planned in my head. If you're interested, we can do my general tour or you can tell me where you want to go, Selena."

"I trust your judgement, and your route seems the best. This is amazingly comfortable," Selena said, happily sinking into the red leather seat. I love to look at cars, and I know a little, so tell me about this fantastic vehicle."

"Well, I don't know where your interests lie, but it's a convertible with a power-folding hardtop. If the day warms enough, we can put it down. It's got 155-horsepower; improved fuel economy; great mileage; lighter weight than previous models; and the latest safety technology."

They chatted about other vehicles, and Selena said, "I enjoy my aunt's – well, my Escape, particularly during the Canadian winters. But this vehicle's a very classy ride."

As they cruised down Maple Lane, Jeremy took the opportunity to swerve over to the Aviation Museum and see the National Research Council buildings.

"See what's there, Selena?"

"That's how close it is to my place. Cool! They have to hire me! They just have to." And she laughed.

"Of course, they do," he said as he joined in her merriment. Jeremy cruised around the area so Selena could get some close-up looks and judge how it would feel to drive over here to work. Jeremy continued the tour, and they drove past the National Art Gallery with its prism-like tower. Selena remembered it was one of the largest art museums in North America.

"Let's head over to Sussex. Would you like to get a glimpse of the prime minister's residence, and we'll go to Rideau Hall?"

"Sure. Rideau Hall amazes me."

"We'll drive around the French Embassy and Notre Dame Cathedral Basilica. Would you like to stop in to see Rideau Hall? We really do have time to go in for a little tour."

"Yep," Selena was thrilled.

"It's still early in the season so we can go in without a reservation."

Even though it was the residence of the Governor General of Canada, it was a stark grey stone building without much pomp and circumstance on the outside. The triangular sculpturing near the roof on the front was very impressive. They parked and walked through the large, landscaped grounds.

There were two areas that Selena found most interesting. One was the entrance hall where the walls were part panelling and part marble. The floor was decorated in lovely mosaic tile. Above, there were two levels connected by a wide white marble stairway. The second area of interest for her was the room that looked like it should have circus animals and acrobats performing. This was the ballroom.

What a wacky idea for a ballroom. I love it cuz it gives the room a fun atmosphere!

Once back in the Miata, Jeremy steered over to the Prime Minister's Residence which was being renovated and then the French Embassy. They could glimpse the windows through the tall stately trees. Next was the Royal Canadian Mint. Then they slowly passed the Notre Dame Cathedral Basilica built in 1846.

"That was so fun! Let's have lunch at the waterfront Major's Hill area" she suggested as her stomach growled.

There was little traffic in this area and Jeremy quickly found a parking spot. He got out and then opened Selena's door.

"You know, I could get used to this kind of valet service."

"Today only, Miss. We stop service at midnight." Jeremy and Selena tugged the items gently from the trunk so as not to scratch his beautiful vehicle. They decided just to take the blanket as it was an easy carry. She left her jacket in the trunk since it was sunny and warm out. They walked the distance to the picnic area overlooking the locks of the Rideau Canal.

"How magnificent the tulips are! From this park, you can see the view of every place we've been today."

They headed to the view of the locks with their supplies. Jeremy spread the blanket out while Selena opened the picnic basket containing a soda and orange juice each, broccoli/bacon muffin-tin frittatas, banana loaf slices, along with heirloom tomatoes, green and purple grapes and cut cantaloupe, two sets of fancy dishes, forks and cloth napkins.

"Gee, Selena, talk about getting used to something. I could definitely get used to this service."

"Today only sir. We stop service at midnight." And they laughed and poked each other, eyes locking for a second before Selena looked away.

The young couple was engrossed in their own lunch and enjoying each other's company so much that they did not even notice the coming and going of several other picnickers and people walking within the park. Car doors opened and closed, and these two were only aware of each other.

Conversation switched to their holidays growing up. Jeremy was a lot like Selena in that his family stayed around Ontario, except for their Saskatchewan visits to see his mom's sister. His family had a cabin up on Georgian Lake. Selena told Jeremy of the boat holidays she and her parents had taken each summer on the Sea Lion belonging to her dad's friend. She expressed how exciting that was as she loved the water, and she indicated she planned to take a tour of the Ottawa River and Rideau Canal on a perfect warm day this coming summer.

"Thanks for the lunch, Selena, and honestly, that was the best picnic lunch ever! Next time, I'll make up the lunch."

"Oh, you're so welcome. I enjoyed it too. Where to next Mr. Driver?"

Walking back to the car, Jeremy wanted desperately to take hold of Selena's hand. Instead, he said, "We'll drive along the Rideau Canal, and then head to Confederation Square, Parliament Hill, Parliament Buildings, Chateau Laurier and the Peace Tower."

"Ottawa is so fortunate to have the Rideau Canal filled with boats in summer and ice-skaters in winter."

Selena had been to the Parliament Buildings and had seen the changing of the Guard. In their tour past these areas, Selena and

Jeremy discussed the Parliament Buildings which were built in 1865 and their stunning Victorian and Gothic stone as well as the shiny copper roof; the Changing of the Guard on the Hill daily each summer morning; the Peace Tower from which you could view the entire city, all the way to Gatineau, Quebec and the Chateau Laurier – how the Chateau was like a medieval castle and that many planned additions had been abandoned because of public disapproval and that perhaps the latest one with twin towers of ten and eleven stories would finally win the day.

"If you're willing, we can head over to drive around the Supreme Court of Canada and the Canadian War Museum."

"I've all the time in the world right now. I've completed my last assignments, studied four hours yesterday, and I'm ready for a day tour."

Pointing to the right, she exclaimed, "There's the War Memorial! You know, I haven't ever seen it. Just look at the sculpture in bronze, and that must be granite for the stone. What a good tribute to the Unknown Soldier." They both paused in admiration and respect.

While stopped at a streetlight, Jeremy said, "On the way back, we can travel to Quebec over the Royal Alexandra Bridge to Gatineau to look at the Museum of History and Civilization. I love how our provinces are only a bridge apart, yet the history, culture and languages are so diverse and distinct."

"I totally agree!"

Having made their way back winding along the Ottawa River and over the Royal Alexandra to Quebec, Jeremy deftly finessed the vehicle around the huge Museum of History and Civilization and down to the group entrance where the buses come in.

"There's a mural at this museum by a famous prairie potter named Jack Sures called *Air, Earth, Water and Fire*. It measures sixty metres long and four metres tall, consists of hollow tubes, open at one end and varying in length. Jack Sures lived in Saskatchewan for most of his life, and, of course, my Aunt Aggie adored his unique pottery and sculptures.

"Cara Driscoll, Jack Sures' wife is also a fabulous potter, and does intricately hand-coiled vessels. Her pieces are extremely lovely. Jack Sures passed away less than two years ago, and he was still teaching art at the University of Regina and encouraging students to take up work in clay when he was in his eighties."

As they stopped, Jeremy pointed in the direction of the piece. "Cool! That's amazing. I'll have to look Jack Sures and Cara Driscoll up on the internet. This massive piece is impressive for sure."

They headed back to her neighbourhood, and Selena asked Jeremy if he would like a lemonade and to come with her and Rufus for a walk if he did not need to get back to work.

Happily, he said, "I've the remainder of the day off, so let's do that." As Jeremy manoeuvered his Miata into Selena's driveway, Karen was out digging in her flower garden. Selena and Karen waved to each other, and Karen walked over, whereupon Selena introduced Jeremy to Karen. Karen shook Jeremy's hand, and said she was pleased to meet him. However, the frown on Karen's face as she shook Jeremy's hand showed she was not entirely pleased to meet him.

"Selena, we've not been out for one of our walks recently. We'll have to do that very soon to catch up everything that's been happening." *Pointedly said,* thought Selena. "I'll get back to my digging, and we'll chat later."

Selena said, "I'd love that, Karen. It's been too long. I hope to see you tomorrow?" They gave each other a smile. Karen barely gave Jeremy a glance, turned away from them both to return to her garden. Selena felt both apprehensive and saddened. She knew that Karen loved that she and Austin had dated, and she supposed that Karen would have liked her to get back together with Austin. However, with news from his own brother about his still having a girlfriend, that was not going to happen. Her distrust of him had grown.

Selena went into the house, let Rufus out and brought out two glasses of lemonade. As they sipped the lemonade, Selena mentioned to Jeremy that she had told Kevin that she might be leaving the Clinic.

"I hope Kevin was all right with that. Yes, I'm sure it'll be fine since it's for the best in your career."

I also hope it'll be okay. Was Kevin going to jeopardize my current work situation? Would he give me a good reference? Should I not have said anything to him spur-of-the-moment like I did?

Look at how my disclosure to him of not wanting to settle down simply burst out. I'm sure he thinks I'm a moron in how I said it. But it was my decision at the time to speak out, and I'm glad it's all said and done.

Ramon was loading the last of his equipment and the refuse in the back of his truck when Selena and Jeremy came to see him. The other workers were getting into their vehicles, doors were slamming, hands waving friendly goodbyes to Selena. She smiled genuinely and waved back to them.

He walked toward her, saying, "I will forward invoice to your accountant as discussed. I am down street ness week working for one of your neighbours who like my work here."

Selena attempted to give Ramon an envelope which he correctly ascertained was a cash tip.

"No, I refuse to take additional money. I charge fair price and I stick to it." He shook her hand.

"Good-bye, Jeremy. It has been good to meet you. You can join my team if you want to give up jour fine computer business. I come in one day to let you sell me a Notebook to keep in my truck for business."

"That would be terrific, Ramon. I'm so pleased that Selena found you to do this work for her."

Selena shook Ramon's hand again and said a final thank you.

As they headed outside to the back yard, Caylie asked to be included on the patio with a "Meow, Murrror, Meoooooowwww" so her leash was also brought out.

"I really enjoy Caylie's spunk. She's a sweet cat".

"She's a sweetheart. She can come out now. Then afterwards, I'll take Rufus for his walk."

Selena mentioned that Caylie's whole name was Caylie Ceilidh Pretty Lady. Sitting and chatting, neither noticed that Caylie had slipped out of her harness and was chasing a leaf. Rufus thought this was great fun and scampered after Caylie, which only spurred her on. Then Selena noticed her kitty heading through the garden with Rufus running behind, wanting to play. Jumping up, Selena, along with Jeremy, moved quickly and were calling "Caylie" repeatedly.

Austin appeared through the bushes from his parent's yard. "I hear you callin' Caylie. Oh, who do we have here? What's this about?"

Running, Selena said over her shoulder, "This is Jeremy. I'll talk later." She and Jeremy each ran around the opposite sides of the garden, Jeremy calling for Rufus at this point. Rufus stopped chasing Caylie and came back to him with his tail hanging down, unsure if he was in trouble. Jeremy hung onto Rufus, which Rufus was happy about while Selena continued on, skirting the garden, coming out on the other side where she saw Caylie slinking down in the lavender bushes.

"Caylie, hello sweetie, come here. There, there -- you're fine. Good kitty." Scooping up the skittish cat, Selena hugged and petted her while walking back to Jeremy and Rufus and a fierce-looking Austin.

Boy, he's fit to be tied about something!

"Hello Austin. Nice to see you. This is my friend, Jeremy. Jeremy, this is my neighbour, Austin."

"Oh, aren't I your friend too?" Austin said, his lip curling so slightly that she was not sure she saw it.

Jeremy came to the rescue with his pleasant reply, "Pleased to meet you, Austin. I've heard so much about you. Are you here for the weekend, then?" quizzed Jeremy, looking quite innocent."

I could hug Jeremy for his cool demeanour.

Standing erect, displaying his firefighter muscles, Austin seemed to sneer, "Yeah sure, I'm pleased to meet ya, too. My mom said there was some guy drivin' Selena home from somewhere. It's good that ya have heard so much about me. Then you'll know that I'm Selena's boyfriend. I've known her since we were kids. We've just resumed datin' which we started in high school. It was good of ya to drive Selena home and help wrangle Rufus and Caylie, but ya must be on your way now, right?"

That was more of an order than a question!

Boyfriend indeed! How exasperating.

"Austin, just stop! I don't know what has gotten into you! Jeremy is a good friend. I've known him for a couple of years. We've been for a drive around Ottawa. In fact, Jeremy has helped me to purchase a tablet and set it up. Don't speak to him like that."

Having known Austin for so many years, Selena could tell he was working himself up to a lather. He continued, "Well, with you inheritin' all your aunt's money, I don't see why this Jeremy should have to help ya ta purchase anythin'. Ya can afford ta do whatever ya want without his bloody help. And I'm sure I can be of more help luggin' a computer around than this guy."

At this point, Selena turned and walked away with Caylie in her arms. She opened the garden door for Jeremy with Rufus right at his heels. Austin followed. Selena then reached to close the door behind her.

"Selena, wait. When this guy is gone, come back. Let's try again."

Rufus turned back toward Austin and did something very unusual for his personality. While looking at Austin, Rufus gave a short "growl" and went into the house. Selena firmly closed the door as Austin got closer, almost in his face and clicked the lock into place.

"That was terrible, Selena. I would have punched him in the nose except he's bigger than me and obviously in really good condition." Selena tried a laugh, failed, put Caylie down and just shrugged what Jeremy saw as her very fine shoulders.

"That put a damper on what was a lovely day, Jeremy. I'm sorry you had to hear any of that with his fake tough guy speech, too. When we were teenagers, he was nice. Or maybe he put on a good act – he's always been a little drama prone. I just don't know, and he upset me beyond belief just now. I'm not going to forget that display of temper and bad manners for a long time. He has had no time for me for the two years since he broke up with me, and now suddenly he wants to be back in my life, or at least that's what he says. That isn't what his eyes are saying. And that temper!"

"Let's take Rufus for a walk out the front door, Selena. I'm not leaving you like this, and Rufus looks very mournful that he didn't get his walk. We'll go the opposite direction from their house, and you can show me your neighbourhood."

"You're good not to cut and run after the display out there. Rufus, would you like to go for a walk?"

"Ruff, ruff!" "Yes, yes!"

"Caylie, here sweet girl, here are a few treats for you. No, not for you Rufus Goofus. Shoo!"

Jeremy brought Rufus' leash, attached it and waited patiently for Selena. "Caylie, sweetie, come here," Selena fussed as she guided the kitty to her treats.

"Meow, purr." "Thank you Selena".

Selena closed the front door behind them, and they set off the opposite direction from Karen and Bud's home, walking close together with Rufus ambling along, being even extra good as if he knew their reflective mood. They had walked several blocks in silence when Jeremy inquired, "Are you okay, Selena?"

"Well, I guess I have a few emotions. I'm angry and embarrassed, but I must admit, not totally surprised. You can have the long version if you want."

"Yes, tell me what you think's happening here."

"There has been something different about Austin this week. My best friend Laura, who is engaged to Austin's twin brother, Theodore, has told me some things that she and Theodore agreed I needed to know about Austin. I told you, he has ignored me in the past two years. After he broke it off with me, it was evident that he had moved on after he relocated to Toronto. Laura told me that Austin has been dating various girls and someone seriously, for a year, and she said they even saw him with her two weeks ago. Suddenly, he shows up for my aunt's funeral, which would be totally normal, but he was insisting that he missed me and loved me and that we had to get back together. Something is so off here."

With his face sad and his voice quiet, Jeremy said, "I'm sure you two will work it out when you get a chance to discuss it together rationally,"

She beamed wholeheartedly at him.

His heart tugged.

"Let's head back. It's not up to you to make it better, Jeremy. I suppose he and I need to talk, but I don't feel about him like he says he feels about me. I yearned for him when we first broke up, but I moved on as well. I love the life I have now, and I'm ready to do lots of new things, travel to new places and to even move to another job. Life just goes on.

"But the thing that bothers me the most is the jab about me being able to afford anything now. That doesn't sit well with me. That isn't any of his business… Unless that's it!" A hard look crossed her features. "That creep! Maybe he wants to make that his business."

As they approached her front door, she said, "I had better explain something to you." She was studying his deep blue eyes and admiring his choice of clothing – khaki pants, cream polo shirt, setting off his tanned complexion. His presence was setting off a higher rate heartbeat in her chest.

Jeremy took her hand. "Hey, Selena, please don't explain anything to me unless you truly want to. You don't owe me an explanation. It's none of my business either. Let's just enjoy the rest of this fantastic day. Would you like me to scratch something together in your pantry and fridge and make you supper tonight or can we make supper together?"

Still keeping her hand in Jeremy's, Selena stroked his wrist and said, "No, Jeremy. Truly, I had a fantastic day. But I just need to have time to myself right now. Will you mind terribly? Since we had such a fantastic day together, I don't want it to be spoiled by me not being in the mood for company."

Goodbyes were said at the door. Selena just prior to closing the door sighed and said, "I'd love to do something with you another day." That led to Jeremy stepping back in and giving her a gentle kiss. He held her face in both his palms and looked deep into her eyes before reluctantly letting her go.

"Selena, I'd like nothing better. I'll text you in the morning just to see how you're doing." That was settled. Selena closed the door with a gentle *swish*, leaned back against the door, blushed and grinned.

I want more of that. What a sweet and gentle kiss.

Jeremy was ecstatic. *I really enjoyed Selena's company. I knew I would. There's just something about her that makes me feel at home, like I've known her a dozen years. I need to have a chat with Kevin to see what he's thinking so I know what my next steps might be. Awesome.*

Selena was in the pottery studio right after her breakfast the following morning, rolling out thin coil strips. As she used Jeremy's technique to roll out and then cut a circle for the bottom of a bowl to put the coils on, she thought of Jeremy and that kiss. *Yum!* When she had about 30 slim coils ready and covered with plastic, along with a small container of water and a sponge, she used an eight-inch bowl form that she had set out as well. Covering the bowl inside in plastic, she placed the cut clay circle at the bottom, scratched each surface of the coil as she was adding them to the layer below using a miniscule amount of water and attached the coils one by one until she had used up all 30 of her coils. She rubbed each layer gently with the dampened sponge to ensure they were attached and then stepped back to admire her project.

This process took her less than an hour, and she still felt energized enough to do a matching piece. She used a sponge to round each top coil, then used her new Tablet to photograph her pieces and texted them to Elizabeth. After everything was covered with plastic, she gave a sigh of contentment. On her middle shelf now sat her tray, slightly covered, these two additional bowls and several pinch pots she had quickly formed in between studies and her daily routines. She smiled thoughtfully as she looked at the ones that Jeremy had created the other day.

After she had tidied up the work surfaces, wiped everything down and mopped stray pieces of clay from the floor, she left the pottery studio wandering back to her home deep in thought.

It's so bizarre and yet amazing even to me that I just saw Aunt Jenny and my parents here – here, but in the past on New Years' Eve, and that they're dead in my time. Will that ever seem normal to me? I still can't believe that she's gone.

Seeing my parents was so fulfilling. I thought I'd never see them again and then seeing them, now that I'm an adult, was a horribly sad, yet gratifying experience. That doesn't do it justice. It was heartwarming, uplifting, tender. Leaving was heartbreaking. A sob escaped and tears formed in the corner of each eye.

Selena attempted to gather her spirits again and found herself wondering if she would tell Jeremy.

I'll never tell anyone until I'm sure of them. I've had so much fun with him – just fun. But, if I wanted a guy in my life, he would be Jeremy. I find I'm so at ease with him. I like him very much. Jeremy would be the one to trust with my secret travel room. With Jeremy being a computer guy, he would be absolutely fascinated.

As Selena walked through the yard and past the garden, she was totally immersed in thoughts of her family. Austin practically jumped out at her. She stared at him. They were quiet for a few beats staring at each other as a car horn honked in the distance. A crow cawed a few times.

When it was silent, Austin said quietly, "I see that *Ramon Silva Roofing* has finished repairin' the roof. I gather everthin' worked out for you. Did he find a lot of other stuff that's wrong? You know, you could sell this place before something else is discovered. Then maybe you could move somewhere else less trouble."

Astonishment registered on Selena's features. Feeling disappointment in this person who had stolen her heart, then thrown it back at her two years ago, who had attempted to highjack it again, she examined him, "Are you trying to be obtuse? What are you trying to accomplish? This is my home. I thought you wanted to get back together. Where is your heart, Austin? What do you want from me?"

He gave an exasperated sigh. "Let's start over now. We can make us a couple again. If only you'd try harder. You know I'm a better choice than any hoity toity doctor or that guy with the computer. They're just not for you."

Beginning to turn away, yet turning toward him again, she said, "Austin, when you feel like being respectful to me, then we can have a decent conversation. We have things we need to talk about, soon." She couldn't stop herself asking a question that she did not even care to hear the answer to, perhaps just to hear what he could come up with. "I'm curious, though, what happened to those two calls you said you would make to me this week?"

Then Austin looked sheepish. "Well, I got busy – there's a hell of a lot goin' on in my life."

With her voice raised and her temper showing, she said, "Oh, and would having a 'hell of a lot going on' in your life have anything to do with the girlfriend that you have been seeing for over a year and that you are serious about?"

"Selena, that is a low blow. Yeah, I had a girlfriend, but that petered out. I ain't with her now. She just wasn't you, and it's only you ... that ... that ... I care about." He would not meet her eyes, and his tone was becoming less sincere with each word. He had flushed an unattractive shade of crimson as he lifted his gaze toward her.

"Really." He tried to make his voice sound heartfelt.

"Austin, is it possible that you only started to pay attention to me when you found out Aunt Jenny had died – that I'd possibly be her sole beneficiary. You certainly ignored me for the last two years. You know you did."

"I need you, Selena. I love you. We can make it work for us."

"No, Austin. I didn't feel you have been truthful since you came to my aunt's funeral. What a disgusting thing to attempt to do on top of my Aunt Jenny passing away. Where did the old Austin go? Everything you've said was just a little too pat, suddenly being attentive to me after two years of not caring one bit. I've moved on with my life and evidently so have you."

At that moment, Karen strode out their solarium door, with Bud walking more warily behind her.

"What's going on here?" Looking bewildered, Karen quizzed, "This sounds like something we should know about – definitely we should know about!" Bud was standing back a little, and Karen noticed that he was not beside her.

"Bud, why do you not look shocked or at least surprised at what we heard just now when we were reading in the house?"

Bud motioned Karen over, and he spoke very quietly to her. "Um, I think part of me knew that Austin had a girlfriend. At least, there was twice when I, um, telephoned, once very early morning and another time, um, quite late at night... You remember, I telephoned that evening to tell Austin that Jenny had passed away? Well, um, a girl answered. Both times it was the same voice. I told her I was Austin's father. I asked her the second time did she mind telling me who she was. Well, um, she said she was Austin's roommate, which did surprise me."

Bud indicated to Austin for him to step closer. Austin, red in face, anger showing, grumbled, "For cripes' sakes", but he complied.

"I tried to, um, talk to you about it when you came home for the funeral, but you brushed me off. Then, when your mother tried to tie you down to something last weekend, I interrupted her so that you could, um, go to Selena. I still thought that there was a chance for the two of you."

Karen threw a withering look at Austin, turned and walked back toward Selena. She gave Selena an affection hug, and said, "Selena, oh my gosh! I'm so sorry that I was short with you yesterday."

Turning again toward Austin, she said, "Austin, would you prefer to discuss this in our house, or should we continue on discussing this in Selena's presence?"

Austin gave a non-committed shrug. He seemed to struggle to say, "Yeah, let's get this done right here."

Karen, again taking charge, said, "And what exactly was going on? Are you in love with Selena or this other girl? How long has she been your girlfriend?"

"About 14 months. Ahh mom! As I was just tellin' Selena, it didn't mean nothin'. She was just not Selena and …"

Karen sighed and said gently, "Austin, as your mother, I can tell your lie a mile away. My concern is: Is Selena right? Are you trying to get Selena to fall in love with you again because she, because she… Oh my heavens, are you wanting Selena because she inherited Jenny's estate? Do you love this other girl?"

"Well, can't I love both of them? Honestly, mom! Ya should just mind your own damn business and leave this alone."

Selena then had enough – again. In a sad and resigned voice, she said, "Austin, I don't care to discuss this further with you." Turning to Karen and Bud, "I found out several days ago that Austin has been involved with someone seriously for quite some time. He was seen only two weeks ago with the same girl. They didn't know she was living with him. I'm going home now. You guys can have a debate about who knew what and when, but I'm not remaining here one second longer. Karen and Bud, I'll chat with you both another time. Austin, goodbye. This time for good!" She turned and marched away.

Austin looked angry. Bud took Austin's arm to stop him from the forward motion he attempted to make to follow Selena. "No, let her go."

His father felt no resistance from Austin, so he dropped his arm. With a jerk of his head, he indicated Austin to go ahead of them. Austin had a scowl on his face as he walked into the house first, followed by his mother treading heavily behind him and then his father, walking much more slowly and morosely.

About that same time, Jeremy drove into Selena's driveway, rang the front doorbell. Since there was no answer, he walked around to the back of the house, just as Selena was turning the doorknob to enter through the garden door.

"Selena, I was telephoning, and then I got worried." Giving her an appraising look, he added, "You look done in! What's happened? May I come in with you?"

Selena nodded.

Walking into the living room and beckoning Jeremy to sit on the other wing chair, Selena relayed to Jeremy what had transpired in the past 15 minutes with Austin and his parents.

He moved toward her, saying, "Selena, I just knew yesterday that there was going to have to be another conversation between you two. Do you want a glass of water?" He was already up and walking toward the kitchen.

Selena murmured, "Yes, please."

When Jeremy came back into the living room, Selena said, "You know, I'm better than I've been in two weeks. Aunt Jenny is gone, and I must get used to that. Austin has been gone from me for two years, and I'm honestly used to that. There has been a tension in me about him since the evening of Aunt Jenny's funeral when he professed his love for me. Now that it's all out in the open, I'm relieved. I didn't love him any longer so you can dispense with feeling sorry for me. I confronted him just now. I don't like conflict, but I'm ecstatic that I got over another hurdle.

"I also want to tell you something else. You heard Austin say yesterday about me now having money. No, don't stop me. I'm the sole beneficiary of my Aunt Jenny's estate. This is my house now, and I'm enjoying that feeling."

Jeremy looked shocked. "I just assumed that she had family. I mean, of course, you're her family, but I meant I didn't realize that she didn't have any children. I didn't know your Aunt Jenny, so I didn't think about it at all. I thought you were fixing the roof from necessity, but that this house would be sold or other family moving in. It's a fantastic house." He leaned over her and kissed the top of her head, laying both hands on her shoulders. "It's unfair and sad how this came about, but you're fortunate not to have to find another place to live. I'm so sorry you lost your Aunt Jenny."

"I am fortunate in that respect. I'm an orphan who would have had to find another home, but this's my home. I love this house. One other thing -- I'm blessed to have you for a friend, Jeremy."

"That is truly kind of you, Selena. I also am extremely pleased that you're my friend. Would you like to take Rufus in your Escape to go somewhere entirely different for a walk? You know that dog will fit better in your Escape."

That evening, Selena had many reflections to make. Predominately running through her mind was that it was wonderful having the companionship that she had missed so much.

I miss my aunt very much. I always will. She was my family all these years. Jeremy is a good man. He's a true friend that I feel completely at ease with, and I like him more than a lot. I trust him.

After Jeremy's suggestion of taking Rufus for a drive, they had piled into Selena's Escape and driven down the Sir George Etienne

Cartier Parkway and over to the Dog Park where Rufus could run and run. He turned to them "Ruff, ruff, ruff, ruff!" Jeremy said, "I think he just said, 'thank you, thank you'!"

Selena remembered saying, "You are starting to sound like me. I'm always thinking I know what the pets are saying." There were benches where Selena and Jeremy sat and watched Rufus running with the other dogs, getting sidetracked with sniffing all the plants, grass, leaves, fences, well anything and everything. He ran and ran, bounding to each corner of the park with the other dogs. As each new dog arrived, the dogs all looked as if they had to show the new dogs the places they had discovered.

Someone unlatched the gate, and Rufus was out of the dog park like a shot, running and then swerving over to the remains of a picnic lunch, the people off in a distance having left their litter behind. He was sniffing it with anticipation when Selena whistled to him. He gave the lunch another sniff, turned to Selena, turned back to the food, then gallantly ran back to her when she called "Rufus, come!"

"Good dog. I told you that nose would cause you trouble, but you're a good dog for coming when I called. You didn't get into any trouble… yet."

He nuzzled Jeremy and let Selena clip the leash around his neck. They walked over to the Ottawa River, sat on the grass and enjoyed another hour, sitting and chatting while Rufus, exhausted, lay on the grass beside them. A squirrel ran right over Rufus' back foot. He lifted his head and then put his head down again and stretched out lazily.

Unbelievable! He's that tired.

Reminiscing of Jeremy's conversation that afternoon, he had begun with, "I came to your house to tell you I talked to Kevin last night. We had a long chat about life and what our futures might bring."

Selena remembered laughing. "Well, what is happening with Dr. Kevin Carey? What is his life and future going to entail?"

"He isn't angry with you, Selena. He probably also tried to call you this morning. He said that when Colleen left the Clinic, he totally misunderstood – thinking she wanted to end their relationship. He has always loved her, and he feels that he may have another chance with her now that they have sorted it out. He knew what he wanted out of life, and his dream of it being Colleen may well come true."

"Kevin was struck by how forthright you were with him. He expected that with your classes that you'd have to go elsewhere sometime soon, even after summer. In fact, he said he was going to suggest that you should start looking at other opportunities when you returned to work."

Once they were back from Rufus Goofus' walk and their discussions, Selena confessed she not taken the time today to plan anything for supper, so she had asked Jeremy if he would want to stay for eggs and hash browns with some bacon.

Jeremy laughed, "I'd love to have breakfast for supper, Selena, so I'll get the dishes and set out the cutlery, but I'll let Rufus out in his dog run so there's no interruptions while we cook and have our supper. Then, after supper, I need to make an early night of it cuz I'll be meeting a client on the other side of Ottawa early tomorrow morning in his offices. I must prepare for the presentation, and I also have to prepare for that conference I'll be at in Montreal next week."

"That'll be fine with me. Honestly, I'll be glad to just snuggle up with a good travel magazine I subscribed to."

In her diary, she had revealed:

> *"It's another relief. Today was full of surprises, all of them good. I asked Jeremy, "Then what's your life and future going to hold?"*
>
> *His reply: "Well, to be honest, I hoped that it might hold you, if that's okay with you? We're having a totally awesome time, aren't we, Selena? It's important to me what you want out of life, but I just want to have you in my future. I've admired you from the moment I met you, and I'm totally head over heels for you."*

I feel so close to him. I've known Jeremy for years as just a friend who came into the Clinic to take Kevin for lunch and spent a little time joking with me. However, recently, I see another side of him. He's fun to be with, but serious, gallant and gentle too. That's a great combination. We'll take this one day at a time.

I wanna hold his hand … hum, hum, hum, laughing in the sun, always having fun, doing all those things without anything to tie me down.

Not true any longer. My future might be to hold this someone's hand, laughing in the sun, always having fun, with Jeremy.

I'm well rid of Austin and his deceitful antics.

I've decided to seek new employment.

I've funds to have some time off if that's how things turn out.

I'm loving Jeremy's wit and twinkle in his eyes when he laughed.

Most of my worries are over.

I love looking at Jeremy. I love being with him, and he's kind of sexy.

Remembering Jeremy's smile as she flirted with sleep, she thought of another portion of that poem she had composed:

"Someone, someone with your big dark eyes
Those that so easily cause my heart to rise
And fall more often than the usual beat
When your eyes and mine chance to meet.
I feel myself upon the threshold of love,
With all of my body aglide as a dove."

Sleep came easily.

PART THREE

27

Connected

A long and very eventful week later, Selena could feel summer was here, which was not to be trusted as weather in Ottawa was never a certainty throughout a given day. She pulled back the drapes feeling the warming sun on her face.

"Ahh, I'll open all the windows to let in the spring air." She walked around the house, airing the winter away and welcoming the sun into her home. Drifting from room to room, she thought: *My home. I'll never tire of calling this wonderful home "my home".*

What she loved most was the feeling of her family. She could feel her Grandmother Olive and her Grandfather Arthur's presence, and she felt the connections to each of them that she had not ever felt before right in this home. These travel encounters had occurred in this house, and that cemented the feeling of tenderness. Having visited with her grandparents, her real memories of being with them when she was a little girl had become vivid in her mind.

"I'm relieved to have some memories back. No more unanswered questions of who they were. I remember them, my feelings for them!"

"I feel Aunt Jenny's familiar presence in this home in hundreds of memories: Aunt Jenny looking after me as a child; who had countless conversations with me; who travelled back in time to be with her own mother and father; who had written many meaningful books; who loved me.

Selena had entered her father's old room several times, sitting and chatting to the memory of her father, feeling her father growing up in this house, of his love for her mother, of their love for her when they were pregnant with her and during her childhood.

"I actually physically feel the love radiating throughout this home – my grandparents, my parents, my aunt, and, quite probably now, Jeremy and me. And on top of all that, my mysteries have been solved. What a tremendous relief! It's a soothing sensation. I am totally relaxed for the first time in years. I think that I have always been sensitive to the vibrations. The mysteries interfered with that. Now I feel everything is settled around me."

Walking upstairs, still feeling the love in *her* home, Selena sank into a lounge chair and let the sensations of the home absorb into her.

Feelings of peace, love – tender feelings.

Caylie thought this was a good time to jump onto Selena's lap, and they sat together in contentment with Rufus lying beside the lounge, snoring.

Reaching for her diary, she added these comments:

"Oh, Aunt Jenny, I wish you were still here. I didn't ever get – no, pardon me – I didn't ever take the opportunity to say, 'thank you for everything you did for me'.

I now understand that Eric Brisbane had been in love with you all those years. He was content just to spent time with you until your death. This home holds that love too. You may not have loved Eric Brisbane in the way he needed you to, enough to marry him. But you loved him in another way – of deep, continuing friendship.

Grandma and Grandpa: This closeness of feeling is because of the time I spent with you both during my trips back to the afternoon in 1968 and 1999 New Year's Eve which are etched into my mind, surrounding me with your love. I'm so thankful for those times together. I'm thankful for the time I would have spent with you as a small child. Thank you for being there for me the night my parents perished in that accident.

I can feel your arms around me as if you're both here with me. With those shocking flashbacks of that night, my real memories of you have intensified, along with the memory of getting ice cream with Grandpa. Selly. That word. That's all it took. Grandpa calling me "Selly".

Mom and Dad: There will never, ever, ever be enough words to say how I miss you. I think that God will have shown you how much I loved and love you. I know you loved me. I'm thankful to have been able to see you and your love for each other and your love for me when you were pregnant. I will remember you until the end of time. I will love you until the end of time."

After time spent absorbing the feelings, of reminiscing and writing in her diary, Selena rose from the lounge, gently moving Caylie onto her kitty blanket with the kitty purring and rolling over. A tummy rub and a chin scratch later, Selena continued on with opening the upstairs windows. She could hear the *tweet, tweet* of Robins and the Blue Jays whistled notes in the garden. She gazed out at the yard that was now coming into full bud. Just then, a family of raccoons scurried across the yard, off on their own adventure.

Selena had watched for several minutes as Eric Brisbane and his nephew had performed magic with the gardens this past week, turning the soil, and Eric had pruned the plants that had to be done in the spring.

She had approached them and said, "Thank you so much Eric and Seamus for doing this work in Aunt Jenny's garden. She would have loved to walk out here with you, Eric, to enjoy what you've done."

Eric had looked carefully at Selena, gauging what she knew, wondering what he could say. He simply said, "Thank you, Selena. That means a lot to me."

Lovingly looking out the window, Selena could see off into the woodlands. The trees swaying in rhythm to the gentle winds. The clouds hanging over top like a comforter.

How fortunate I am to have these woodlands as my home backdrop, framing in the rest of the yard and garden.

She admired the view, the budding trees and shrubbery, the remains of the crocuses poking out above the grizzled grass, the birds singing and flitting from branch to branch, the bees looking for a flower to sink into. Her outside world was grasping at and pulling itself toward a splendid Ottawa summer.

28

Moving On

Jeremy had been away at an IT conference in Montreal for three days this week, which gave Selena a chance to be on her own to handle her complex and busy week.

Selena thought over how she had returned to work this past Monday, refreshed and ready to handle her week of exams, her interview with National Research Council and the possible meeting with Doctors Carey and Kothare.

I studied extensively during my time off work. My exams were difficult and involved. I believe I passed them with no worries. That new tablet is the best purchase – ever.

Following her interview with the National Research Council, and having received a verbal employment offer, Selena had arranged to meet with Dr. Kev for lunch last week.

Kevin had said during lunch, "I'm glad, Selena, that we had the opportunity to talk on the phone on the weekend. It's important to me that we meet today so that you can let me know your plans prior to any meeting with my father and Dr. Kothare."

"I'm confident that I passed my examinations this week. I've been accepted at the National Research Council. They couriered me my offer letter at work this morning. In fact, I just received it at 11:00 a.m. today. I apologize for the manner that this has worked out. I feel that I'm being presumptuous, and I apologize for my timing…

But I'll be submitting my letter of resignation this afternoon, hoping that you will allow me … Well, two weeks to work while you find someone to replace me."

"No apology necessary. You'll be starting in two weeks at the NRC?"

"No, actually, that's why I hesitated for a moment when saying two weeks. I want to apologize and explain. My start date is June 1st. They're organizing a transfer of staff in my department. With your agreement, I'll give only two weeks' notice to the Clinic."

"It isn't ideal, but I can perfectly understand you wanting additional time off between working at the Clinic and starting your new employment. A lot of things have been happening in your life. You had mentioned before that you might arrange a tour of the British Isles this summer. Is that what you plan to do during May?"

"I've arranged a tour with *Girl Travel Tours*. I have my itinerary and have given them a deposit on a tour; however, I can work for three weeks if you wish."

"No need. We've seen this career move coming – no hard feelings on our part. We'll put out the ad for your position and go from there."

"Kevin, do you feel comfortable chatting about Colleen?" He nodded, indicating she should proceed. "Good. She and I met for supper the other evening, and she said that you and she have come to an understanding. By-the-way, Colleen said she's fine with me chatting with you today. It's sad that the two of you hadn't understood each other when she left the Clinic, and that you thought she was making a move away from you as well."

A small grimace had passed over his face. "Even though we met for some suppers and lunches, I didn't know that she still felt the way she does for me. I didn't stop loving her. I just didn't understand, and we're enjoying our new-found relationship. Then a slight smile played across his face, an inward thought crossing his mind. He had looked thoughtfully at Selena and revealed, "It's time that I looked for another place to live closer to Colleen, and we'll take it from there. I think everything will be permanently settled between us before the new year."

"That makes me happy since she's a dear friend. Well, I'd like to get back to the Clinic so that I can have the meeting with you, your father and Dr. Kothare. I'll let them know what will be happening regarding my employment at *The Caring Medical Clinic*."

I feel confident and am still in awe of how more capable I feel than several weeks ago. So much has happened and who knows what my future may involve, but I feel ready for it.

Now back from lunch, Selena picked up the letter from the National Research Council to again look at it. She ran her hand down the wording, feeling all the emotions that came with her acceptance at the NRC. She would have a one-year term position with possibility of extension. Her job would be in the department accessing information in health science, research, emerging biotechnology and nanotechnology research.

As she sat in her office, she contemplated, *Am I scared, worried, concerned? I'd be foolish not to feel a little of that. Mostly, I'm feeling excited and ready for this new path. I'll only be assisting at the NRC and continuing part-time in September with year three at the University of Ottawa.*

Pausing, with a real smile of satisfaction, she added, "Grandma and Grandpa, I'll be working where you were working so long ago."

Selena knocked on Dr. Brent Carey's office door. He opened it, ushered her in and gave her a firm handshake, congratulating her on her new job before she even spoke. Selena had wondered what she should expect; however, as she glanced at Dr. Kev, she knew he had smoothed the way for her. She smiled as all three doctors agreed that Selena would be much better employed where she would get more experience for her BSc degree in Biochemistry.

Dr. Carey Sr. said, "Selena, there will never be any hard feelings on this. You've been through quite a lot in the past weeks. When Kevin brought to my attention how your career path will improve with changing jobs, I can only be glad for you and to wish you luck in your career. Kevin has also explained that you'll be staying on for two weeks giving us time to interview and hire someone to fill your shoes. Thank you for that time."

He gave her perfunctory pat on the back and said, "Good luck, Selena. I know you'll be here for another two weeks, but I just want to add that you have been an excellent and involved employee."

Selena noted Dr. Bethany Kothare nodding her approval at her, and she shook her hand as well. Tears of appreciation in her eyes, Selena left and closed the door behind her, looking out at her co-workers. She had let them know what had been transpiring. Emotionally, all she could manage was the 'thumbs up' sign to them. They came forward and congratulated her.

Now, back to work doing this job that I still feel a little nostalgic about leaving behind. And I'll meet with these guys occasionally for after work drinks.

The last two weeks of work had moved by quickly with Selena finishing up the majority of her workload. Her replacement started working with Selena for her last two days. There had been preparatory planning to give the new Medical Assistant an easier start and show her the way the doctors liked the work completed. Nalini Varma had just completed a year of classes. Nalini, first in her university class, olive skinned and beautiful, was eager and ready to start her career. Selena felt a connection with the young lady, and they got along well.

As Selena left the Clinic the final day, the staff all gave her hugs, and she reciprocated, but her mind had already moved on to her future. She would miss her co-workers, but "Forward and Onward" was her mantra.

"So, are you all ready for your trip, my sweetheart?" Jeremy radiated that smile that Selena knew came from deep within his heart, and that smile caused her own heart to flutter faster.

She went to him and hugged him. "Yep, I've already packed a suitcase to ensure that I have everything I need, along with passport, waist money belt, credit cards and just some currency. These foreign euros are quite neat to look at. Scotland doesn't use them, but Ireland does. I'll keep a few as souvenirs when I get back.

"You have been supportive to me throughout all these weeks, and I'll miss you so much. It's a shame it didn't work out for you and me to take a tour together this time. Hey, I've been looking at what could happen in September. There's a week-long tour to Paris coming up which could fit around the long weekend. I've checked out the details. Hopefully, it will work for both of us. I'll have earned some holidays, and the NRC indicated that they're flexible."

Jeremy came closer toward her, caressed her cheek and took her by the shoulders. Selena reached for his hair, pulled his head toward her, and they kissed. Smiling, they then moved even closer. He was almost as excited for her about her trip as she was.

"Selena, this tour is perfect for you. I love you, and I'll miss you, but I'm happy that you're going to get one of your dreams to come true. Every time I check out your itinerary, this is just so you! Scotland and Ireland!"

Reaching a brochure off the table without letting go of Selena, he read, "Edinburgh, Scottish Highlands, seeing the Irish Sea, Belfast, Galway, Circle of Kerry and Cliffs of Moher. The Leprechaun Museum; King of Vikings Exhibit; Bunratty Castle & Park; and Kilbeggan Distillery all sound fantastic!"

"It's very exciting, and I can't wait for the next three days to pass so that I can fly to Toronto and then on to Edinburgh. Two weeks sounds heavenly, and I'm floating."

He reached for her hand again, leaned in kissed her neck and said, "I'm ecstatic for you."

Selena pulled him closer, "Me too! I will be texting you throughout because I'll miss you terribly, but not enough that I won't go," she added giggling. "This tablet is also coming with me. With your business booming, you'll have a lot of high school students wanting to get devices before their own finals come up, and I know that you're the best store in all of Ontario and Quebec."

Sitting down together, they embraced tightly like they did not want to ever let go. They both knew that their feelings for each other ran very deep.

Jeremy whispered to her, "When you return, this will be the beginning of our life together."

Selena reflected --

This is what real love should feel like:

"Trust; acceptance of who I am and of whom I want to be; feeling comfortable and confident in the love that I give and love I receive. I just did not know what I was missing."

Before bed that evening, Selena moved her aunt's French Louis XVI cane bench from the library to a spot directly under her bedroom window so she could look at the stars, and she wondered what was happening at her travel destinations at that moment.

I'll see the same moon wherever I travel. I'll see the same moon on my vacation that Jeremy will be looking at from here.

This entry was added to her diary:

> *"Jeremy has been a fantastic support and so much more than a friend over the past five weeks. Our relationship has bloomed into love.*
>
> *He's a regular fixture in my life.*
>
> *I love his sense of humour which occasionally reminds me of my dad's humour.*
>
> *Jeremy agreed with me that he'll move here while I'm away. That was why everything fell so easily into place. Rufus Goofus loves, loves, loves Jeremy. If we're sitting down close together, Rufus lies right by Jeremy's feet and*

puts his head on my feet so that he's sharing himself with both of us.

When Jeremy became the one to feed Caylie, she meowed to him when she wanted a treat. She would rub herself up against his leg, "Meeoowww", suggesting it was time to be given the evening delicacy.

I'm happy to know that I can count so fully on him. It's been a whirlwind romance for us this spring. I've been contemplating a travel tour for many months, and I'm finally going to live part of my dream.

I told Jeremy a new dream for me is knowing that he'll be here when I return, and then we can continue where we leave off. I also told him he was the best thing that has ever happened to me. I love him dearly.

Waking up on the day of her airline flight, Selena thought again how much she would miss Jeremy. She was going to pick up her cell to chat. Instead, she wrote down another poem for him to find while she was gone. She put the poem on the bed in Aunt Jenny's old bedroom so he could see it the first night she was away.

I knew you a time as only a friend.
The time came for those feelings to end.
You are more now since we met again
And when we are apart, my tears do stain
On my pillow where I lay my head,
Crying for you all alone in my bed
Where no one can even a whisper hear
Of my thoughts of you, nor see my tear.

Darling, thy name alone sets astir my heart.
How much longer must we stay apart?
My every thought is centered on you.

All of my actions, whatever I do.
I wish to see you, that you know.
Come to me; set my heart aglow.

When saying goodbye at the airport, for one last hug and one last moment together, Jeremy said, "I'll be waiting for your texts, and I'll also be waiting to hear in person all about your galivanting when you return."

One of Selena's texts came to Jeremy as he was having his supper.

"This week, I'll be dancing the Irish jig, sampling Guinness, munching Shamrock & Sour Cream chips and eating at Durty Nell's Bar & Restaurant. Doesn't that sound great?"

He readily replied:

"Oh Selena, how happy I am for you. See you soon, but not soon enough, sweetheart."

On the last day, he received:

"Green grass and green trees and pretty flowers
Which you could stroll through for hours and hours.
When the trees are in bud and the flowers in bloom,
It's a time of colour and a day in Athlone."

His reply:

"Tomorrow, I'll hug you until you beg me to stop!"

Hers:

"I'll never beg you to stop!"

29

Beginnings

PURE SUMMER HAD ARRIVED bringing warm, humid, lovely weather. Selena relished the heat with every fiber of her body – healing, inviting, loving, deep and visceral.

Selena had come home from a fantastic holiday to an incredibly happy Rufus and Caylie. Rufus danced, pranced and "ruffed" and Caylie scampered and "meoooowed". The pets were crazy with happiness that Selena was there. Selena's tablet had allowed them to see her face and hear her voice many times in the past two glorious weeks.

Jeremy had himself danced and pranced prior to Colleen Kirsch bringing Selena home. When she arrived, he grasped Selena, swung her around, and hugged her fiercely while having tears in his eyes and love in his heart.

"Selena, I've missed you so much. The pets and I got along great, but they missed you as you can see."

There had been a few moments during the fabulous vacation that Selena had lamented their separation. Her holiday had been consuming her days, evenings and dreams. However, she thought of Jeremy often.

Jeremy would like this.

Wouldn't it be fun for Jeremy to be here too?

I thought I saw someone that looked like him in the crowd.

I wonder how Jeremy is doing at work right now.

Karen had come over to the house to see Selena the day after she returned from her holiday. Selena had cried as Karen hugged her.

Karen has been as close to a mother as I've had had in almost 13 years. Never replacing my own.

"I couldn't wait any longer to come to see you, Selena. You have matured so much over these past months. I watched you grow from a young child. I've observed how you have handled the loss of Jenny and the decisions that you've had to deal with. I'm amazed, yet I also felt deep down that you would become who you are, with time. I'm sorry it had to happen so suddenly, but you're a capable woman now, Selena."

"Thank you, Karen."

"I've loved you like a daughter for so many years, and I feel awful for doubting your choices with Austin. He's currently a lost soul, but Bud, myself and his girlfriend will work with him to get through some of his recent decisions. She's obviously not happy with what his plans had been regarding you and your inheritance." Taking a sorrowful breath, she continued, "Somewhere along the line, Bud, Austin and I lost sight of each other, but it'll be okay, I know. Sometimes our children grow away from us, but, almost always, they come back."

Selena said, "Karen, I had a poem come into my mind during the flight home. I had to write it down. Take it with you, and read it when you're alone, maybe with a glass of wine in your hand."

Karen walked home with the poem Selena had slipped into her hand. A little while later, she carried a glass of wine for herself and one for Bud, into their living room. She read the poem aloud to Bud, having to stop occasionally, tearing up at parts of it. She was desperately hoping the last stanza would come true someday soon:

Child, where are you?
Where is the child that I remember?
The child that was happy to be near.
I used to know who you were.

You were the sun and the stars.
You were the happy, sunny boy
Who cheered my heart and soul.
I used to know who you were.

You were not annoyed at me.
You loved me. You loved our family.
You were a friend to us. Accepting us.
I used to know who you were.

You used to care about being family.
Care about what we thought.
Care about what we felt.
I used to know who you were.

You thought we had the right ideas.
You thought we knew a thing or two.
Then you changed. We stayed the same.
I used to know who you were.

We spoke – you listened, and you felt
We might be right; we might be wrong.
But you did not judge. You loved us.
I used to know who you were.

You moved on to new ideas and thoughts.
This is what you should do – we agree.
This is good, but we stayed the same.
I used to know who you were.

We speak. You listen and you judge.
We cannot be right. We are wrong.
But you cannot love us the way we are.
I used to know who you were.

You try to change us by not talking.
By ignoring us when we are near.
You hurt our feeling to show us what you think.
I used to know who you were.

Years went by as we all grew older.
You love and accept us once again.
Thank God! You're back, and we are happy.
And now I know who you are.

Jeremy's parents had met Selena when she came back from her holiday, insisting that they could tell their son felt the earth began and ended with Selena and they wanted to meet this young woman.

They had been on holiday in the United Kingdom in their 30s, and they felt that it was time for them to return there. Both sets of Jeremy's grandparents had been born in Ireland, i.e. County Cork and County Galway (both areas where Selena had travelled), moved to Canada and had met each other at an Irish gala in Ottawa. Selena had a quick thought that Jeremy and herself, along with the McGregors, could go there in a future year.

Wouldn't that be terrific to go to Ireland with someone who knew about the history and had family there?

His parents had conversations with Jeremy along the lines of:

"Jeremy, this woman is exactly whom we would have picked out for you."

"Isn't that fabulous?"

"We agree that she's the one for you."

Jeremy had known that his parents would love Selena as he did. He watched as they spoke with her, and he could see that she was amazed and taken with them as well.

Isn't life grand!

This entry was added to her diary:

> *"I can't believe how wonderful love is. We love each other and enjoy all our time together. We're much farther along than just taking it one day at a time.*
>
> *We delight in each other's company, can't do enough for each other.*
>
> *We both feel the same about decisions and the future.*
>
> *Jeremy told me - 'I feel captivated by you – good, gentle, kind, yet a fierce spirit if you see a cause worth fighting for.'*
>
> *I'm enchanted with how genuine and caring he is. He's so handsome, and his smile makes me smile."*

Theodore had taken Laura to his parents' home in June. He had advised them that he and Laura were engaged. His parents were not entirely surprised; however, they did express their reservations.

"Mom and dad, how old were you when you became engaged?"

Karen stopped short at that comment as she and Bud had been young as well. "Okay, that does make me realize that I should take a slightly different view of this. But you must be sure! Are you thinking of being engaged for a little longer prior to getting married?"

Both Laura and Theodore said that they had not set a date, but it would be within the next year. Karen hugged Theodore and then gave Laura a warm, welcoming hug.

Karen and Bud were content with Theodore's choice. Through Selena, they had watched Laura grow up, and they did admire her and knew how hard she had been working to get her Bachelor of

Science in Nursing. Both Theodore and Laura would be finished their studies and be working by next spring.

They're growing up so quickly, thought Bud, and he gave each of the young people a brief hug of approval.

As July approached, Selena had spoken with the editors and excited publishers regularly and Aunt Jenny's *History in the Making* was unfolding. The book had been submitted and a couple of minor revisions made. Julian had the reservation of an accountant though, and he expressed these to Selena.

"As I mentioned, I like your plan to donate to the writers' groups. It's a fabulous idea. However, I believe your aunt's book will generate a great deal of money. Your aunt's past book popularity ensures this – particularly for classroom sets. Selena, you may want to consider donating the proceeds to other worthy charities as well."

"I'm pleased that you brought this up. I've been speaking with Elizabeth and Mary from the Clinic. They suggested charities such as Food Banks, shelters for the homeless and second-stage housing for women could be other worthy groups."

Julian also suggested, "Ensure that if any of your donation recipients close and are no longer in operation, that you have clauses reverting the sums back you to redistribute."

As it happened, Jeremy's mom had a good friend who was able to advise Selena about two of the charities as she was on their boards. Selena researched the additional possibilities thoroughly, and she felt strongly about donating to them. After discussing this with Tessa and Julian, tentative plans were made dependent on when *History in the Making* came out and what amounts were gleaned from the sale as time went on. They would do a percentage donation to each chosen group.

Jeremy told her, "I'm extremely proud of you for these decisions."

In her bedroom later, Selena remembered the phrase *in loco parentis*, in place of the parent – that was her Aunt Jenny.

Talking aloud to her aunt, "I sense your approval, Aunt Jenny, and I'm happy that through your dedication and hard work, we can make life easier for so many. Thank you for helping me to become the person that I am. I'm confident these are good choices."

Selena had been at her new job at the National Research Council for all of six weeks. It took a little while to get in the rhythm of new responsibilities; however, everything went smoothly enough with few hiccups. Her employers and co-workers were very accommodating and guided her in every way she needed. The transition was marvellous for she was working in evaluating formulations for induction of immune response and response validation (antibody, cell-mediated, immune memory, functional assays). She had assisted with another area regarding efficacy studies in challenge models for both infectious disease and cancer vaccines.

It's my perfect job. I love the ever-evolving challenges.

Her former co-worker, Elizabeth, had called on the last Saturday in June, and she and Selena had placed Selena and Jeremy's fun pieces of clay into the kiln for the bisque (first) firing. Selena's breath caught in her throat.

"I'm just beside myself with excitement. My first pieces!" Elizabeth ensured Selena set the kiln for low firing as per the clay type. The kiln would take over 12 hours to reach temperature and another 12 hours to cool enough to open the kiln ensuring the pieces did not crack or shatter with the air hitting them upon opening. With that in mind, Elizabeth arrived again the next day at 3:00 p.m., and, with Elizabeth's coaching and assistance, Selena had unloaded her first pieces from the kiln.

Thankfully, all the pottery turned out successfully and, after rinsing, they were ready for Selena to experiment with glazing. Elizabeth had encouraged Selena to fire some unglazed test pieces with that first load. Then Selena could put strokes of each glaze on those bisque clay pieces to keep a record of what the colours turned out to be after the final firing.

Days later, after the second (glaze) firing was completed, Selena and Jeremy saw how the shades turned out that she had chosen with her heart (and Jeremy with his chutzpa choices).

Selena was already thinking of more piece ideas for her next firing and glazing. "I'll attempt that large bowl with "What Defines Art" written inside it. I'll do more than attempt. I'm going to do it!"

Jeremy glowed and announced, "Wait until Aunt Aggie sees this post of these glazed pieces."

While Selena had waited for the first bisque firing to cool on that Saturday, she wondered, "How can I keep myself busy while the kiln is cooling because I can hardly wait! I know – bake something." Jeremy was at *JM Computer & Consulting* for a few hours, so Selena had decided to make her favourite pie recipe, a Chocolate Pecan Pie.

Oooooh! I love this recipe!

While the pie was baking, Selena formed a plan.

We'll have a party and invite everyone in our lives! Sure, it's my house, but we're a couple.

Selena began a list in her head:

Laura and Theodore; herself and Jeremy; Colleen and Kevin; Bethany Kothare; Penelope Sanchez; Brent Carey; Elizabeth; Mary; Tessa; Gavin; Julian; Nalini (the new employee at the Clinic); Eric Brisbane; Karen and Bud Semple; and Josephine Owens, her veterinarian and friend; Dr. Robertson, as well as their guests/spouses.

Jeremy will add to this list too.

"These are all people who have been in our lives for the past several months, a few since childhood and some from Aunt Jenny's life."

What about Austin? Yeah, what about Austin? Oh brother! Austin came by one day, and apologized in a surly manner, but it's time to put that to rest and get on with our new lives. His girlfriend (I assume) was standing a little back. He didn't introduce her, but her expression and demeanour made her look like a nice person. Patient enough to stick around for him to grow up.

Ding, ding, ding, ding. "The timer for the pie!" Just as Selena had taken the pie out of the oven, Jeremy had come in the door, giving her a hug and then quickly heading for the pie as soon as he smelled the enticing odour. Selena put forth the party and guest ideas to Jeremy. "You must add to this list I started."

"That is an awesome idea, Selena. A par-ty!" Selena shared with him her ideas and asked what he would prefer. "It all sounds awesome. I'll invite three of my co-workers."

"Yes, you should invite Ben, Jean and Pat from your work, as well as your sisters and your parents. I can do an invitation to email out, not too fancy, but I want to include spouses/dates as well. The yard and garden are looking so gorgeous this time of year for a patio BBQ, and the sun will be up until after 10:00 p.m. Jeremy, this will be fun! If it happens to rain, well, then this house is large enough for the guests."

"Don't you want to invite anyone from your job?"

"Not for this party – next time. I won't invite them even though I admire and respect them. I want this to be those who've been in our lives during our friendship and courtship. Isn't that a fun old word? Courtship!"

Jeremy had smiled in total agreement, loving her more each day, if that were possible. Her excitement and enthusiasm were contagious. Selena thought of the words from another stanza of the poem she had written. She felt the words were appropriate right now.

Someone, someone, gentle and kind
I know not if you and I should bind
Ourselves in the bond of matrimony,
But if you feel as I do earnestly,

There would be no doubt in my heart
That could possibly keep us apart.
Tell me, darling, oh please tell me true,
Can you love me as much as I love you?

The wonderful thing was that she did know the answer to this!

Epilogue - August

On a weekend in mid-August that same year, Selena had been thinking and thinking about everything that had happened over the past five months.

"At that BBQ, I think everything turned out to be fun for everyone. What a great party."

All the invited came, except one couple, unsurprisingly. This absence was felt with a small amount of relief by both Selena and Jeremy, and, if truth be known, Laura and Theodore. Austin and his girlfriend had been unable to attend.

The BBQ had fallen on a glorious day in July – a sunny, hot day with slim wispy clouds. Selena's home had perfect landscaping for a party with shade on the patio where the main party was held, and evergreen shade near the gazebo and lounge area. Karen and Bud had rolled over their own BBQ and brought eight lawn chairs to add to those Jeremy had brought from his parents.

Prior to the meal being served, Selena and Jeremy mingled with all their friends and had conversations with everyone. Many introductions were made, and it seemed that the guests had a lot to chat with each other about. Selena took an opportunity to discuss her new employment and how rewarding that was. Of course, she was also queried about her recent holiday. After Selena recounted the highlights of her Scotland and Ireland trip, Jeremy beamed, "Selena and I will be taking a Paris vacation in September."

Selena added, "After the fantastic time I had on my holiday, we genuinely want to go on a trip together. The one we plan includes the long weekend in September, so that is only four days off from work."

Kevin jovially quizzed his best friend on how he and Selena were getting on, and, not to be outdone, Jeremy quizzed Kevin on his and Colleen's future cohabitation. The two friends joked more, and Jeremy turned to Colleen.

"Colleen, have you and Kevin decided on the plan you were discussing last week?"

"Yeah, our plan is confirmed to travel to Germany and then on to Switzerland. The trip is scheduled for three weeks in September, at about the time you're getting back. The four of us world travellers will have a lot to chat about at the end of September." Selena caught a wink between Colleen and Kevin.

What's going on with them that's a secret? What are they planning on their September vacation? A lot to chat about at the end of September... Hum!

Jeremy and Theodore had barbequed steaks, wieners and sausage on one BBQ, while Kevin and Colleen cooked the potato/carrot/onion/celery trays. Selena and Laura had overseen appetizers, salads and glorious desserts that had kept showing up as guests had arrived. Buns and condiments, plates, cutlery had all been set out on the pop-up tables and covered with a fine tablecloth to discourage any hovering insects. Drinks and glasses had been placed on a separate table with ice coolers below.

Everything is working out so well, including my life.

The guests had roamed and mingled, investigating the blooming orchard of fruit trees and the woodland conservation park, admiring the size of Selena's planted garden with tidy vegetable rows she had put labels on. Plants were growing high above the warm ground.

Jeremy had set out the Bluetooth portable speaker now playing one of their Spotify lists: Adam Levine, followed by Adele, Calum Scott, Taylor Swift, Selena Gomez and Ed Sheeran. It was set to randomly play those and their other favourite artists.

Selena had been involved in many conversations, but she also heard tidbits of conversations among the guests, some friendships forming, and others renewed. In turn, everyone milled around the food tables where Selena was serving, conversations running every direction.

Julian and Josephine, had seemed to get along extremely well, discussing her veterinarian business, his expertise in accounting and movies they would like to see.

Together?

She had overheard Tessa and Jeremy's sisters, Jane and Eva, having a chat about Apple watches and Fitbit coming out with a heart arrhythmia monitor. Bethany and Penelope had chatted with two of Jeremy's co-workers, Ben and Pat, about sporting events.

Selena was happy to remember that Nalini, the new medical assistant, smiled while engaged in a conversation with Jeremy's co-worker, Jean. They had strolled toward the woodlands where the raccoon family had passed by minutes before.

She grinned at the remembrance of Jeremy's parents discussing young love with Karen and Bud Semple.

A titillating conversation that had truly grasped Selena's antenna much more sharply than any other conversation had been between Eric Brisbane, Gavin Perrault and Dr. Robertson, who were all earnestly discussing time travel and the changes in the body's molecules during time travel.

What!!!?? How???!! What's going on here?

Dr. Robertson had seemed to be sharing his knowledge! Selena heard Eric mention worm holes.

Maybe they knew about Aunt Jenny and her travels!! That can't be a coincidence. But Aunt Jenny didn't even know about the travel machine until my parents died and her parents then told her their plans.

It was possible that they knew. They were all old friends. Perhaps Aunt Jenny had even discussed it with Dr. Robertson in respect to her health.

Oh, no!

Oh, wow!

Selena had leaned forward trying to catch more of their conversation; however, they walked away while talking. They were out of earshot now.

Selena seriously pondered – *Maybe I could follow them. Now what! I must find out! I wonder if I'll get a chance to find out what's what with those three. If they approach me, what would I say to them?*

Sliding her mind back to the present, she relaxed.

I don't need to think about Aunt Jenny's friends. 'It will all come out in the wash'.

But I've thought constantly of sharing with Jeremy my discoveries in this house: the machine that my grandparents built in the time travel room; their travels; them travelling to and staying in 1967 to re-live their lives; Aunt Jenny's travels; and, goodness, my travels as well.

I can't seem to put into the appropriate words to engage with him about all of it these past weeks. With Jeremy being a Bachelor of Science in Electronic Systems Engineering and a total computer geek, I know he'd be fascinated – even understand the possibilities of travelling in time. Not that I've definite feelings one way or another about entering into any further travel, I simply need and want to share with him. I've been in that closet since my last travels, and I feel a pull toward the idea of travelling – maybe one more time…

Later that day, following all her reminiscing about the BBQ, Jeremy came into her bedroom. He had been working on some renovations in Aunt Jenny's childhood bedroom. He drew Selena's attention to a pamphlet he had found stuffed into a folder on a bookshelf.

"What do you think this is about?"

Selena glanced at the pamphlet as he handed it to her and then sat bolt upright.

I'm stunned. I'm certain I saw lightning flash!

The title on the booklet cover was: "*Invisible Travel*". Selena fought off yelling out "Eureka".

"Invisible Travel," she whispered as she flipped the instructional pages.

Where was this all those weeks ago?

Invisible travel. Invisible travel would be a fantastic idea. Oh, that would be ideal!

It's a good opener. I'll consider saying, "Jeremy, this is a very long story".

With that she realized that it was August.

Holy mother!

Her thoughts sped through her mind:

And that 'long story' should be right now because my grandparents could easily just 'poof' arrive here any day now that it's almost the third week in August!!!! I will be so, so happy to see them again. They can meet Jeremy.

I'm not letting this opportunity to go away. Maybe if I start with "Once Upon a Time".

Totally ignoring her ringing cellphone, she looked up at him and said, “Jeremy, could you take a break and come sit here with me? I have some things that I’ve wanted to share with you and to show you, and no time like the present.”

Or was it no time like the past?

(THEIR BEGINNING)

NOTE FROM AUTHOR, MOIRA DARRELL

Character speech notes:

Austin – Since his parents and brother speak well, his intonation is just a manner of speech he adopted as his persona.

Ramon – In researching the Spanish Language, I chose to use only a small amount of dialect issues in English. I wanted to maintain good communications and show that Ramon was an educated, professional business owner.

Grandma/Grandpa Jenkins and Aunt Jenny – Their words are well formed and spoken in a more formal old-world way, and their education is reflected in their manner.

I had started this book 30 years earlier with 3,000 words. Then I became busy with my own family, moving, living, working full time, recovering from neurological west nile virus. I had put the book in a folder which moved from home to home with us until one day during the time of the 'damndemic', I could not get the book out of my mind.

Since this is my first book, I didn't know how it usually worked for Character Development. As I parachuted myself back into Selena's story, the characters seemed to line up and introduce themselves to me. Each one indicated to me, not I to them, how they wanted to be portrayed, and they showed me what to say and the actions to take on their behalf. As time went on, I decided they could just "not shush up" at night when I should have been sleeping.

I am the great, great niece of a good and prolific author from the 1800s, David Christie Murray. He could write a story! Maybe someday, I will find talent like his. I'll keep trying.

ABOUT THE AUTHOR

Moira Darrell has been a daughter, a sister, a wife, a mother, a grandmother, a legal secretary (22 years), a school admin secretary (12 years), a poet, a hand-sculpting potter in many techniques, dabbled in drawing, painting and, recently, is the writer of *SELENA AND HER MYSTERIES.*

Born in Saskatchewan, Canada, she has travelled to distant places – using modern modes of transportation. There has been no time travel at the time of writing this book.

She loves nature and nurture, has had many pets – two closely resembling the animals in this particular book, has loved them all, and she currently does have a kitty named Caylie Ceilidh Pretty Lady – really. Her English Springer Spaniel, Snickers, now passed away, knew the hand commands described in this book.

Moira now lives closer to the mountains in Alberta with her husband and kitty. Some family members are close by; others so far away that it brings tears to her eyes. Such is life.

She had volunteered for various groups throughout her life, such as community associations, city zone board, a women's shelter and a housing project, an arts committee. She believes in giving to charity by time or donation if you are able.

PERMISSIONS:

Permission received for mention of the following:

Jack Sures and Cara Driscoll, potters (from Cara Driscoll)

Girl Travel Tours, Marah Walsh - Girltraveltours.com

Writers' Union of Canada - writersunion.ca

Canadian Authors' Association

Laura Smart "What Defines Art?" and "I See a Tiny Golden Light"

Purrmission received from Caylie Ceilidh Pretty Lady to relate stories which depict her.

ORIGINAL POEMS AND DREAMS SCENES

WRITTEN BY THE AUTHOR

Poems written as a teenager:

Ecstasy
Where Is the Wind?
The Wind is Blowing All Around
Saskatchewan Seasons (only a portion of poem herein)
Someone, Someone Love Me (only portions of poem herein)
Loneliness Without You
Green Grass and Green Trees

Poems written as an adult:

Winter is Gone; Spring is Here – written after my grandmother's passing.
I Used to Know Who You Were

The Dreams:

Totally Alone
The Storm

The following was written by Laura Smart (*reproduced with permission*):

I See a Tiny Golden Light

What Defines Art? (which I have written in hand-crafted pottery bowls)